Energy of fai...
results in ...

"But when God, who set me apart from birth, and called me by His grace, to reveal His Son to me so that I might preach Him among the Gentiles, I did not consult any man."

Gal 1:15

Christian Faith and Beliefs

Christian
Faith
AND
Beliefs

MORRIS
ASHCRAFT

BROADMAN PRESS
Nashville, Tennessee

4216-03

ISBN: 0-8054-1603-X

Dewey Decimal Classification: 230

Subject Heading: THEOLOGY

Library of Congress Catalog Card Number: 83-71872

Printed in the United States of America

Unless otherwise noted, Scripture quotations are from the Revised Standard
Version of the Bible, copyrighted 1946, 1952, © 1971, 1973.

Scripture quotations marked (KJV) are from the King James Version of
the Bible.

Library of Congress Cataloging in Publication Data

Ashcraft, Morris.
   Christian faith and beliefs.

   1. Theology, Doctrinal—Popular works.
2. Baptists—Doctrines. I. Title.
BT77.A84   1984   230'.6132   83-71872
ISBN 0-8054-1603-X

To my faithful wife and companion,
Anna Bernice Haley Ashcraft

Acknowledgments

During the preparation of this manuscript several persons were especially helpful to me. I express to them my special thanks. Marc Mullinax, my student and research assistant, made many trips to the library for me, read several chapters of the manuscript, and made helpful suggestions. Debbie Hill and Diane Stewart, who work for me at the seminary, gave many hours of painstaking care in typing and reading the manuscript. Carolyn Bailey, Evelyn Carter, and Mary Lou Stephens, secretaries for the faculty, gave of their time and expertise in typing the manuscript. Carolyn Bailey and Linda Smith Lee copied the manuscript. I am indebted to my student and research assistant, Bill Bridges, for the preparation of the index. To all of these I express my deepest thanks.

Foreword

It has been my privilege to teach classes in theology for thirty years. Most of these were in the seminary classroom. Many, however, were in churches in which laypersons contributed to me with their questions and ideas, as have my students in the seminary classroom. I am grateful to all of these for the exchanges, but especially to a large number of laypersons to whom I have taught Christian theology.

In this volume, I have attempted to state what I consider the major beliefs of Christian faith as I have encountered it and studied it. It is obvious that my outlook is that of the Free Church tradition in Protestantism.

The honor of my life has been the privilege of teaching in the seminary classrooms of three Southern Baptist theological seminaries and in one Baptist university. It is no small honor to be entrusted with the theological education of the future ministers of the churches.

This volume is intended to state the beliefs so that persons lacking formal theological study may work their way through their own thoughts, doubts, and beliefs to sound Christian commitment.

MORRIS ASHCRAFT
Wake Forest, North Carolina

Contents

1
Introduction

The title of this volume speaks of two distinct, but related, realities. The term *Christian faith* in the singular is not intended to overlook the numerous interpretations of what Christian faith is. Definitions will be given later, but the intent is to distinguish between personal faith or commitment and the intellectual statements which one may make "about" the content of that faith.

The word *beliefs* has been chosen in preference to the term *doctrines* for the simple reason that a belief sounds more personal and confessional. A doctrine could be taught by one who did not really believe it was true. The term *beliefs* is intended to convey the idea that the person who has Christian faith also holds certain convictions, which can be expressed clearly and coherently.

This volume is a presentation of those beliefs which I believe and think represent well the meaning of the Christian faith. As such, it is a book of theology. Theology is about God. The word is composed of the Greek words *theos* (God) and *logia* (word about). It is necessary for us to look at a number of definitions if we expect to gain understanding. After all, how do we speak of God? Before we look at those definitions, however, it will be helpful if we look at the subject "Christian faith" in terms of its origin and nature.

Jesus of Nazareth

Christian faith had its origin in Jesus of Nazareth. It remains "Christian" only so long as it remains faithful to him.

On a spring morning in the year AD 28 or 29, on the first day of the week following Passover, a small group of women went to the tomb in which Jesus of Nazareth had been buried. They reported that he had been raised from the dead. Later, others reported that they, too, had seen him. Christian faith could have begun at this point. There is evidence, however, that it had already begun.

For many months, perhaps as long as three years, Jesus had led a small band of disciples, had taught them, and had worked wonders in their presence. They had followed him from Galilee through Perea, Samaria, and Judea. They had witnessed his death on a cross outside the north wall of Jerusalem. It appeared to have been all over until the resurrection.

Many months before the crucifixion, Simon Peter, who was a leader among the disciples, had confessed to Jesus, "You are the Christ, the Son of the living God" (Matt. 16:15). That confession of faith in Christ appears to be close to the heart of what we call Christian faith even though it was made before the cross and resurrection.

When the disciples confessed faith in Christ, they believed in him, followed him, learned from him, and lived in an awareness of God's presence and majesty. They certainly did not form a new religion. They already had more religion than they could live with. They had witnessed many religious people coming to Jesus to find fault and to oppose him for healing on their religious days. But the disciples believed in Jesus and followed him.

Jesus had stated in severe terms that those who followed him would have to forsake all else, that they might lose their lives, and that they would have to walk a narrow way.

Believing in Jesus was a way of life resulting from a commitment to God whom the disciples had met in Christ.

Revelation and Reconciliation

In Jesus Christ, the disciples had encountered the presence of God in a personal way. They entered a new relationship with God which we shall call reconciliation (being made right with God and others).

The theological question, How do we know God? raises the prior question, How do we know anything or anyone? We know objects by observing, measuring, investigating, and describing. We know persons in a different way—the way of personal encounter. Those disciples knew God through the personal disclosure in Jesus Christ.

If God is, and if persons can know him, then nothing else is nearly so important. And so the disciples, believing they had encountered God, left all to follow Christ.

The Origin of Christianity

The movement, later to be known as Christianity, had its origin in Jesus of Nazareth and the events related to his life, death, and resurrection. The small band of disciples formed the nucleus, but they were soon joined by many others. During Pentecost, following the cross and resurrection, there was a most unusual event. The Holy Spirit came in great demonstration of power and inspired the disciples to proclaim their beliefs. Thousands were moved to believe in Jesus Christ (Acts 2:1 to 4:37).

The sermon recorded in Acts (2:14-40) offers a rather clear insight into what these people believed. They believed Jesus Christ had fulfilled hopes from the Old Testament, that God had affirmed him with mighty works, wonders, and signs. They believed that his death was a human crime but a redeeming act according to God's plan. They believed God had raised Jesus from the dead and had exalted him to the right hand of the Father and made him Lord. They believed that through repentance people could receive the forgiveness of sins and the gift of the Holy Spirit (Acts 2:1-38). The amazing element in the belief in forgiveness was that Peter was speaking to the crowd in which the crucifiers of Jesus stood (2:23), and the same forgiveness was offered to them. God moved to save the crucifiers by means of his grace through their own crime? It would be rare, indeed, for people to invent such an idea.

The event on the Day of Pentecost portrays the coming of many individuals to believe in Christ, who in their coming formed a community of faith or were added to the community of faith. Their individual faith made them members of the community of faith that was forming in response to Jesus.

It is very significant that this reconciliation of persons with God and each other resulted from, or was the conclusion of, God's revelation of himself in Jesus Christ the Son. These people believed God was very real and was acting in their presence.

The Origin of the Church

The church had its origin in Jesus Christ and the events surrounding his life. If one takes the position that Jesus founded the church, it will be necessary to acknowledge that only after the crucifixion and resurrection was its gospel complete. If, on the other hand, one dates the origin of the church after the resurrection, say at Pentecost, it will be necessary to acknowledge that even in the lifetime of Jesus the embryonic church was real. There was a nucleus, or congregation. They had a mission and a message. They practiced baptism and participated in the Last Supper, two celebrations which universally identify the church.

The church in the New Testament, which originated in the life of Jesus and surrounding events, was both a local community of believers and included all of the believers in Christ wherever they were.

Church and Christianity

The church in the New Testament was not an organization or institution; rather, it was just people called together in a community on the basis of their common faith in God. It was to be expected that they would later develop order and structure within the communities. This developing order was present during the time of the writing of the New Testament, but it was secondary in importance to the church as a people.

Christianity is the name of the religion that stands alongside the other great world religions. The word is also used in a cultural sense. Sometimes it designates the faith itself. Consequently, we will have to endure the ambiguity in the word *Christianity*. It designates the movement, the religion, and later the church and has even developed political and geographical connotations. In this study, *Christianity* will be used in the general sense to designate the Christian faith.

The purpose in this study is to clarify the Christian stance which is a personal and community faith in God which does issue in several "beliefs" which can be identified and defined.

The Expansion of Christianity

After the stoning of Stephen, persecution scattered the Christians (Acts 8:1). Wherever they went, they told about Jesus of Nazareth and the things which had happened to him and them in Jerusalem. Prior to the first missionary journey of Paul and Barnabas (Acts 13), there were Christian communities in Judea, Samaria, Galilee, and Syria. The movement spread into Egypt and southward very early, to the east beyond Damascus, and north and westward. There were Christian communities in Rome before AD 49. The expansion of Christianity during the next two centuries was phenomenal. Kenneth Scott Latourette wrote:

> Never in the history of the race has this record ever been equalled. Never in so short a time has any other religious faith, or, for that matter, any other set of ideas, religious, political, or economic, without the aid of physical force or of social or cultural prestige, achieved so commanding a position in such an important culture."[1]

The Christian religion had grown in size and influence until in the early fourth century it became the official religion of the Roman Empire.

Factors in the Expansion

The central event of Jesus Christ was the primary factor in the vitality of the Christian movement. A galaxy of events surrounded him, but he gave them their meaning. The Holy Spirit's coming at Pentecost gave the Christians a conviction that God was present with them. This sense of God's providence injected their movement with purpose and power. They were a new people held together by a strong bond; wherever they went, they found other Christians and enjoyed a family-type relationship with them. The message they proclaimed, the gospel, had a power in itself to transform lives. This called people to a new way of life, a commitment which endowed life with meaning. They had the Old Testament Scriptures with them. These writings gave a world view with unity and purpose that constituted a powerful influence among the peoples to whom the Christians witnessed.

The Formation of the Bible

In addition to the Old Testament, which the Christians claimed as their Bible in the beginning, new Christian writings emerged. These writings appeared quite early in the life of the Christian movement. The letters of Paul to the churches were probably the earliest. They were followed by the Gospels; the Acts; the other letters; and the Apocalypse of John, Revelation.

Incidental notes within these writings indicate that the churches circulated their letters to others. At least the author of Colossians suggested that the addressees pass their letter on to the church in Laodicea and in return read his letter to the Laodiceans (Col. 4:16). There is an interesting note in 2 Peter about the writings of Paul which may suggest a growing awareness of the importance, if not the inspiration, of these Christian writings (2 Pet. 3:15-16).

The formation of the Christian Bible is a special study. A brief discussion will appear in the chapter on revelation, but a few comments seem necessary at this time. When the early Christians wrote, circulated, and evaluated the writings which were appearing, they evidently did not think they were forming a Bible. The canonization of the New Testament writings came about over a period of time. A writing was respected if it were (1) related to an apostle, (2) faithful to the life and teachings of Jesus, and (3) well received when read in public worship. These criteria speak of the trustworthiness of such writings because the apostles were the primary witnesses and Jesus was the final norm of religious truth. Also the worship response to such a writing indicated its inspiration since the Holy Spirit led the listeners to hear God's message in the writing.

One cannot understand the Christian faith apart from a grasp of the significance of the writings which came to form the New Testament. The Bible is the primary source of information for Christian beliefs and the chief source of guidance for Christian living and inspiration.

Different Expressions of Christianity

There are at least four major divisions or families of Christian communities: Eastern Orthodoxy, Roman Catholicism, Protestantism, and sectarian Christianity. There are numerous Christian communions not directly affiliated with Eastern Orthodoxy or Roman Catholicism which are, nevertheless, included in these general divisions. Each division includes groups with practices and beliefs which are incredibly diverse.

The present study stands in the Free Church tradition of Protestantism. Honesty and gratitude, however, require an expression of appreciation for the understanding, traditions, and writings which have come down to us from the Eastern and

Roman traditions and Protestantism and for the numerous contributions which continue to appear in our own times.

Historical Influences on the Present Theological Task

One cannot speak of interpreting Christian faith and beliefs apart from those historical and cultural factors which have shaped the modern mind. It would be a preposterous presumption for one to think these factors could even be listed, let alone discussed, in so brief a study. On the other hand, it would be calculated neglect to move on to the interpretation without some mention of these currents of thought. Dale Moody has called these "Main Currents of Modern Theology" and "Current Trends in Christian Theology."[2]

The Protestant Reformation

The Reformation changed not only the church but also the history of Europe and the world. The Reformation included several historical movements. Of primary importance are the German Reformation led by Martin Luther (1483-1546), the Swiss Reformation led by Huldreich Zwingli (1484-1531) and John Calvin (1509-1564), the Anabaptists, and the reformation of the Church in England. The Lutheran, or Evangelical branch, and the Swiss, or Reformed branch, contributed the most to the making of the Reformation emphases.

All Christian groups believe in the one God who has been most fully revealed in Jesus Christ and who is present as the Holy Spirit. They all speak of atonement, forgiveness, grace, salvation, eternal life, the church, worship, prayer, and so forth. All hold the Bible in high regard and speak of a Christian way of life, and they all have some kind of missionary emphasis.

Protestants, however, are distinct from other Christian groups for a number of beliefs. They insist that God is known *only* though Jesus Christ's revelation. They uniformly assert that our justification with God is by faith in Jesus Christ and not by works. They believe in the priesthood of all believers which asserts direct access to God, responsibility for others, and a measure of liberty. They base their beliefs on the Scriptures which are the authority above church or creed. Their views of the church, and hence of the ministry, are different from Roman Catholicism and Eastern Orthodoxy.

Negatively, Protestants reject papal power, the demand for confession to official priests, purgatory, monasticism, the veneration of Mary, a celibate clergy, and vows of poverty.[3]

The spirit of Protestantism according to Robert McAfee Brown includes these following affirmations: the centrality of grace in the Christian life; the authority of Scripture; the sovereignty of God and biblical election; the priesthood of all believers; the calling of the Christian person; loving God with the mind; and, the private and public worship of God.[4]

Protestant Orthodox Theology

Philip Melanchthon (1497-1560), a disciple of Luther, wrote the first systematic theology in the Evangelical tradition of Luther. It was entitled the *Loci Communes* and appeared in 1521. The classic statement of Reformed theology was John Calvin's *Institutes of the Christian Religion* which appeared first in 1536 and was revised five times before the last edition in 1559. Zwingli's writings were not as systematic, even though they were influential. All of these writings are available in translation in publications such as "The Library of Christian Classics."[5]

Calvin's *Institutes* has been one of the most influential theologies ever written, perhaps because of its thoroughness and comprehensiveness. Along with the other publications cited, these writings resulted in a kind of "Protestant orthodoxy" which prevailed until the challenge of the Enlightenment and theological Liberalism.

Liberalism

Theological Liberalism had its origin in the thought and writings of Friedrich Schleiermacher (1768-1834). His major works were *On Religion: Speeches to Its Cultured Despisers* and a systematic theology entitled *The Christian Faith.* Liberalism produced many great scholars. In theology they were in two groups: the evangelical liberals who stayed as close to traditional Christianity as modern learning would permit; and, the modernistic liberals whose first loyalty appeared to be twentieth-century learning but who retained as much of the Christian faith as they could and still give primary allegiance to modern learning.[6]

Evangelical Liberalism produced scholars such as William Adams Brown, Harry Emerson Fosdick, Walter Rauschenbusch, Albert C. Knudson, and Eugene W. Lyman. Modernistic liberals were men such as Shailer Matthews, D. C. Mackintosh, and Henry Nelson Wieman.

To attempt a summary of Liberalism's emphases is to engage in crass oversimplification, but it is necessary. They tended to emphasize the immanence of God more than the transcendence; they placed Jesus in a central position, but it was the Jesus of history apart from Christological complexities. They had an appreciation for science and scientific method which led to questioning such subjects as miracles and the virginal conception of Christ and to an appreciation for Darwin's theory of evolution. They interpreted Christian faith primarily in ethical terms and sought social reforms. They had a high estimate of human life and a parallel lack of appreciation for the orthodox doctrine of sin and depravity. Since sin was not so serious, their view of atonement was usually a subjective one, that is, the cross only changes our attitude toward God who would have forgiven us apart from the cross.

One cannot understand the modern theological climate apart from an appreciation of Liberalism and its contribution, even though its optimistic view of man was so inadequate (as proved by two World Wars which show us the depth of our sin and the necessity for God's grace).

Fundamentalism

A powerful theological movement had its roots in the last quarter of the nineteenth century. Its primary reason for existence was to fight Liberalism. The theology of Fundamentalism was a restatement of Protestant orthodoxy with one additional feature, the inerrancy of Scripture. Fundamentalism as a theological movement should be distinguished from Conservative or Orthodox theology which held essentially to the same theological views. The difference is that Fundamentalism was a belligerent movement without a social concern.[7] The contemporary Orthodox or Conservative theology differs on both counts.

The name *Fundamentalism* appears to have been derived from the appearance of the twelve books (pamphlets) which were published under the title *The Fundamentals: A Testimony to the Truth* between 1910 and 1915.

Historians list variations of these "fundamentals," and the Niagara Bible Conference of 1878 published a creed of fourteen points, but, generally, they agree on the "five fundamentals" which appear with slight variations. They are these: (1) the inerrancy of Scripture; (2) the virgin birth of Jesus; (3) the substitutionary view of the atonement; (4) the bodily resurrection of Jesus; and (5) the physical return of Christ.[8]

Fundamentalism opposed Liberalism, fought any form of the idea of evolution, opposed the use of literary criticism in biblical study, and began to decline after the infamous Scopes trial (1925) on teaching evolution in the public schools. Liberalism declined when its optimism died as a result of the wars of the twentieth century.

Neoorthodoxy

A new theological movement emerged after Karl Barth published his commentary on Romans in 1921. The theologians of this group included Reinhold Niebuhr, Barth's counterpart in America; Emil Brunner of the University of Zürich; H. Richard

Niebuhr, and a host of others who had previously been in the Liberalism movement. They moved out because they recognized its bankruptcy, but their return to orthodoxy was not merely a reaction. They retained what they had learned in Liberalism and tried to restate the orthodox doctrines in the full light of modern literary and historical research.

The movement has been known as the New Reformation Theology, Dialectical Theology, as well as Neoorthodoxy. It placed a heavy emphasis on biblical authority, the transcendence of God, the seriousness of human sin, and the revelation in Jesus Christ, the Word of God. The movement was influential in both Europe and America but has since declined as a movement. The influence continues, however, through the writings of these and other theologians of the group.[9]

New Conservatism

Since World War II, a new group has emerged answering to various names, such as Evangelicalism, New Conservatism, or simply Orthodox Theology. Edward J. Carnell wrote the "Case" book for this theology.[10] This movement of conservative theology has been very influential in America. It has produced a large share of candidates for the ministry and missions.

The theology of this movement is the same as that of Fundamentalism with the following differences. These theologians are not belligerent as were the Fundamentalists, and they have a social concern which the Fundamentalists did not. Also, the theologians of this group utilize to an increasing extent historical and literary critical methods in the study of the Bible and have a more friendly attitude toward modern science.

Persons associated with the movement include Carl F. H. Henry and Billy Graham.

Recent Trends in Theology

The scene has changed rapidly during the last three decades. America witnessed a great religious revival in the 1950s. Record numbers of people joined the churches. National news magazines displayed religion prominently. Billy Graham was at the height of his popularity. Norman Vincent Peale appeared before great audiences of American readers. Roy Eckhardt described these two figures as representatives of a trend he wrote about in *The Surge of Piety in America,* published in 1957.

The 1960s were turbulent years. Martin Marty called it the "unhealthy" decade. National leaders were assassinated. There was Vietnam. Riots erupted. Public officials and their constituents were troubled by credibility gaps. John A. T. Robinson published *Honest to God.* This little book popularized a secular approach to theology.

The most radical form of this secular theology was "The Death of God" movement associated with Thomas J. J. Altizer, William Hamilton, and others. The less radical forms suggested a secular theology in terms of Dietrich Bonhoeffer's religionless Christianity. In his *Letters and Papers from Prison,* he had spoken of our faith in secular terms. He advocated a Christianity without religion. He saw religion as an artificial system toward God and maintained that Christ taught a simpler way of life which was essentially secular. The good Samaritan, for instance, just helped a person in a purely secular way. This is what God really desires. Unfortunately, the fragments which survived his imprisonment and found their way to his friends did not clarify fully what Bonhoeffer meant. Nevertheless, these fragmentary writings have been the happy hunting ground for both the secularizers and the "Christian atheists."

During the sixties and into the seventies, we had the emergence and development of futuristic theology. *Theology of Hope* was one of the works of Jürgen Moltmann on the subject. Wolfhart Pannenberg was one of the most prolific writers on this theme. Ernst Bloch of Tübingen was the philosopher of hope who included elements of Marx and Hegel. Johannes Metz is perhaps the best-known Catholic scholar of this group and is known for his volume *Theology of the World.*

Liberation theology has been very influential in Latin America. Theologians, such as Gustavo Gutierrez with his *A*

Theology of Liberation, have produced many volumes, most of which have disturbed the church. Many theologians in Europe and America have become interested in this liberation theology. Black theology and feminist theology are American examples of liberation theology.[11]

Some theologians are working on a Process theology based on Process philosophy related to the thought of Alfred North Whitehead. Process philosophy sees reality in terms of process rather than traditional terms of creation. These theologians are blazing new trails and will continue to make contributions. Process thought, however, is not understood well by those lacking study in philosophy. And, like Existentialist theology (outlook based on the idea that reality is more nearly seen on the basis of total human existence rather than reason or some specific part of existence), it may remain somewhat obscure to the masses.

Why Study Theology?

The study of theology is regarded by many as uninteresting, by others as unnecessary. Occasionally, a person will say that all one needs is the Bible and that the formulation of doctrine may actually distort the faith. That person is not thinking or speaking clearly. One does not read the Bible without formulating theological beliefs. The question is how carefully and systematically one does so.

There are several reasons which require us to study theology and articulate our beliefs: (1) our experience of faith in Christ is the greatest event of our lives and we must speak about it; (2) we are rational beings and by inner necessity must organize our beliefs into some kind of coherent whole; (3) we cannot teach anyone else the meaning of our beliefs unless we have carefully studied them; (4) we must speak clearly as we share our faith with unbelievers; and (5) theological reflection and statements purify our personal faith and beliefs, thereby preventing us from falling into or cherishing our superstitions and prejudices.

Definitions in the Study of Theology

The purpose of Christian theology is to study and state the meaning of Christian beliefs. The study involves not only the individual beliefs but also the whole body of beliefs and the relationships existing among the beliefs. Since the purpose is to achieve understanding and share it, we must use language and concepts which are clear.

Definitions

Paul Tillich stated, "Theology is the methodical interpretation of the contents of the Christian faith."[12] Gustav Aulen used the words, "Systematic theology is therefore that discipline which has as its purpose the study and investigation of the Christian faith."[13] John Macquarrie began, "Theology may be defined as the study which, through participation in and reflection upon a religious faith, seeks to express the content of this faith in the clearest and most coherent language available."[14]

Several factors are necessary in a definition of the task of theology: (1) it is an intellectual discipline; (2) it seeks to understand the contents of the faith; (3) it is a discipline which can be done only by a participant, or believer; (4) it must state these beliefs in clear language.

Acknowledged Limitations

We acknowledge certain limitations at the outset. Note that Macquarrie spoke of using the "clearest and most coherent language available." He approached theology from an existentialist perspective. An existentialist appreciates reason but does not elevate human reason to the supreme judge of reality as would have been the case with a theologian following the philosophy of Hegel. Liberal theologians had a tendency to elevate human reason above revelation. Albert C. Knudson, for instance, began his volume, "Theology may be defined as the systematic exposition and rational justification of the intellectual content of religion."[15]

The "rational justification" may rule out a number of elements, such as miracles, all of the supernatural, and even the incarnation of God in Christ. Christian theology must be dealt with rationally, but it cannot be reduced to a rationalism if it is to remain Christian. Theology must be reasonable, or rationally stated, but it cannot justify all of its beliefs before the bar of human reason.

Another approach was that of "historicism." This approach as found in Albrecht Ritschl would limit Christian faith to the historical. Faith would be able to maintain as its doctrines only those which could pass the test of historical verification. While Christian faith is certainly grounded in history, it bases its entire faith on the belief that Jesus was the Son of God, which historians can neither verify nor refute.

In the work of theology, we shall work with the historical, the rational, the existential, and so forth, in our quest for understanding and clarifying the beliefs. We must, however, employ a method capable of embracing the larger area of truth.

Faith, Beliefs, and Doctrines

Faith is the comprehensive term which designates our trusting relationship to God. We believe in him, and we think we embrace him through faith as he embraces us.

Beliefs are the convictions that we hold about God, ourselves, creation, the meaning and destiny of our lives. They are personal and confessional. They are intellectual and conceptual. They come from inward reasoning and reflection, from the confessional conversation with other believers, from the questions of unbelievers, from history, philosophy, and all other disciplines which seek to know and understand truth.

Doctrines are beliefs stated formally. Doctrines are the theological statements of the church. In some types of churches, they have a binding effect on the adherents.

In a sense, doctrines are formulated by a review of past

events. Faith comes first as personal commitment. Of course, the person who comes to faith already has religious opinions and ideas. The difference, however, is that in faith these opinions and ideas are refined and personalized into beliefs. The systematic and coherent formulation of these beliefs need not remove the personal and confessional nature.

If you wish, you may argue that my beliefs are no different from doctrines. I would like to attempt, however, to maintain the distinction so that faith and beliefs will remain more personal and confessional. Also, I would like to avoid the idea that doctrines are the official statements which are to be accepted. I don't know how you can accept something like a religious belief unless you have come to believe it for yourself, and that requires individual reflection.

The task of formulating a methodical and coherent statement of these beliefs is not the individual's task; rather, it takes place in the community of faith where there can be conversation, clarification, and understanding.[16] This conversation includes not only the contemporary community of believers but also those of the past who have spoken with us (not merely to us) in their writings. What we declare as our beliefs must also be stated as clearly as possible for those not yet in the community of faith and those yet to be born.

Kinds of Theology

Systematic theology has been customarily used as the title for this broad discipline which seeks to study, understand, and make a coherent statement of the doctrines of the Christian faith both in their individual meanings and in their relationships to one another and to the whole. It is a contemporary study; that is, it is made at the present time for the present generation in light of all that has gone before. It acknowledges, however, that future generations will have to repeat the process in their own times. This is due to the fact that systematic theology is an interpretation of the doctrines intended for understanding at the present time. The European theologians have used the term *Dogmatics* in the same sense as "Systematic Theology."[17] Theological schools today tend to use "Christian Theology" in the same broad sense of "Systematic Theology." Systematic or Christian theology is the broad area and is vitally related to the other theological disciplines.

Biblical theology is a study of religious beliefs and is limited to the Bible or to some part of the Bible. The study may be an Old Testament theology, a New Testament theology, or the theology of Paul. The point of definition is that the study is limited to the Bible or a designated part of the Bible. The biblical theologian seeks to articulate the beliefs as they were stated by the writers at the time of the writings. While the biblical theologian may illustrate from church history or philosophy, the point is to clarify the meaning of the text at the time of writing. It is obvious that systematic theology is vitally related to and dependent upon biblical theology. Examples of biblical theology would be *Old Testament Theology* by Gerhard von Rad and *The Theology of the New Testament* by Werner Georg Kummel and *Theology of the New Testament* by Rudolf Bultmann.

Historical theology is the discipline which seeks to clarify the historical development of the doctrines of the church in the life of the church. This study would, for instance, include a study of "The Doctrine of the Trinity." Examples of historical theologies are Bernhard Lohse, *A Short History of Christian Thought;* Otto W. Heick, *A History of Christian Thought,* two volumes; and Adolph Harnack, *History of Dogma,* seven volumes.

Apologetics is a theological discipline developed and written from the standpoint of persuasion. The Christian beliefs are presented so as to be persuasive to a nonbeliever. Studies in "Science and Religion," for instance, would be apologetics if they sought to present Christian beliefs in terms that would be most clearly understood by persons whose primary mode of thought was scientific. Examples would include Ian G. Barbour, editor, *Science and Religion;* Bernard L. Ramm, *A Christian Appeal to Reason;* and Alan Richardson, *Christian Apologetics.*

Systematic theology always has an apologetic interest even

though it is primarily a discipline within the church. When the theologian directs his appeal to those not yet in faith, he is dealing in apologetics.

Philosophy of religion or *Christian philosophy* is a discipline which investigates religious beliefs utilizing the philosophical method. The theologian in this instance will limit the discussion to what can be said about the belief on the basis of philosophical method. He or she would not be free to utilize the authority of revelation, for instance, but would be required to say only that which could be sustained by the rational method of philosophical study. Examples are Frederick Ferre, *Basic Modern Philosophy of Religion,* and F. R. Tennant, *Philosophical Theology.*

Christian ethics is a theological discipline which seeks to apply the meaning of Christian beliefs to the daily issues and problems of life. Obviously, any serious study of theology will eventually get to the matter of such application.

Practical theology includes a number of disciplines which seek to specialize in a particular way by making the beliefs understandable, meaningful, and applicable. Examples include Christian ethics, pastoral care, preaching, missions, evangelism, and religious education.

Christian Theology and Nontheological Disciplines

Christian theology seeks to understand truth as it is discovered in all disciplines and to relate that truth to its beliefs. I have already mentioned that the study of philosophy is always necessary for the theologian. Philosophy is the discipline which clarifies our thought and expression of truth. It provides the structures through which communication of truth is possible. Theologians need also to be philosophers.[18]

The conflict between science and religion was a disastrous mistake. During the Fundamentalist-Liberal controversy, conflict focused on evolution. Both scientific method and theological study aim at the discovery of and clarification of truth in their respective areas. If we believe in God as Creator of the universe, then we believe in a unity of reality. If the scientist

discovers any truth in the universe, it should be of interest to
the person of faith. On the other hand, if the persons of faith
are in touch with truth, no true scientist will be indifferent to
that truth. The question reduces down to the matter of
whether statements in each discipline are true.

The scientific study of religion, languages, literary documents and their transmission, for instance, have been of in-
valuable assistance to the theologians. Biblical scholars almost
uniformly depend on literary historical criticism and its
methodology in their study of the biblical texts.

The Sources of Christian Theology

The sources for the study of Christian theology may be
divided into two: (1) the primary and (2) the secondary.

The primary source for the study of Christian theology is the
Bible. The canonical writings of the Old and the New Testaments are the first source to which the theologian goes for
knowledge of the beliefs of Christians. Christian beliefs must
be grounded in the biblical teachings; they must certainly not
be in conflict with clear biblical teachings.

The secondary sources include (1) the history of the church
with its creeds and confessions; (2) human reason as it appears
in philosophy, for instance; and (3) human experience.

Since God is living and since the Holy Spirit is present in the
church as teacher, the church will increase its knowledge of
Christian beliefs and articulate them more clearly now than it
was able to do in previous times. Human reason is God's gift.
With the Christian view of humanity as God's creation, human
reason will provide additional insights that indeed affect doctrinal statements.

If Christian life is a pilgrimage in faith, as indeed it is portrayed in the primary source, then it follows that those who
walk its way will learn through Christian experience more
about their faith and its beliefs. This experience itself constitutes a secondary source.

Paul Tillich, for instance, listed three sources for Christian theology: (1) the Bible, (2) church history, and (3) the history of religion and culture.[19]

The secondary sources sometimes appear to be complementary or derived interpretations rather than sources. The creedal statements, for instance, are not additional to the biblical teachings (or should not be), but rather, are interpretations of those beliefs at a given time. John Macquarrie has chosen to speak of "formative factors" rather than "sources." He lists these formative factors: (1) experience, (2) revelation, (3) Scripture, (4) tradition, (5) culture, and (6) reason.[20]

It is obvious that since the data from the Bible, church history, and experience in faith is so voluminous we must follow some principle or norm in the evaluation and arrangement of the theological beliefs. This necessity prompts a discussion of the method and the norm in theology.

The Method of Christian Theology

Theologians, like other interpreters, develop their statements in keeping with some rationale, whether they specifically state it or not. There are theologians who hold to a view that the Bible is the revelation, that it is in some sense inerrant (usually limiting inerrancy to the original writings which no longer exist), and that the Bible is really all the theologian needs. A study of their theologies, however, reveals that there was in fact a rationale underlying the way they approached the Bible. Edward J. Carnell is a good example.

Carnell started with the statement, "Orthodoxy is that branch which limits the ground of religious authority to the Bible. No other rule of faith and practice is acknowledged. Orthodoxy is friendly toward any effort that looks to Scripture; it is unfriendly toward any that does not."[21] The uninitiated would get the idea that one has only to go to the Bible and find the doctrines.

The Bible, however, is a large and complex collection of writings which were written over a period of many centuries. There are cultural developments and changes which make earlier parts of it extremely difficult for later times. The "eye for eye, tooth for tooth" idea of the Old Testament was clearly contradicted by Jesus who repeatedly said, "But I say to you, . . ." (Matt 5:38 *ff.*).

In the case of Edward J. Carnell, there was a rationale or method which he followed that allowed him to get at the theology of the Bible, but which upon investigation turns out to be quite surprising in light of his opening statement as quoted. He stressed that revelation is "progressive," thus allowing for the changes. Then he stated five rules governing biblical interpretation: (1) the "New Testament interprets the Old Testament"; (2) "the Epistles interpret the Gospels"; (3) "systematic passages interpret the incidental"; (4) "universal passages interpret the local"; and (5) "didactic passages interpret the symbolic."[22] This rationale led him to make the statement: it "remains true that Romans and Galatians are the highest ranking sources in theology."[23] The rationale which guided all of his theological beliefs was the doctrine of the inerrancy of Scripture but the Scripture must be interpreted by the doctrine of justification by faith in Christ as it is articulated in Romans and Galatians.

Paul Tillich developed and followed what he called the method of "correlation." In this method the theologian, who is also a philosopher, analyzes the human situation and thereby uncovers the existential questions and then shows how the revelation provides the answers to these questions. Theology, therefore, is the correlation of questions from human reason and answers from divine revelation.[24] His theology is also what we call existentialist theology. It is grounded in a view of human existence. The understanding of human existence is the guiding norm for understanding reality.

Gordon D. Kaufman sought to follow a "historicist" method. He referred to his method as "radically historicist" and sought to interpret faith "within the limits of history alone."[25] It should be obvious that such a methodology would rule out the traditional Christian belief in a life beyond history.

Kaufmann, following his historicist method, saw no reason to believe in individual personal existence beyond death or in such things as last judgment, heaven, or hell.[26]

Karl Barth followed a dialectical method, Rudolf Bultmann a method that was existentialist interpretation. Dale Moody, whose theology for the most part is Evangelical and conservative and very biblical, speaks of a "dialogical method" by which he means that the theologian must maintain a critical conservatism in theology but listen to both critical and conservative scholars in theology and to be in dialogue with modern science and society.[27]

Each approach to theology has contributed insights of value. The existentialists, for instance, have provided clarifications in the understanding of faith, human estrangement, and so forth. No single approach like correlation, historicist, or existentialist appears to do justice to the whole.

In this volume, we shall begin with the Christian beliefs which are held and have been held by the Christians over the centuries. Then we shall examine their biblical foundations to determine if they are grounded in the primary sources. Thereafter, we shall give consideration to the statements of the church through its interpretations, creeds, confessions, and hymns to determine how the beliefs have been understood. Then we shall consider basic objections which may have been raised by human reason, and consider additional justification which may have been provided by human reason. Then some thought will be given to the meaning of these beliefs in human life. Throughout this process, we shall be guided by one norm.

The Norm of Christian Theology

The ultimate standard by which Christian beliefs must be built and judged is Jesus Christ the revelation of God.

Christian faith is belief in God as revealed in Jesus Christ. Consequently, Christ determines not only what we think and say about God, and hence, about all other related subjects, but he is the way through which we know God. Therefore, Christian beliefs may be illustrated and clarified by information from many sources, but the final question is, Is it a belief that is faithful to Jesus Christ as the disclosure of God?

Summary

The method previously stated does not require that each single belief be discussed in the sequence of steps as outlined. They should be included at some stage. In some cases, the application may be so obvious as to need no mention; sometimes several beliefs are so related that a statement in one will suffice for all.

In the study of theology, the reader needs to be reminded that all theological beliefs are intertwined with all of the other beliefs. One cannot speak of God, for instance, without implying humanity. One cannot speak of creation, for example, without implying consummation or eschatology. Consequently, any apparent repetition is necessary to keep the relationships clear.

Since Christian faith is belief in God as revealed in Jesus Christ, we must begin our study with Jesus Christ, the Son of God.

Notes

1. Kenneth Scott Latourette, "A History of the Expansion of Christianity" *The First Five Centuries,* (New York and London: Harper and Brothers Publishers, 1937), p. 112.
2. Dale Moody, *The Word of Truth* (Grand Rapids: William B. Eerdmans Publishing Company, 1981), pp. 17-37.
3. Winfred E. Garrison, *A Protestant Manifesto* (Nashville: Abingdon Press, 1952), p. 176.
4. Robert McAfee Brown, *The Spirit of Protestantism* (Oxford: The Oxford University Press, 1961), pp. 53-156.
5. The Westminster Press of Philadelphia began publication of *The Library of Christian Classics* in 1953. The general editors were John Baillie, John T. McNeill, and Henry P. Van Dusen. Luther's works (not complete) will be found in volumes 15-18; Melanchthon's in 19; Calvin's *Institutes* in 20 and 21,

and some of his other works in 22 and 23; Zwingli and Bullinger's works are in 24.

6. Kenneth Cauthen, *The Impact of American Religious Liberalism* (New York and Evanston: Harper & Row, Publishers, 1962), pp. 27-30. For a statement of contemporary liberal theology see L. Harold DeWolf, *The Case for Theology in Liberal Perspective* (Philadelphia: The Westminster Press, 1959); for a brief summary of the various contemporary theological views see William E. Hordern, *A Layman's Guide to Protestant Theology,* 2nd. ed. (New York: Macmillan Publishing Co., Inc., 1968).

7. Edward J. Carnell, "Fundamentalism," *A Handbook of Christian Theology* (New York: Meridian Books, Inc., 1958), pp. 142-143.

8. Morris Ashcraft, "The Theology of Fundamentalism," *Review and Expositor,* 79, No. 1 (Winter 1982), pp. 31-44. Also, see Stewart G. Cole, *The History of Fundamentalism* (New York: Richard R. Smith, Inc., 1931), p. 67; Ernest R. Sandeen, *The Roots of Fundamentalism* (Chicago: The University of Chicago Press, 1970), p. 246; James Barr, *Fundamentalism* (Philadelphia: The Westminster Press, 1977); Norman Furniss, *The Fundamentalist Controversy, 1918-1931* (Hamden, Conn.: Archon Books, 1963).

9. William Hordern, *The Case for a New Reformation Theology* (Philadelphia: The Westminster Press, 1959).

10. Edward J. Carnell, *The Case for Orthodox Theology* (Philadelphia: The Westminster Press, 1959).

11. James H. Cone, *A Black Theology of Liberation* (Philadelphia: J. B. Lippincott Company, 1970); Gustavo Gutierrez, *A Theology of Liberation,* trans. Sister Caridad Inda amd John Eagleson (New York: Orbis Books, 1973); Letty M. Russell, *Human Liberation in a Feminist Perspective—A Theology* (Philadelphia: The Westminster Press, 1974).

12. Paul Tillich, *Systematic Theology,* 1 (Chicago: The University of Chicago Press, 1951), p. 15.

13. Gustaf Aulen, *The Faith of the Christian Church* (Philadelphia: The Muhlenberg Press, 1948), p. 4.

14. John Macquarrie, *Principles of Christian Theology,* 2nd. ed. (New York: Charles Scribner's Sons, 1977), p. 1.

15. Albert C. Knudson, *The Doctrine of God* (New York and Nashville: Abingdon-Cokesbury Press, 1930), p. 19.

16. Tillich, p. 3; Emil Brunner, *The Christian Doctrine of God: Dogmatics I,* trans. Olive Wyon (Philadelphia: The Westminster Press, 1950), p. 78.

17. Brunner; Karl Barth, *Church Dogmatics,* trans. G. T. Thomson (Edinburgh: T. & T. Clark, 1936 *ff.*). Barth's *Church Dogmatics* was planned to be five volumes (with multiple parts), but only three and most of the fourth were finished before Barth's death.

18. Tillich, p. 18-19.

19. Ibid., p. 40.

20. Macquarrie, pp. 4-18.

21. Carnell, *The Case for Orthodox Theology,* p. 13.

22. Ibid., p. 53.

23. Ibid., p. 66.

24. Tillich, pp. 18-28.

25. Gordon Kaufman, *Systematic Theology: A Historicist Perspective* (1969 BIP-1969 pap.) (New York: Charles Scribner's Sons, 1968), p. xii-xiii.

26. Ibid., p. 479-480.

27. Moody, p. 3.

PART I
Belief in God

"In the beginning God . . ."

"In the fullness of time, God . . ."

"In the end God . . ."

Capacity to Believe

This capacity to believe is the most significant and fundamental human faculty, and <u>the most important thing about a man is what he believes in the depth of his being.</u> This is the thing that makes him what he is; the thing that organizes him and feeds him; the thing that keeps him going in the face of untoward circumstances; the thing that gives him resistance and drive. Let neutrality, confusion, indifference, or skepticism enter this inner place, and the very springs of life will cease to flow.

—Hugh Stevenson Tigner

2

Jesus Christ

"God was in Christ, reconciling the world unto himself" (2 Cor. 5:19, KJV).

Jesus Christ is central or foundational in Christian faith. Christians believe that through him they have come to know God and have a continuing relationship with God. They also believe that Jesus Christ reveals the very nature of God so that they know what God is like. It is on the basis of Jesus Christ's revelation that they make statements about God.

This affirmation does not imply that Jesus Christ brought the first knowledge of God. Those who first believed in Jesus Christ already believed in God. They stood in the Old Testament tradition in which the Hebrews had for centuries worshiped God. In a covenant relationship with God, the Hebrew community knew God. They served him through obedience to the law and by observing the ethical concepts proclaimed by their great prophets. They also had developed a complex sacrificial and ritual religious practice. The first Christian converts in Galilee and Judea were participants in that tradition.

Although Jesus was born to a Jewish mother and cradled in the tradition of Israel, his disciples concluded rather early that God as revealed in Jesus Christ was now more fully revealed. They thought that in Jesus Christ God had so revealed himself that previous revelation was preliminary and preparatory. There was a fullness, a uniqueness, in Jesus Christ that included both continuity and discontinuity with Israel's tradition.

The discontinuity derived from the belief that Jesus Christ

is the Son of God. This belief was and is central to the Christians; yet, it ran against the very grain of Jewish thinking both then and now.

Beginning the discussion of the doctrine of God with Jesus Christ appears to be natural. A glimpse, however, at the tables of contents in many Christian theology books will show that most writers do not do so. For instance, John Calvin in *Institutes of the Christian Religion* discussed "The Knowledge of God the Creator" in Book 1, and "The Knowledge of God the Redeemer in Christ" in Book 2.[1]

It is impossible to discuss the beliefs in chronological order and not altogether in logical order. It is certainly impossible to discuss them all at once, which would be desirable in view of their interrelatedness. Since one belief is foundational to all the rest, one could build a strong case for discussing that belief first. That is the approach in this volume.

Beginning, Center, and End

John, in the Apocalypse, spoke of Jesus Christ as the "Alpha and the Omega" (Rev. 1:8; 21:6; 22:13) the "first and the last" (Rev. 1:17). By the time John wrote the Apocalypse, the Christians had recognized the uniqueness of Jesus Christ and believed that the understanding of God was determined by him.

In the words of Emil Brunner, the "Christian Faith is simply faith in Jesus Christ. Therefore the whole of Christian theology is simply the explication of faith in Christ."[2]

Otto Weber also understood Jesus Christ as the beginning and foundation of Christian faith. He wrote, "Christology is nothing other than theological thought about the encounter with Jesus Christ which establishes and supports our faith."[3]

Christian faith began with Jesus Christ. The beliefs of Christians are all founded on Jesus Christ and related to each other in terms of their relationship to him. Christians tend to reject as religious principles those which do not find their origin in Jesus Christ. They certainly reject those which are incompatible with him.

Christian faith also culminates in Jesus Christ. The early Christians cherished a hope that Jesus Christ would return to the earth to bring their salvation to a triumphant conclusion. It seems that they expected that Parousia, or coming of Christ (sometimes called "Second Coming"), during their lifetime (1 Thess. 4:13-18; 2 Thess. 2:1-12). Apart from the time of his coming, Christians throughout the ages have drawn support from the belief that Christ who came to reconcile us to God would come again to bring all things to completion in accordance with God's purpose.

The Christian hope for God's ultimate victory over evil and the complete salvation of those who believe in him are anchored in the expected coming of Christ. The eschatological hope of Israel pointed toward a future event in which God would both judge and vindicate his people, the Day of the Lord. The Christians see all eschatological hope in terms of a fulfillment related to Jesus Christ. We believe that in the resurrection of Jesus Christ from the dead God established a basis for our hope that beyond this life we have an eternal destiny with God (1 Cor. 15:20-28). So, Jesus Christ is the goal—the future of Christian faith.

Paul, whose writings are the earliest Christian literary compositions to come down to us, believed that Jesus Christ was not only the center of Christian faith but also the center of history. Paul's theological beliefs began in the idea that God was the Creator who had not only brought all things into existence but also guides them toward their ultimate goal. As such, God is an invisible participant in history.

In response to the shattering event of Jesus Christ, Paul saw history as a continuum in which Jesus Christ stood at the center, giving understanding to all that had preceded and all that was yet to come. Paul wrote to the new converts in the Roman province of Galatia, "But when the time had fully come, God sent forth his Son, born of woman, born under the law, to redeem those who were under the law, so that we might receive adoption as sons" (Gal. 4:4-5).

From almost any perspective, historical or theological, Jesus Christ is the center of the Christian faith. John Hick, who argues for a revolution in Christian thinking so that Christians will cease placing their own religion in the center of their thought and will place God at the center, stresses that, "The centre of Christianity is also its starting-point—Jesus of Nazareth." He wrote that this is true "both of Christianity as a whole, . . ." and also for "the Christian faith of any individual in any age."[4]

Jesus of Nazareth was a Jew in nationality, culture, and religion. His first disciples were also Jewish and seemingly thought of themselves as being faithful to the faith of their fathers. The early Christian congregations were at home in the synagogues and in the Temple for a decade or two. By the middle of the first century of the Christian era, however, the Christian faith was distinct from Judaism in its beliefs about God. The difference was Jesus Christ.

The centrality of Jesus Christ means more, however, than that he is the center of history. Christian belief in Christ means that we understand him to be the fullest revelation of God in history. In him we know God; apart from him we cannot speak meaningfully of God. The subject of Christology is central in our doctrine of God as well as in our understanding of history. D. M. Baillie, in his superb volume entitled *God Was in Christ,* convincingly argued that Jesus Christ, as the midpoint of history, gives meaning both to the beginning and the end of history.[5]

This belief in Jesus Christ requires a radical rearrangement of theological beliefs around the new center or on the new foundation. So Christian theology is quite different from general discussions about God and from other specific doctrines of God. Christian theology is determined by this belief in Christ. In other words, while there is continuity between the Israelite view of God and the Christian view of God, there is also discontinuity. There is only one God; but since Jesus Christ is the Son of God revealing God most fully, it follows that the

"Christian" doctrine of God is not identical to the Hebrew view. In fact, it is quite different.

Encounter and Confession

About halfway through the ministry of Jesus and in the district of Caesarea Philippi, Peter made the great confession to Jesus, "You are the Christ, the Son of the living God" (Matt. 16:16). There is a sense in which every believer in Christ has a similar encounter with God and makes a similar confession, whether audible or not. Christian faith, in the strict sense of the word, is always encounter and confession.

When Peter expressed this confession, he and the other disciples had already been followers of Jesus for many months. They had heard the teachings and had witnessed the wonders and the healings. One might think that Jesus would have already told them fully who he was, but evidently that was not the case.

Jesus asked them, "Who do men say that the Son of man is?" (v. 13). They responded with various answers: John the Baptist, Elijah, Jeremiah, some other prophet. Jesus put the question in a very personal way: "But who do you say that I am?" (v. 15).

The crucial question throughout the ages remains the one Jesus asked: "But who do you say that I am?" One does not learn the right answer to this question merely from study or reflection. Nor does someone else teach a person the right answer to this question. In fact, this is not the kind of question that calls for an answer; rather, it calls for a confession which is not solely the achievement of the confessor. There was an element of God's involvement in the confession, a revelation.

This is the reason Jesus had not told the disciples clearly who he was and what he was about. Surely the disciples had discussed the basic question when he was not with them. Such questions and discussions constitute a part of the capacity to grasp the meaning at a later time. When Peter confessed his faith in Jesus Christ as Son of God, Jesus congratulated him and said, "For flesh and blood has not revealed this to you, but my Father who is in heaven" (v. 17). Jesus meant that Peter's confession was not a human achievement or a doctrine taught to him by another; rather, it was a confession, a conviction of faith, born partly of his own reflection on events and their meanings but aided by a mysterious or spiritual power. God, himself, had been at work in Simon Peter's struggle. A confession includes a work of God as well as a free response of the human confessor.

This kind of confession grows out of an encounter with God. It is more than a religious conclusion or conviction. It is a personal, deeply personal, conviction that involves more than mere intellectual assent; it involves the whole of the individual believer's life. An encounter with God may be compared to a meeting with a human person. Do we not perceive and respond with feelings as well as thoughts? Personal acquaintance is more than an intellectual encounter despite the importance of the rational element. In theology, we speak of this encounter with God as an existential encounter.

Existential thought came to the fore in modern times through the writings of Sören Kierkegaard who lived and wrote in the first half of the nineteenth century. Kierkegaard, however, actually learned his "existentialist" perceptions from the New Testament. Rudolf Bultmann, utilizing the philosophical terminology of Martin Heidegger, popularized existentialist theology in modern times. Paul Tillich, with a new ontology of his own, developed a kind of existentialist theology. John Macquarrie produced the most complete and readable existentialist theology in his volume, *Principles of Christian Theology*.[6]

The existentialists see human existence (*Existenz*) as the area of reality in which we know. Reason is but one part of our ability to perceive. Some of our knowledge, and perhaps the most important part, is nonrational. We know anxiety, love, faith, hope in our existence. They are as real and as important as our ability to reason. Truth in some areas may be nonrational. Existentialist thought tends to reduce one's dependence on the historical and the rational. While there are dangers in such an approach, there are also helpful insights.

An existential encounter is personal, individual, subjective, and involves one's total existence. Involvement and commitment are characteristics of such an encounter. One could reach a historical conclusion about the deity of Jesus Christ and yet remain unchanged. One could presumably learn such a belief from someone else and repeat it in the sense of accepting it without question, but that is quite different from the kind of confession that Simon Peter made. Peter's entire existence was changed by his faith.

Christians believe that we hear a word from God when we hear the gospel of Jesus Christ and are guided by the mysterious inward presence of the Holy Spirit. The conviction or belief voiced in our confession is not our conclusion—not something we investigated, learned, or proved; rather, we understand it as an encounter with God. Our confession is our response assisted by his illumination.

Each individual, regardless of his or her previous religious instruction or lack of it, comes to a point of affirmation in which he or she confesses this faith. This is credible because we believe that God as Holy Spirit continues with us, that he loves us and desires that we know him in this encounter. On this basis, Christians believe that when the good news is shared with others they may hear a word from God and respond in confession. The hearers have an encounter with God themselves.

Christian faith always returns to this foundational encounter with God by faith in Jesus Christ. We can discuss the faith historically and theologically, but we always acknowledge the mystical encounter with God.

Therefore, since Jesus Christ is the Alpha and the Omega, the beginning and the end—and the center and foundation, we test all doctrines by their faithfulness to Jesus Christ.

The Primary Sources

The primary written sources for information about Jesus of Nazareth are the writings of the New Testament. Matthew, Mark, and Luke provide most of the historical information. The Fourth Gospel, while certainly containing much historical information, is intentionally theological. There are, of course, historical details about Jesus found in the other writings of the New Testament; but these other writings appear to assume a knowledge of the information found in the Gospels, and these references add no new factual information.

While there are early nonbiblical references to Jesus, these do not contribute any additional historical information to that which we already had in the Gospels. The Jewish historian, Josephus, included a vague reference to Christ.[7] Tacitus (AD 60-120) in the *Annals* mentioned the fire in Rome which Nero blamed on the Christians.[8] Suetonius (AD 75-160) repeated the same information in his *The Twelve Caesars.*[9] Pliny (the Younger) (ca. AD 62-113), while writing about the interrogation of Christians in Bithynia (ca. AD 112), gave information about the early Christians; but he did not include any historical information about Jesus which we did not already have.[10]

The New Testament documents are historical documents; they convey genuinely historical information. At the same time, they are theological documents; they convey the convictions of faith written by believers. The Gospels, as they have come to us in literary form, were written three or four decades after the death of Jesus. The primary witnesses remembered the information about Jesus; they circulated it orally and perhaps in some written forms that have not come to us except as they are incorporated in the Gospels.

Apart from our views of inspiration of Scripture, we have strong reasons for believing in the accuracy of the records. Witnesses still living when the writings were first circulated would have remembered. We have many witnesses and from different perspectives. We do need to note, however, that much of the information is not the kind of data that can be verified historically; there is a large element of theological interpretation in the documents.

Since this proclamation about Jesus Christ is "the power of God for salvation" (Rom. 1:16) as Paul wrote, then its oral form is no less the gospel than its written form. In fact, when Paul wrote Romans, he spoke of a gospel transmitted orally; the Gospels as we know them had not been written.

The written record is of paramount importance to us. We need to correct our religious traditions with the Scriptures. The primary witnesses, the apostles, are our primary sources whether they come to us in written documents or in the spoken traditions of the community of faith.

The Historical Jesus

During the last few decades it has been rather commonplace for theologians to make a distinction between the "Historical Jesus" and the "Christ of faith." This new division appears to have run its course and a new unity may be emerging, but let us look at the terms.

Sören Kierkegaard preceded Rudolf Bultmann by a century and argued that Christian faith is not dependent on the historical Jesus but rather on faith in Christ. Bultmann consistently maintained that we not only cannot know the real historical truth about Jesus but that it really doesn't matter. Our faith is grounded in the post-Easter faith of the disciples that Jesus was alive and with them.

The "Historical Jesus," or the "Jesus of History," has become a rather technical term identifying the Jesus who can be known by modern historical research. It has nothing to do with the question of whether Jesus lived; no serious scholar doubts that the man Jesus lived. The distinction really goes back to the old "Quest of the Historical Jesus."

During the eighteenth and nineteenth centuries, scholars utilized their newly forged tools of "scientific" historical research to investigate the life of Jesus. They wanted to know

Jesus as he actually was in history. They wrote numerous biographies or "Lives of Jesus."

Albert Schweitzer summarized and evaluated these "Lives of Jesus" in his classic volume known in English as *The Quest of the Historical Jesus.*[11] Schweitzer concluded that the "quest" was futile; it failed because the documents of the New Testament were primarily theological documents, and historical method does not deal with the belief that Jesus Christ was the Son of God. Strangely, Schweitzer concluded his volume with a brief statement that sounds like his own "Life of Jesus."

The old quest was conducted by scholars who, under the influence of a developing scientific methodology and also a scientific understanding of nature, came to regard history as a closed system similar to the current view of nature. In fact, they seemed to think nature and history were the whole of reality.

Schweitzer established that the "Lives of Jesus" were more nearly autobiographies of their authors than biographies of Jesus. Schweitzer's volume of biographies included those "Lives of Christ," beginning with the one by Reimarus and ending with the one by Wrede as indicated by the German title of the "Quest," *Vom Reimarus zu Wrede.*

In 1896, Martin Kähler published *The So-Called Historical Jesus and the Historic, Biblical Christ.*[12] Kähler thought the sources were not suitable for the kind of historical research being attempted. He objected to the attempts to psychoanalyze Jesus and thought that we have adequate grounds for believing in Jesus for the forgiveness of sin.

In the mid-fifties, former students of Rudolf Bultmann opened again the quest for the "Historical Jesus." James M. Robinson summarized this new quest in a volume entitled *The New Quest of the Historical Jesus.*[13]

The issue at stake in the "quest" is whether modern historians can produce a scientific biography of Jesus with their method and the New Testament sources. We have learned that faith does not depend on historical validation but that the

historical information about Jesus is more important than Bultmann appeared to think. We have learned that our faith does
in fact depend on Jesus Christ but that he is not a different
person from Jesus of Nazareth. We have learned to admit that
we don't have all the historical information about Jesus we
would like to have but that what we have is adequate.

We know when and where Jesus was born; the names of the
other members of Jesus' family; the basic outline of his travels;
the content of his teaching; the charges brought against him at
his trial; the names of those who tried him; about when, where,
and how he was put to death. We also know the names of
many of those who saw him after the resurrection. That is
historical information by any reasonable standard.

Theologians at present appear to have gone beyond the
"old" and "new" quest for a rigid "historical" photograph of
Jesus. The man Jesus, about whom we have a limited but
reliable historical knowledge, is in continuity with the Christ
in whom we recognize the revelation of God. He is at once the
historical figure who walked the trails of Galilee, Perea, and
Judea and the Son of God who cannot be known by historical
research but can be known in the encounter of faith. Our faith
is identical to that of the first disciples.

At the heart of Bultmann's distinction was his sharp contrast
between *Historie* and *Geschichte.* These two German words are
hard to translate into English. Bultmann insisted that *Historie*
designates the kind of history that actually happens ("happenedness" is the point), and *Geschichte* is the kind of history
that continues to have an impact on later persons and events.
An event of *Historie* would be historical; a *Geschichtlich* event
would be historic. Some events would be both, like the signing
of the Declaration of Independence. So the event of Jesus
Christ would be both historical and historic.

Cross and Resurrection

The crucifixion and resurrection of Jesus Christ have always
stood at the center of the Christian message. In the middle of

the sixth decade of the first Christian century, Paul summarized the gospel which he had preached:

> For I delivered to you as of first importance what I also
> received, that Christ died for our sins in accordance with the
> scriptures, that he was buried, that he was raised on the third
> day in accordance with the scriptures, and that he appeared (1
> Cor. 15:3-5).

Theologians have traditionally distinguished between the
person of Christ (Christology) and the work of Christ (atonement). The distinction is helpful for discussion, but the person
and work of Christ constitute an inseparable unity. We know
him through his work of salvation; his saving event reveals to
us who he really is. In a sense, the cross and resurrection are
inseparable.

The cross and resurrection are the two most important
events in the gospel, if indeed we make any comparison. There
can be no doubt but that the cross and resurrection set Jesus'
life in a new perspective. If the cross had been the end, we
would have to regard him as an idealist who failed and suffered
the injustice of crucifixion at the hands of an occupying power
prompted by angry and threatened religionists, agitated by an
unthinking mob, and permitted by weaklings in political office.
The resurrection, however, transformed his death into victory.

The witnesses to the resurrection were surprised when they
heard it had happened. They had been defeated; their leader
was dead. The resurrection of Jesus, however, was the light of
a new age. To them, it vindicated their faith that he was indeed
the Son of God. They went forth to share that good news with
the world. They believed that in his death and resurrection
they had been reconciled to God, forgiven of their sin, and
restored to their original destiny.

It is obvious that they did not understand clearly what had
happened in their midst and within them. The cross was a
strange kind of victory. It seemed strange that God would win
his victory by the death of his own Son rather than by destroy-

ing his enemies. The disciples would have fought for Jesus on the night of his trial; one had drawn a sword and tried to fight. Jesus had forbidden him to do so. Peter stated the amazing interpretation in his sermon following Pentecost.

Peter told the "Men of Israel" that Jesus of Nazareth "a man attested to you by God with mighty works, and wonders and signs which God did through him" in their midst was actually "delivered up according to the definite plan and foreknowledge of God," but they had "crucified and killed" him by the "hands of lawless men. But God raised him up." Peter concluded his sermon by offering forgiveness of sins and the Holy Spirit to the perpetrators of the crime, "in the name of Jesus Christ" (Acts 2:22-38).

It is distinctively "Christian" that God forgives the sinners through the death of Jesus Christ on their behalf. It is also distinctively "Christian" that God is this kind of God. It is through Jesus Christ that we know the God of love who loves us because of who he is and not because of who we are or what we may become.

Jesus Christ the Image of God

The Commandments begin, "I am the Lord your God, . . . You shall not make yourself a graven image, or any likeness of anything that is in heaven above, or that is in the earth beneath, . . . you shall not bow down to them or serve them" (Ex. 20:2-5.). Idolatry was a constant threat to Israel's faith, and this Commandment did not remove the threat.

In the New Testament, Jesus Christ is the image of God. Christians believe that God disclosed a clear portrait of himself in Jesus Christ who "is the image of the invisible God, the first-born of all creation" (Col. 1:15).

This means that the eternal God is like Jesus Christ. The word is *eikōn* (image). In the passage cited, the author was dealing with a form of angel worship or veneration which, at least for them, was threatening to replace the Christian worship of God through Christ. The author insisted that Christ was the agent of creation through whom these angelic beings or principalities had come into being if they really existed. Christ was the "fulness of God" in human form (Col. 1:19). Again the paragraph closed with the affirmation that reconciliation happened through Jesus' death on the cross. This is what God is like.

The glory of God is seen in Jesus Christ. The idea of glory is often associated with the image of God and with the holiness of God. Glory suggests the radiance or the majesty of God. Sometimes it is the holiness of God reflected back to God by faithful and obedient creatures.

Paul wrote about those who would not believe,

> In their case the god of this world has blinded the minds of the unbelievers, to keep them from seeing the light of the gospel of the glory of Christ, who is the likeness of God. For it is the God who said, 'Let light shine out of darkness,' who has shone in our hearts to give the light of the knowledge of the glory of God in the face of Christ (2 Cor. 4:4,6).

The word is *eikōn* and again stresses that Jesus Christ is the image of God. The Christian faith responds to the question, What is God like? by saying, "Look at Jesus Christ; God is like him."

The author of the Letter to the Hebrews also noted that Jesus Christ the Son "reflects the glory of God and bears the very stamp of his nature, upholding the universe by his word of power" (Heb. 1:3).

Jesus Christ is the revealer of God. Numerous passages speak to this theme, but none is clearer than Paul's statement "In Christ God was reconciling the world to himself" (2 Cor. 5:19). God is like Jesus Christ. He comes to reconcile us to himself.

Jesus Christ is the Word of God incarnate. The best-known statement of all is in the prologue to the Fourth Gospel: "In the beginning was the Word, and the Word was with God. And the Word became flesh and dwelt among us, full of grace and truth; we have beheld his glory, glory as of the only Son from the Father" (John 1:1,14). The author of Hebrews, however, spoke in the same vein without using the term *logos* which John used. He wrote,

> In many and various ways God spoke of old to our fathers by the prophets; but in these last days he has spoken to us by a Son, whom he appointed the heir of all things, through whom also he created the world. He reflects the glory of God and bears the very stamp of his nature, upholding the universe by his word of power (Heb. 1:1-3).

Biblical faith depends heavily upon the term "Word of God." The writer of Genesis understood and stated that God created the world by his word. "God said, let there be. . . . ," and it was so. The Hebrews thought of the spoken word as being a kind of extension of the person who said it as we might say today, "his word is his bond," or "his word is good enough for me." We mean that a person's statement is as reliable as the person because of the character of the person. The prophets of the Old Testament saw God's word as an abiding and powerful reality.

Isaiah spoke of God's word in this manner: "so shall my word be that goes forth from my mouth;/it shall not return to me empty,/but it shall accomplish that which I purpose,/and prosper in the thing for which I sent it" (Isa. 55:11). God's word is as real as God; he stands behind it; it is powerful and abiding. God's promises and covenants are given in his words. They are dependable because God is faithful.

In this tradition, Jesus was seen as the Word of God in the flesh. God had spoken before to his people; but in Jesus Christ, he has spoken his fullest and clearest word. What is God's message to the world? Jesus Christ is his Word. God not only spoke the world into existence but also speaks to his creation. Jesus Christ is his message.

The Humanity of Christ

The belief in the deity of Christ prompted the early Christians to raise the question of his humanity. Obviously, they faced a world with a message that immediately evoked such a question.

The writers of the New Testament books did not discuss the question of how Jesus could be both human and divine; rather, they spoke quite naturally of his fully human life and also spoke of his deity.

Mark, for instance, spoke quite naturally of Jesus' anger when the people criticized him for healing the man with the withered hand (3:5). Jesus responded with amazement and surprise (6:6); he displayed human emotion at the sight of the throng (6:34). He was disappointed in his disciples (8:17; 9:19); he became indignant when they forbade little children to come to him (10:14). Jesus was tempted to sin as are other human beings; he "was in the wilderness forty days, tempted by Satan" (1:13). Near the end of his narrative, Mark wrote the brief report of Jesus' death, "And Jesus uttered a loud cry, and breathed his last" (15:37). These genuinely human characteristics, particularly temptation and death, leave no doubt but that Mark regarded Jesus as a fully human person.

Luke and Matthew repeated the same, or similar, details about Jesus' humanity and included some additional themes. They both included long accounts of the temptation and death. Luke commented on Jesus' growth in childhood or adolescence, and noted that "Jesus increased in wisdom and in stature, and in favor with God and men" (Luke 2:52).

Luke and Matthew included lengthy narratives about the virginal conception of Jesus. There can be no doubt about the intent of both Matthew and Luke in reporting that Jesus was born of Mary without impregnation by a human father.

The obvious problems related to the idea of a virginal conception have led to various attempts to get around such a belief. The text has been repeatedly subjected to intense criti-

cal study, but there is no documentary evidence strong enough
to reject the text or modify it. Matthew and Luke had sources
of information that convinced them the narrative should be
included. Since the other New Testament writers did not mention the virginal conception, some interpreters have concluded
that Matthew and Luke were in error or else included reports
from their sources whether they believed them or not. Luke
was a physician and would likely have had as many problems
with the idea of a virginal conception as any would have had.
Other interpreters have tried to prove the credibility of a virginal conception by arguing that such things have actually
happened in very rare cases. That interpretation certainly is not
what Matthew and Luke are talking about. Jesus certainly was
not a freak of nature.

The opponents of the early Christians circulated a story that
Jesus was the son of Mary by a Roman soldier, but these
reports are not related to any primary sources and are obviously the kind of reports which originate in heated controversy.[14]

The fact that Paul did not mention the virginal conception
has received more attention than other objections. Did Paul not
know about this report? Or, knowing it, did he disregard it as
untrue? Or did he believe it but found it unimportant for the
case he made about Jesus? Paul wrote before the Gospels were
written in the form that they have come to us. Is it possible that
belief in the virginal conception of Jesus had not received
widespread acceptance by the time Paul wrote?

By any standard of evaluation, the virginal conception of
Jesus must be regarded as a miraculous event or one that never
happened at all. If it were a miraculous event, then no explanation can be made. Attempts to do so lead to absurd conclusions.
For instance, if we argued literally that the Holy Spirit had
sexual intercourse with Mary to produce the pregnancy, then
Jesus would literally have been half God and half human—a
heresy in terms of the church's interpretation and a being
neither fully human nor divine.

The importance of the virginal conception is seen in the fact that it was included in the early creeds of the church. It was, however, as much to speak of the humanity of Jesus—born of Mary, as of his deity. During the Liberal-Fundamentalist controversy, it was the final test for believing in the deity of Christ. Fundamentalists regarded any statement about the deity of Christ to be useless unless a person believed literally in the virgin birth of Jesus.

The virginal conception of Jesus is an element of faith; it comes to us in the primary sources; it was included in the early creeds; it has continued as an emphasis in the confession of the church. It is a doctrine that can neither be proved nor disproved. Historical research cannot deal with unique events, and this is certainly a unique event,[15] if it is an event at all; and Mary would be the only primary witness who could speak on the subject.

The doctrine of the virginal conception does not guarantee either the humanity or deity of Jesus. It does speak for Jesus' uniqueness. Opponents of the doctrine sometimes show that it has fostered an ascetic attitude with a negative valuation of human sexuality, and it has also encouraged an erroneous view of sin as something which can be biologically transmitted from one generation to the next. Emil Brunner saw the doctrine as an encouragement to Mariolatry,[16] but whether his observation is true or false is irrelevant; one does not judge the truthfulness or falsity of a statement by later uses or misuses of it.

The earliest Christian proclamation which has come down to us simply presented Jesus as a fully human being, "a man attested to you by God with mighty works" (Acts 2:22). While Paul did not write on the subject of Jesus' humanity, he referred to Jesus' Davidic descent "according to the flesh" (Rom. 1:3); Jesus was "born of woman" (Gal. 4:4); and Jesus was "in the likeness of sinful flesh" (Rom. 8:3).

The Deity of Christ

Along with their statements about Jesus' humanity, the Gospel writers spoke of Jesus as "Son of God" (Mark 1:1;[17] 3:11;

5:7). Mark reported that the Roman soldier at the crucifixion used the term "Son of God" in speaking about Jesus (15:37).

We have previously noted statements about Jesus Christ being the very image of God. They called him "Lord," using a term which usually designated God. They called him "King," "Master," the "Holy One," the "Savior," and the "Alpha and Omega."

Jesus Christ was seen as coming with "the fulness of God" in his person (Col. 1:19). The great hymn in Philippians voices the Christian understanding that Jesus Christ was in the very "form of God," but he came "in the likeness of men" and was obedient even to "death on a cross." But God raised him from the dead and exalted him to heaven, and people worship him as "Lord" (2:5-11).

The deity of Christ is a religious belief; it is related to historical events and witnesses, but it cannot be proved or disproved. It should be noted that a person is not related to God by believing *that* there is a God, and one is not a Christian by believing *that* Jesus Christ is divine. Rather, one becomes a Christian by believing *in* Jesus Christ—trusting one's life to Christ.

Historical Interpretations of Christology

Jesus and the first disciples were Jewish; they believed that God is one. Monotheism was the distinctive contribution of Judaism to world religions. When the first Christians called Jesus the Lord, they apparently did not think of God in terms of plurality. The Spirit of God, for some reason, did not present any challenge to the unity of God. To speak of Jesus Christ as Son of God did.

When the early Christians proclaimed their faith in Christ as Lord, they were asked, and began to ask themselves, What does this mean for the unity of God? Numerous answers were proposed during the first few centuries.[18] Most statements since that period have repeated those early views.

Docetism was an early interpretation which sought to exalt the deity of Christ by stating that he was not really a human being but only "seemed" (from *dokeō,* to seem) to be. Jesus, according to this view, would have been God or a ghostlike being, appearing to be human. If he were God, then he could not have suffered. This view was encouraged by an emerging form of gnosticism and was viewed as heretical by the church. While it sought to do justice to Christ's deity, it destroyed his humanity. The church could not accept this view.

Monarchianism was a Christological approach which sought to preserve the unity of God and maintain a place for Jesus Christ in terms of adoption or modalism.

Dynamic Monarchianism, or the Adoptionists, held that Jesus became the Son of God by adoption, not by birth. At some point, perhaps at the baptism or resurrection, God adopted Jesus as Son. Prior to that time, Jesus would have been merely a man. This interpretation, therefore, preserved a version of both humanity and deity, but the Christians could not reconcile this view with the New Testament witness.

The Modalists held that Christ was but a temporary manifestation (mode of existence) of God's appearance. Sabellius (in Rome, AD 215) was the famous advocate of this view, and the heresy often bears his name, "Sabellianism." The view holds that God has appeared in a sequence, Father, Son, and Holy Spirit. God's modal, or successive, appearances would thereby remove the humanity of Jesus. What would Jesus' prayers be? Soliloquies? If God controls the universe and answers prayers, who was in charge while God was on earth as Jesus Christ?

Arianism preserved the unity of God by teaching that Christ was not eternal but created. Arius advanced his views about AD 320. He evidently taught that Christ was a divine being but reserved eternity for God only. He was condemned as a heretic because he taught about Jesus Christ, "there was [a time] when he was not." In other words, Christ would have been a being in between God and humanity and perhaps neither fully God nor fully man, despite Arius' protests to the contrary.

Apollinarianism was named for Apollinarius, bishop of Laodicea until about AD 390. The church had seemingly settled on
the true deity and true humanity of Jesus Christ by the end of
the Arian controversy. Now the discussion focused on the
manner in which the deity and humanity were related, the
question of his "two natures." Apollinarius taught that in Jesus
Christ the human soul was replaced by the divine *logos*. What
kind of man would Jesus be if he did not have a human soul?[19]
Would this Christ be either human or divine? Apollinarius
later modified his position to say that Jesus was human in both
body and soul, but the reasoning spirit within him was replaced by the divine *logos*. The church could not accept this
view because of its implications for the humanity of Jesus
Christ.

In the first half of the fifth century, Christological discussion
focused on the two natures—the human and the divine—and
how they could be related in Christ. Nestorianism, named for
Nestorius, bishop of Constantinople (AD 428-431) and Euty-
chianism, from Eutyches, appeared as interpretations of the
two natures. Nestorius preferred to call Mary the "Mother of
Christ" rather than "Mother of God." The word *Theotokos*
meaning "God-bearer" was not quite as shocking as the
English "Mother of God." The Greek word stressed the deity
of the Son rather than the privilege of the mother. Whatever
Nestorius meant, his opponents understood him to say that
Christ born of Mary was not divine as well as human. Nestorius claimed to believe in both natures but was understood to
teach that they remained separate in Christ almost like two
individuals who in a marriage remain individual though "one"
in union. This view was condemned as heretical.

Chalcedonian Christology

The controversies previously discussed culminated in the
Council of Chalcedon in AD 451, the Fourth Ecumenical
Council. Actually, no answers were found for the perplexing
problems raised in the controversies. The council, however,

agreed that Christians believe in both the humanity and deity of Christ. While no explanation can be given that will satisfy reason, the church concluded that our Lord Jesus Christ is

> truly God and truly man, consisting also of a reasonable soul and body; of one substance [*homoousios*] with the Father as regards his Godhead, and at the same time of one substance with us as regards his manhood; like us in all respects, apart from sin; ... recognized IN TWO NATURES, WITHOUT CONFUSION, WITHOUT CHANGE, WITHOUT DIVISION, WITHOUT SEPARATION; ... one person and subsistence [*hupostasis*].[20]

The Chalcedonian Definition of AD 451 has been normative for most Christians. Obviously, it does not deal with the question of how Jesus Christ could be both human and divine; rather, it states the faith as a confession of paradox.

Paradox and Incarnation

The term *paradox* designates a statement that appears to be contradictory in terms of common sense but may in fact be true. Donald Baillie entitles his major chapter, "The Paradox of the Incarnation."[21] He recognized the danger of using paradox as a hiding place for ignorance or illogical thought and yet considered this an appropriate category for discussing certain truths. Of course, the statement that Jesus is both human and divine contradicts our normal way of thinking and speaking. Any miraculous event does so.

Baillie cited other paradoxes which we accept as expressions of truth. The doctrine of creation, for instance, speaks of creation out of nothing. This is inconceivable to human reason; human reason cannot conceive of a time when "nothing" existed. Nor does it mean creation to a human being if we presuppose a preexisting reality like matter, and yet we think it true that God created.

We also speak of God's sovereignty and human freedom. These two are paradoxical or are at least in tension. There are polar concepts which may assist us in seeing the truth in paradox. The positive and negative poles of an electrical circuit are opposites; and yet, in their polar relationship, they complement each other and produce a very workable and useful reality.

The paradox of grace[22] consists of the facts that Christians believe any good in them is the gift of God's grace but that any evil in them is their responsibility. It is paradoxical that we hold ourselves responsible for our evil but attribute to God's grace any good within us.

Christians unashamedly confess that they believe in Jesus Christ as Son of God, holding to the belief that he is fully human and fully divine.

Christ as Contemporary

Christian faith rests on the historic event of Jesus Christ. The entire biblical faith is grounded in history. We speak of historical revelation and depend on it. History, however, is not confined to the past.

There is a mystical element in Christian faith even though it would distort Christian faith to change it into a mysticism. After all historical and rational statements are made about the beliefs of Christians, there is the matter of inward awareness of a direct relationship with God through Christ. This direct relationship is usually very private and sacred. Paul spoke of his life as being "in Christ"; that is a mystical statement.

We think of Christ as a historical person who lived almost twenty centuries ago; we also think of him as our contemporary. He said, "I am with you always, to the close of the age" (Matt. 28:20). We believe he is with us. Doctrinally, we usually speak of the presence of the Holy Spirit when we speak of God's contemporary presence. The revelation of God in Jesus Christ, however, has not left us with a modalistic view of God. To be sure, the Holy Spirit is present. God is Father in heaven in every age, and Jesus of long ago is Jesus the Christ today. We, too, are his disciples.

The Finality of Christ

It is not adequate to speak of the uniqueness of Christ. In a sense every person is unique, so I choose to use the expression the "finality of Christ."

The word *finality* appears to have emerged in the encounter of Christianity with other world religions.[23] When the term was used in the World Council of Churches when it met in New Delhi, "The Finality of Jesus Christ in the Age of Universal History," it included two ideas: finality designated the end of a series and a "depth and completeness beyond which one cannot go."[24]

In this discussion, *finality* is used in that sense. It means that Jesus Christ was the climactic event of revelation at the end of a long series of events (Heb. 1:1-2.), and it means that we regard Jesus' revelation of God in history as having reached a depth and completeness beyond which one cannot go.

We have already noted the great Christological passages in which Jesus Christ appears as the fullness of God's disclosure.[25] There is also a New Testament emphasis in the expression "once for all." Christ "died to sin, once for all" (Rom. 6:10). The author of Hebrews noted that the priests made daily sacrifices and the high priest made an annual sacrifice, but Christ "entered once for all into the Holy Place, . . . securing an eternal redemption" (9:12). Christ "did this once for all when he offered up himself" (7:27). Again, "by that will we have been sanctified through the offering of the body of Jesus Christ once for all" (10:10).

Another form of this term "once for all" appears in 1 Peter. "For Christ also died for sins once for all, the righteous for the unrighteous, that he might bring us to God" (3:18).

There are other claims in the New Testament that Jesus Christ is the final revelation of God. Luke wrote, "There is salvation in no one else, for there is no other name under heaven given among men by which we must be saved" (Acts 4:12). Paul wrote, "For no other foundation can any one lay than that which is laid, which is Jesus Christ" (1 Cor. 3:11), and there is only one gospel for salvation (Gal. 1:7). John spoke on numerous occasions of Jesus as the single way to God or disclosure of God. Jesus said, "I am the door" (10:7,9), "I am the good shepherd" (10:11), "I am the way, and the truth, and the life; no one comes to the Father, but by me" (14:6). John also quoted Jesus as claiming "I am the resurrection and the life" (11:25). Perhaps John's strongest statement is "I and the Father are one" (10:30).

The primary witnesses believed that God had done something in Jesus Christ which was "once for all," unrepeatable, adequate, and final. We have noted the basic affirmation of Christian faith, "God was in Christ." This certainly does not say that God is nowhere else, but it certainly does claim that there is a fullness here not known elsewhere.

There is an exclusiveness in this statement of Christian faith. If it degenerates into the statement, "my religion is better than yours," then we have probably denied Christian faith. The exclusiveness is accompanied by an all-inclusiveness. Jesus Christ loved all persons and gave his life for all persons. His followers believe that their mission is to give this message to the world if it involves their giving their own lives.

Such exclusivism would indeed be insufferable if the adherents of the faith saw their relationship with God as a privilege to be enjoyed or their election to imply a rejection of others. They are probably denying that they know the spirit of Jesus Christ. Christian exclusivism is the exclusivism of the all-inclusive death of the righteous for the unrighteous. Jesus' death on the cross means that all salvation comes at the price of the death of the innocent for the guilty. Perhaps if that awareness determined the attitude of believers, persons in other religions would not be so offended. It is certain that the dialogues among those of different theological persuasions would be of a different kind.

Christian theology is grounded on the event of Jesus Christ who is understood as the fullest and final revelation of God in human history. This unrepeatable event happened for the whole world. To be sure, God was known before Christ came. Paul acknowledged a general revelation of God outside the Old and New Covenants (Rom. 1:20 to 2:16). It is up to God to decide about our contemporaries who have not heard of Christ and, in the process, to decide about us who have. It is, however, Christian theology precisely to the degree that Christ determines its content.

Notes

1. John Calvin, "Institutes of the Christian Religion," *The Library of Christian Classics,* 20, 21, ed. John T. McNeill (Philadelphia: The Westminster Press, 1960).

2. Emil Brunner, *The Christian Doctrine of Creation and Redemption, Dogmatics II,* trans. Olive Wyon (Philadelphia: The Westminster Press, 1952), p. 239.

3. Otto Weber, *Foundations of Dogmatics,* 2, trans. Darrell L. Guder (Grand Rapids: William B. Eerdmans Publishing Company, 1983), p. 26.

4. John Hick, *The Center of Christianity* (San Francisco: Harper & Row, Publishers, 1978), p. 15.

5. D. M. Baillie, *God Was in Christ* (New York: Charles Scribner's Sons, 1948), p. 74.

6. John Macquarrie, *Principles of Christian Theology,* 2nd ed. (New York: Charles Scribner's Sons, 1977).

7. Flavius Josephus, *The Life and Works of Flavius Josephus,* trans. William Whiston (Philadelphia: The John C. Winston Company, n.d.), *Antiquities of the Jews,* 18 chapter 3, paragraph 3; 20, chapter 9, paragraph 1.

8. Tacitus, *Annals,* 15, 44.

9. Suetonius, "Claudius," *The Twelve Caesars,* Book 24, chapter 4.

10. Henry Bettenson, *Documents of the Christian Church* (New York and London: Oxford University Press, 1947), pp. 3 *ff.,* gives full information on these sources and the quotes about Jesus.

11. Albert Schweitzer, *The Quest of the Historical Jesus,* trans. W. Montgomery (New York: The Macmillan Company, 1948).

12. Martin Kähler, *The So-Called Historical Jesus and the Historic Biblical Christ* (Philadelphia: Fortress Press, 1964).

13. James M. Robinson, *The New Quest of the Historical Jesus* (Napierville, Ill.: Alec R. Allenson, 1959).

14. For a complete discussion of these narratives about Jesus' being the son of a Roman soldier, see Joseph Klausner, *Jesus of Nazareth,* trans. Herbert Danby (New York: The Macmillan Company, 1925).

15. See Dale Moody, "Virgin Birth," *Interpreters Dictionary of the Bible,* 4, p. 789 (hereafter referred to as IDB) for a detailed study of the biblical materials and alleged parallels.

16. Brunner, p. 355.

17. Some ancient manuscripts omit this phrase and therefore some contemporary versions do not include it. But these manuscripts do use the phrase in Mark 3:11 and 5:7.

18. See Bettenson for listing and summaries on these heresies and the Council of Chalcedon.

19. Note that this view presupposes the Greek understanding that human life is dichotomous, physical body inhabited by a soul which is a separate entity.

20. Bettenson, p. 72-73.

21. Baillie, pp. 106-132.

22. Ibid., p. 114.

23. See Morris Ashcraft, "The Finality of Christ and the World Religions," *Southwestern Journal of Theology,* 21 (1979), pp. 23-40; Paul Tillich, *Systematic Theology,* 1 (Chicago: The University of Chicago Press, 1951), p. 135.

24. Ibid., p. 23.

25. John 1:14; Hebrews 1:1-4; Philippians 2:5-11; 2 Corinthians 5:19.

3

Revelation

A concept is an idea arrived at rationally. A doctrine is a teaching quite often intended for someone else. A belief is a religious conviction and happily admits that it is a response to a perceived action of God and is not merely a creation of human reason.

The doctrine of revelation is sometimes called the Christian epistemology—the theory of knowledge by means of which Christian theology does its reflection. Christians believe that Jesus Christ reveals the true nature of God. The belief is the Christian answer to the question, How does one come to know God?

There are different ways of knowing. In the subject-object relationship, we human beings are the subjects who come to know objects by observing, hearing, touching, or analyzing them. We know persons in a different way. In the subject-subject relationship, we come to know persons by self-disclosure. To be sure, one can learn something *about* another person by observation, but true personal knowledge of another is received as the person chooses to reveal the self.

Friends or spouses after many years of close acquaintance often speak of a startling revelation the other has made which came as a complete surprise. Persons cannot be truly known merely by the subject-object approach. The existentialists have taught us that we know some of life's most valuable realities not by reason but by involvement and personal encounter.

Christian belief in God is based on this personal kind of

knowing. It is our belief that God who is personal has revealed himself to his creatures so that we can both know and worship him. It is our belief that the Holy God cannot be known unless and until he chooses to disclose himself.

The word _revelation_ means "removing the veil" and designates the belief that God has disclosed himself to human beings in the course of history. It implies that the disclosure is of something or someone previously not known, or only partially known, but now more fully disclosed. Revelation often involves the disclosure of what was formerly a mystery. A mystery, however, does not lose its mysteriousness even when revealed;[1] we speak of God as mystery even after he is known in revelation.

In most Protestant theology, there is the belief that with our limited resources and sinfulness we are not able to discover God or know God apart from his self-disclosure.

Theoretically, there could be two ways for knowing God: either we could know God by our effort and achievement through prayer, reflection, reason, or good works or we could know God by receiving and responding to his revelation of himself.

Of the great world faiths, Judaism, Christianity, and Islam were built on beliefs in God's revelation. The other faiths, for the most part, are reflective systems of thought, ethics, and life built primarily on human striving and reflection.

Christian theologians have differed widely concerning the role of human reason in our knowing God. Thomas Aquinas, the great medieval theologian, utilizing the reason of Aristotle, worked out a rational approach to God that stood for centuries as a very persuasive argument. On the other hand, the Reformers in general, and Martin Luther in particular, had a low estimate of human reason in terms of its ability to know God. Luther appeared to belittle philosophy.

In the twentieth-century New Reformation theological revival, the difference is still obvious. Karl Barth, for instance, stressed the "special" revelation of God through his Word.

Barth denied (for decades) any "general" revelation, that is, revelation outside this historical disclosure. Emil Brunner insisted just as strongly on the special historical revelation of God but acknowledged a "general" revelation. Brunner argued that Paul, in Romans (1 and 2), taught such a general revelation. *Revelation and Reason* indicates Brunner's belief that reason has a place but that it is in second place to revelation.

Revelation as God's Self-Disclosure

In recent decades, the discussion about revelation has focused on whether revelation is to be understood as personal or propositional. Does God reveal himself, or does he reveal information about himself? The real issue behind this distinction is the view of Scripture. Those theologians who hold to a view of the inspiration of Scripture as assuring inerrancy or infallibility, even of the autographs, tend to regard Scripture as revelation. They, of course, equate the Bible with revelation; to them, the Bible is revelation. On the other side, theologians understand revelation as God's self-disclosure, with Scripture, the record of revelation, as the primary source of our knowledge of the revelation.

Carl F. H. Henry has insisted on equating the concept of revelation with propositional truth. The Bible is revelation in this sense. One notes in Henry's more recent work a heavy insistence on revelation as God's personal self-disclosure, but he remains very skeptical about theology that refuses to understand revelation as disclosure of propositional truth about God. He continues to insist that revelation includes truth divinely given.[2]

John Baillie, in *The Idea of Revelation in Recent Thought,* pointed out that the "way of defining revelation as communicating a body of knowledge"[3] had endured for a long time without challenge.[4] John Baillie, who regarded the center of revelation as "The Mighty Acts of God" with Jesus Christ being the peak of the mountain range, went on to present revelation as "The Divine Self-Disclosure." The disclosure was from God, from

the divine subject to the human subject; the disclosure was also
"of subject to subject." So revelation is God's self-disclosure
and the content of revelation is God himself rather than some
information "about" God.

. There is rather strong agreement, except for the theologians
in the contemporary "Evangelical" or ultraconservative group,
that revelation is best understood as God's self-disclosure.
That self-revelation is found in the Bible.[5] This revelation is
the "self-disclosure of God" and is God's act in which he
reveals the mystery of himself for our salvation.[6] Dale Moody,
who holds also to a wholesome view of general revelation,
defined special revelation as an event in which "God discloses
himself" to people ready to receive him.[7]

Revelation in Nature

If God is the Creator of the world, it would seem reasonable
for us to expect to find his fingerprints in nature. If God is our
Creator, then there should be some capacity in the human
mind to know God. Since God is the Creator of the world and
our Creator, natural revelation designates the disclosure of
God, or human perception of God, outside of or apart from the
special revelation of God in the historical events recorded in
the Bible. Such a view of revelation means that some persons
can detect the presence of God in nature or can "discover" God
with unaided human reason.

There is a biblical basis for such a view. The psalmist declared, "The heavens are telling the glory of God;/and the
firmament proclaims his handiwork" (Ps. 19:1; also see Ps.
104). Cyrus, who was not among the covenant people, appears
in Isaiah as one with whom God was dealing outside the covenant (44:28; 45:1). The clearest teaching of all is Paul's section
in Romans on the universality of sin and condemnation. He
argued that the Jews were condemned because they had been
unfaithful to the covenant and the Gentiles because they had
worshiped idols instead of the true God. Paul said, "For what
can be known about God is plain to them, because God has

shown it to them. Ever since the creation of the world, his invisible nature, namely, his eternal power and deity, has been clearly perceived in the things that have been made" (Rom. 1:19-20). Paul apparently believed that people outside the covenant should have recognized God in nature or in their reason. If so, he believed in a general revelation or natural revelation but this does not necessarily mean that he thought it was adequate for salvation. Obviously, it was not.

Rather generally, Catholic and Protestant theologians have thought it necessary to acknowledge both a natural and a special or historical revelation. Often the revelation of God in nature, or reason, was prerequisite and preparatory, making it possible for persons to perceive the special revelation when it happened. The rather widespread, if not universal, phenomenon of religion is understood to be an indirect confession that humanity, by nature, recognizes the fact of God. But many authorities would not use the term *general* or *natural* revelation since they understand revelation to mean the act of God which we encounter. *Revelation* is too strong a word to use for the dim awareness "that" God is there somewhere.[8]

Natural revelation raises the question of natural theology. Is it possible to build a theology on the basis of natural reason without the aid of historical revelation? The classical proofs for the existence of God—cosmological, teleological, ontological, moral, and so forth—stand as monuments to that effort. Contemporary philosophers continue to insist that we can speak meaningfully of God on the basis of reason. Christian theology, while based on the special event of Jesus Christ and consequently concerned primarily with special revelation, has no need to fear philosophy. Rather, gratitude requires the Christian theologian to acknowledge a deep indebtedness to the discipline of philosophy.

Revelation Through History

Special revelation designates the belief that God revealed himself in a series of specific historic events which are recorded in the Bible. These events happened at a specific place and time (whether or not we know the exact details) to specific persons. So special revelation is historical revelation.

Biblical faith is inextricably intertwined with history. One cannot understand Hebrew or Christian faith apart from the historical setting of the events. The belief is that God really acted in the Exodus and incarnation and other events.

Revelation as Historical and Biblical

Revelation is historical revelation and has come through the historical events recorded in the Bible. These are the events through which we believe the revelation came. The belief does not necessarily exclude other historical events from revelatory possibilities, nor does it deny the possibility that God may in some way be disclosed in all history. Those questions are for other discussions. The belief before us is that God disclosed himself specifically in these events recorded in the Bible.

Revelation as Personal Encounter

These special events took the form of a personal confrontation: God appeared to human beings. A common factor appeared in these events whether we speak of the call of Moses or Isaiah or the encounter with Jesus by Peter or Paul. If we take the call of Isaiah (6:1-8), for instance, we find an appearance of God to Isaiah in the Temple. Isaiah was overwhelmed by the presence of God; he was aware of his own unworthiness in God's presence; he confessed his sins; he became aware of God's forgiving reconciliation; and he committed himself to the purpose of God made known in the experience.

Revelation Is Reconciliation

In all of these events, God reveals himself to reconcile his people to himself. The reconciliation of the individual always leads to the life of the community of faith to which the recipient of the revelation is related: Moses to the Israelites, Isaiah to Judah, Paul to the Christian community. Revelation is for the purpose of salvation; God apparently never revealed himself merely to answer human questions about himself.

Human history is the medium through which God makes himself known. We see in this historicity a vertical and horizontal dimension.[9] We have no basis for limiting God's activity to these few events recorded in the Bible; nor do we have adequate basis for establishing what God may be doing in certain other events of history. We do have adequate reason, however, for believing that God acted decisively in these historical events. Jesus Christ as the center gives meaning horizontally to the history preceding and following, and vertically to God.

Response to Revelation

The revelation through historical event included human response. The individuals to whom the revelation came trusted God and spoke the Word of God to God's people. The Word of God was not decided by a vote of any people. The hearing in successive generations of Hebrews and Christians clarified, or allowed the Spirit of God to clarify, God's Word in a historical setting. Our indebtedness to these peoples is incalculable. In their historical pilgrimage, they heard the Word of God and struggled to understand and follow. History is the medium through which God has chosen to disclose himself to his people.

The Mighty Acts of God

We have already noted certain specific biblical events and indicated that they were revelatory events: the Exodus from Egypt and Jesus Christ, the incarnation of God. In these events God acted to make himself known. This is the integrating and unifying theme of Scripture: God's revelatory redemptive work within his people. The event of Jesus Christ is regarded as the greatest of all revelatory events, the one which gives meaning and a kind of validation to all of the others.

In the account of the Exodus from Egypt, there are many

exciting narratives of heroes and other events. The story of Joseph, for instance, contains all of the elements of a great saga. But the purpose for the inclusion of these narratives is that they show that God was active in history, guiding the destiny of his people.

Joseph's slavery was a crime committed by jealous older brothers—not a work of God. Joseph's rise to power included considerable administrative ability and possibly some scheming. Joseph's eventual forgiveness of the older brothers was not an act of charity prompted by familial sentimentality; rather, it was prompted by Joseph's awareness that God had a purpose for his family, himself, and the other brothers included. Indeed, they had meant evil for Joseph, but God had a purpose for good (Gen. 50:20).

The Hebrews had no weapons and no military training; the Egyptians had a well-equipped, highly trained army with chariots. The Hebrews escaped. They regarded this as God's deliverance; Pharaoh may not have so regarded it.

Revelation in Jesus Christ

Jesus Christ the Central Event

The central event of biblical revelation is Jesus Christ. When Peter confessed at Caesarea Philippi, "You are the Christ, the Son of the living God" (Matt. 16:16), he had been a part of God's greatest revelatory act. This event is discussed rather fully in the previous chapter. Jesus came to be regarded as the Word of God "[in the] flesh" (John 1:14) in whom "all the fulness of God was pleased to dwell" (Col. 1:19). While we attribute to Jesus Christ a fullness and a finality, we are obliged to acknowledge that his centrality in revelation involves a previous revelation and a following revelation.

Brunner has correctly understood this series of events in which Christ is the central event. While discussing "The Basis of Christian Doctrine: Revelation," he pointed out that the central revelatory event, Jesus Christ, was preceded by Old

Testament revelation of promise and prophetic Word and followed by the revelatory events in the New Testament. This included the record which bore witness, the teaching of the church, the response of faith, and the future hope.[10]

Christian belief is that God disclosed himself in Jesus Christ in a fullness unprecedented and unrepeatable. This is indeed the foundation of Christian faith and theology. In Christ we believe we know God and that God is like Jesus Christ.

The Witnesses and the Interpretation

Revelation is historical, but it is not identical with the historical event. There is another factor. In every revelatory event, we encounter a human response. These human recipients or witnesses were led to hear the Word of God or recognize his revelation in the event. Apparently, not all bystanders saw the revelation of God. Pilate did not; the mob at the crucifixion did not. The apostles did. How did they arrive at or receive this interpretation of the event? Jesus had said to Peter at Caesarea Philippi that God had made it known.

Consequently, a view of inspiration naturally follows the view of revelation. The prophets in the Old Testament and the apostles in the New Testament stood in a special relationship to the revelatory events. They witnessed the event; the Spirit of God led them to see the meaning. So Peter at Pentecost could interpret the crucifixion of Jesus, a crime of men, as a work of God for the salvation of those who would repent and receive forgiveness.

The interpretation, as inspired of God, receives some of its credibility from the community of believers who hear the interpretation. They believed it to be God's act and live their lives accordingly, thereby testing and providing a kind of affirmation for it.

The Hebrews retold the story of the Exodus when their children asked the meaning of religious observances (Deut. 6:20-25). When the Hebrew leaders sought to rally the people,

they reminded them of God's work which delivered them from
Egypt (Judg. 6:13; Josh. 3:5). The Hebrew hymnbook directed
this theme to the memory of the people in song and worship.
God had begun his deliverance at the Exodus (Ps. 66:6). He had
done mighty works in Egypt (Ps. 77:11,15). The prophets called
the people to repentance by citing the Exodus (Amos 2:10;
3:1-2; 9:7). Hosea proclaimed the faithful love of God for Israel
by comparing God's love to that of a husband for his betrothed
(Hos. 2:14; 11:1; 12:9). Jeremiah, in the dark days of decline and
in the shadow of the Babylonian invasion, reminded the Hebrews of God's previous mighty act of deliverance (Jer. 16:14-
15; 23:7-8; 31:31-32; 32:16-25).

In this community of faith, the event which had really happened in the past continued as a motivating factor in the
present. In that sense, it continued to be revelatory; so in a
sense revelation is contemporary.

The event of Jesus Christ occurred in history. Any casual
bystander could have witnessed the crucifixion. But the interpretation that he was the Son of God and that his death has
a bearing on our forgiveness was not obvious to all spectators.
Those interpretations are theological. We believe they are true.
We believe the Spirit of God led the witnesses to perceive this
truth. When the story of the cross is repeated in the life of the
church, the revelatory event becomes contemporary. If the
Spirit of God led the original witnesses to perceive the word
of God in the event, it follows that the same Spirit can lead the
hearers of today to hear this word again.

Revelation and Response

The only worthy human response to revelation is hearing
and trusting. This is due to the sequence of events: God takes
the initiative and acts; human beings respond; God completes
the revelatory encounter. *take step out in faith*

Response by Hearing

The human response of hearing and believing may not be

two separate responses but a single response. We discuss the response in this way for clarity. In biblical faith, "hearing" receives special attention; it is more than receiving and recognizing sounds. It designates "listening" which is hearing with an attentiveness or alertness for more than surface meaning. The Hebrew Shema begins with the words "Hear O Israel." The prophets announced God's condemnation of the people because they would not hear (Jer. 7:13) and called the people to hear God's word (Isa. 1:10; Jer. 2:4; Amos 7:16). Jesus spoke about hearing with responsibility in his repeated charge, "He who has ears to hear, let him hear" (Mark 4:9). The apostle Paul, believing the gospel was the Word of God for salvation, wrote, "So faith comes from what is heard, and what is heard comes by the preaching of Christ" (Rom. 10:17).[11]

Response as Trust

The only worthy human response to revelation is personal trust. If God is addressing us, his word is more than a greeting or the passing of information; it is a command and more because he is God. He addresses men and women not because of his need but theirs. Therefore, we do not respond with questions or opinions; we bow in trust and obedience. Note the response of Isaiah in the Temple, Peter at Caesarea Philippi, Saul on the road to Damascus.

Trust, or faith, has often been compromised into assent. We come to know something about God, then perhaps agree that it is true. But faith goes beyond assent to personal trust or commitment.[12]

This kind of response to God in revelation establishes a relationship, a communion. It is a beginning, and this is why salvation is always a restoration of the lost person to God. This is why salvation is always by faith. What else can a person do but trust God? God reveals himself to his creatures precisely for this reason.

Revelation: Word and Spirit

In our previous speaking of revelation, we have been required to deal with the Word of God in revelation and the presence of the Spirit of God who illumines the witnesses to perceive or hear God's word. This apparent necessity led Hendrikus Berkhof to write of the "Duality of Revelation: Word and Spirit" and the duality and "biunity" of Word and Spirit.[13]

Since God's revelation is personal encounter with other persons, it involves always a communication which the Bible calls "Word." The biblical term *Word of God* is more than a sound; the Word of God carries with it the power and reality of God since God said it. In creation, God said, "Let there be . . . ," and it was so. Isaiah knew the Word of God as a power that would achieve the purpose of God (55:11). Jesus Christ was called the "Word" incarnate (John 1:14).

Human reports of that revelation constitute words of God. This is possible because God's Spirit does not replace our human spirits but illumines us to hear and respond to God.

In terms of revelation, Jesus Christ is always the highest expression of the Word of God; he is the Living Word. The words spoken about him, and written, when guided by the Spirit, are the Word of God. It is appropriate to speak of the Bible as the Word of God because it is about the Word of God Incarnate.

The term *Word of God* is complex. Paul Tillich, for instance, saw six different meanings. It is the principle of God's self-revelation; it was the medium of God's creation; it is the revelation of God in the history of revelation; it is the manifestation of God in Christ; it designates the Bible; and the message of the proclaiming church is the Word.[14]

Revelation and the Bible

The Christian view of revelation recognizes Jesus Christ as the central event of faith and theology. Jesus Christ, as the personal disclosure of God, stands in the position of pulling all other revelatory events into orbit around himself as the center. This means that the Bible is authoritative to Christians because the Bible is the collection of sacred writings which transmits that information about Jesus Christ.

Before the New Testament writings were canonized and included in what we know as the Bible, the Christian Scriptures were the Old Testament. Jesus had held it in high regard and indicated that he did not come to nullify but to fulfill it (Matt. 5:17) and seemingly recognized the role of the Holy Spirit as inspirer in the Old Testament (Matt. 22:43). Paul indicated his conviction that the Old Testament contents were the "oracles of God" (Rom. 3:2).

The most significant, and most often quoted, New Testament passages regarding the inspiration of the Old Testament writings are in 2 Peter and 2 Timothy. "First of all you must understand this, that no prophecy of scripture is a matter of one's own interpretation, because no prophecy ever came by the impulse of man, but men moved by the Holy Spirit spoke from God" (2 Pet. 1:20-21). The other passage reminded Timothy,

> how from childhood you have been acquainted with the sacred writings which are able to instruct you for salvation through faith in Christ Jesus. All scripture is inspired by God and profitable for teaching, for reproof, for correction, and for training in righteousness, that the man of God may be complete, equipped for every good work (2 Tim. 3:15-17).

An interesting passage in 2 Peter indicates a high regard for certain writings of Paul then known to the readers (3:15-16).

While these other statements pertain to the Old Testament Scriptures and since the New Testament had not been formed at the time, they may well express the sentiment Christians would later express toward the New Testament writings.

By AD 49 or 50, Paul had written the letters to Galatia and Thessalonica. His other letters appeared between that date and AD 64. To the best of our knowledge, the Gospels were written between AD 65 and 85. Most, if not all, of the New Testament writings appeared before AD 100 with Revelation dated around AD 95. Some scholars would date two or three of the writings after AD 100.

We know that Paul wrote his letters to the churches in times of need or concern related to a human situation. This would be the human side of that for which inspiration would be the divine. During these decades, the early Christians proclaimed their message on the basis of memory, oral tradition, and perhaps documents which we do not have except as they may be incorporated in the gospels which have come down to us. It needs to be noted that this "good news," which is the power of God for salvation (Rom: 1:16), exercised this saving power when narrated orally as well as when it was later written.

The process by which the New Testament writings were collected and preserved as a body of sacred writings was practically complete by AD 200. At this time, both the Old Testament and the New Testament had achieved essentially their final content. However, the churches had lingering doubts and differences for centuries. The first list of New Testament writings that has come to us just as we have it was in the Easter letter of Athanasius, dated in AD 367. But the process was, for all practical purposes, complete by 200.

This collection, the canon (*canon* means the "rule"), grew by the process we call canonization. The process was informal. There are some indications within the New Testament itself that Paul's letters were passed from one church to another. The recognition of their wider usefulness and the public reading led to a circulation of the writings which formed one step in the process. To the best of our knowledge of the historical process, at least three factors were prominent in the canonization: the writing had to be associated with the name of an apostle, the writing commended itself by its faithfulness to Jesus and his teaching, and the writing was well received when read in public worship.

The apostles, as they were called after Paul's ministry, had been the eyewitnesses of Jesus' life from the time of his baptism and had witnessed his resurrection. The early Christians recognized that their entire faith was determined by Jesus Christ, so the witnesses were very important. While Paul had not been one of those first apostles, he had somehow become included with them.

The churches judged writings on the basis of their "fidelity to Jesus." A writing was accepted as of value if it faithfully represented him. This means, of course, that there was a well-known oral tradition about Jesus that was a basis for evaluating the writings. Numerous writings of the era have come down through history. A cursory reading of many of them will show why they were not included in the canon. They presented an unworthy view of Jesus.

The reading of writings in public worship afforded an excellent opportunity for the inspiration to be recognized, though it had not been planned that way. When members of a congregation heard Paul's Letter to the Romans read in public, they responded with affirmation. They believed it was a word from God that ought to be preserved and shared.

Concentration on the inspiration of the writing at the time of writing has often led to the neglect of the canonization process. Since God inspired the original writers, it seems reasonable to have some appreciation for the possibility that the Holy Spirit may well have played a part in the preservation and selection of the New Testament canon.

Christians mean no disrespect or lack of appreciation for the Hebrew faith and its Scriptures when we state that Jesus Christ is the beginning, the center, and the end of Christian faith. This is the distinctive Christian understanding. The Old Testament itself was accepted as a part of the Christian Bible because it was understood as predicting Christ and providing a preparation for him. There are elements in the Old Testament, ethical teachings and imprecatory psalms, for instance, which have always been a problem for Christians. Paul was apparently the Christian theologian who wrestled with the relationship of

Christ to the Old Testament and presented a rationale that not only permitted acceptance of the Old Testament but also required it.

The understanding of and appreciation for the Christian view of biblical inspiration and authority are possible only if one understands the earthshaking event of Jesus Christ. Christian faith is not a version of "Judaism and Jesus too." Christian faith is deeply indebted to Hebrew faith, but Christian faith is a radical departure from Judaism. Jesus Christ is that point of departure.

Hans von Campenhausen, who has written the superb historical study *The Formation of the Christian Bible,* concluded by saying,

> The Christian Bible—and this is the first and absolutely unshakeable fact that we know—comes into existence from the start as the *book of Christ.* The "scriptures of the Lord" testify to the Lord—the Old Testament prophetically, the New Testament historically. Christ speaks in both Testaments and is their true content. This alone is what makes the Bible the Christian Bible, the book of the Christian Church.[15]

The early Christians had the Old Testament (it was not called that until later) as their Bible. They came to understand it as a prophetic witness to Christ. During the second Christian century, a different problem arose concerning the law. Again, this problem was settled by their Christology; in addition to the prophetic witness, the Christians understood Christ to have come in such a way as to have united the "old" and the "new" era. There was one salvation-history, covering both, and Jesus Christ linked it together. The New Testament did "not emerge as a supplement to or continuation of the Old. Its content is the historical message about Christ, and its purpose is to safeguard the oral tradition of the Church in its original form against the threat of distortion."[16]

When the inspiration of the Bible is focused exclusively on the point of the writing, there is a danger that the emphasis will lead to a neglect of other vital factors. If we speak, rather, of the role of the Holy Spirit in the process, we can see clearly both the human and divine participation. Paul wrote the Corinthians in response to questions they had posed. It was a human response. Both Paul and the Corinthians, however, were following Jesus Christ and seeking to know his way in their lives. The Holy Spirit was the companion of both, and he was the presence of God in the human process of canonization. Can the Spirit not also be the invisible presence when believers later read 1 Corinthians seeking to know his way and will for their lives?

John Calvin, who had perhaps the most rigid view of inspiration among the Reformers, and certainly is quoted most often in support of something like "verbal inspiration," expressed a most wholesome view when he argued that "Scripture must be confirmed by the witness of the Spirit."[17] While discussing the "witness of the Holy Spirit," he argued that "the highest proof of Scripture derives in general from the fact that God in person speaks in it."[18] Again "the testimony of the Spirit is more excellent than all reason."[19]

Calvin stated, at least in these sections, that the view of inspiration includes the present work of the Holy Spirit with the reader or interpreter of Scripture.

The theories of the inspiration of the biblical writings fall into two groups: the subjective and the objective. A subjective theory focuses inspiration on the writer, the subject, who wrote on the basis of his own understanding, in his own language and culture. An objective theory focuses on the writing itself with less emphasis on the writer. The most extreme objective view is the dictation or mechanical theory in which the human author was no more than a scribe. While most persons holding to such a view today object to the terms *dictation* and *mechanical,* this view appeared quite early and found expression in both Augustine and Gregory the Great.[20]

Theories of inspiration of biblical writings tend to focus too narrowly on a single idea to the neglect of the whole process.

A view of the inspiration of Scripture should include several elements. One should recognize the centrality of Jesus Christ in revelation. Due attention should be given to the original witnesses as accurate reporters of what Jesus did and said. The role of the Holy Spirit in the lives of the persons involved in the revelatory events and in their following Christ needs to be heeded. The community which heard, responded, and preserved the Word from God is a part of the process. We must see the relationship of the Holy Spirit to the "hearing" of God's word today when the Scriptures are read.

In 1759, George F. Handel wrote in a period of three weeks what we know as the *Messiah*. He took the words from the Bible and wrote them along with the music symbols on pages of paper. Today we listen to a choir, which has practiced for weeks, sing the *Messiah*. We hear. Would it not be absurd to say, "It's Christmas, I think I'll read the *Messiah?*" It is equally absurd, and ungrateful also, to overlook what happened between Handel's writing and our hearing it. Thousands of music teachers in every generation sat for hours with children drilling into them the relationship of the sounds with the symbols on the pages. Countless millions in a living tradition heard and recalled both the sounds and the meaning of the words and themes and told others the meaning. We "hear" on that basis.

The Spirit inspired the prophets and apostles, who stood as witnesses to the revelatory events, to understand and record God's Word to his people. Between them and us are those throngs who lived on the meaning of this Word from God in the presence of the Spirit. When we read and worship today, we hear God's Word only because others kept alive the understanding of the meaning of the symbols (these cannot be learned completely from the dictionary) on the pages and because the Holy Spirit works with us just as he did with the first witnesses.

The Bible is and will remain the primary source of knowledge for the faith of Christians. As long as it is read under the guidance of the Spirit and in the fellowship of believers, it will be the Word of God to them, a lamp to their feet and a light to their path. Indeed, "All scripture is inspired by God and profitable for teaching, for reproof, for correction, and for training in righteousness" (2 Tim. 3:16) because "men moved by the Holy Spirit spoke from God" (2 Pet. 1:21).

Revelation and Authority

A discussion of authority may appear unnecessary after the previous statements about the Bible, but there are several distinctions which need to be made. Among them are two that are vital: authority in faith and theology is quite different from authority as understood in other settings, and the authority of the Bible is more than a theory of inspiration of the Bible as many appear to think.

The most common debasement of authority results when it is understood in terms of power. Jesus was confronted by disciples arguing over which one of them would be the greatest. His response acknowledged that in governmental hierarchies people exercise lordship and authority, but he drew attention to the Christian standard that service is greater than exercising power over others (Luke 22:24-27). The use of coercive power is alien to the Christian spirit.

In Christian faith and theology, the final authority is God. Since we know God through his revelation in Jesus Christ, Jesus Christ as God's revelation is the authority for our faith and the theological doctrines we develop about that faith.

When Jesus spoke in the synagogue of Capernaum, people were astonished at his teaching and commented that, "he taught them as one who had authority, and not as the scribes" (Mark 1:22). The word for "authority" was *exousia,* and it designated an authority "out of his own being" in contrast to the scribes who had authority only insofar as they quoted others who were recognized as authorities. In the Christian sense, authority is related to the kind of personal truth that evokes trust and belief from the hearers or witnesses. We modern people tend to think of authority as the power or the ability to command, or to coerce if necessary, because we have military, governmental, economic, or other power to enforce our commands.

Authority is personal. A person has knowledge or character which calls forth respect from other persons who listen. If authority were force and not personal, then all actions and decisions would be merely a weaker force yielding to a greater force. Coercion employs force, whether physical, emotional, or social, and can become brainwashing. Authority evokes a willing response from the will of another, willing because the other person is convinced it is of truth.[21]

In Christian faith, authority must be seen in the personal and spiritual sense. Authority derives from Jesus Christ, the revelation of God who has ultimate authority over all.[22]

In the process of canonization, we noted how the apostles also had authority; their authority was related to their eyewitness relationship to Jesus Christ. They could give a faithful witness; therefore, they were respected. This is authority.

The medieval church claimed a supreme authority for itself in matters of religious faith. This claim did not lead the church to reject either the Bible or the Spirit but rather to subordinate them. The Reformers, in seeking to break the authoritarian control of the institutional church over the minds and lives of people, elevated the Bible as the supreme authority. The Reformers were also seeking to correct what they considered another abuse, the excessive appeal to the inner word or spirit with which some persons disregarded the disciplines which usually guided the faith.

The emphasis of *sola Scriptura,* the Scripture alone, was declared in the context of the Roman Church's claim that its councils and creeds had binding authority over believers because of the authority of the Church. *Sola Scriptura* means that in cases when the creeds, councils, or church differ with the clear teachings of Scripture, the Scripture by itself has more authority than all of the others and is to be followed.

Obviously, *sola Scriptura* led to an excessive emphasis on the authority of the Bible at the expense of the church and the Spirit. In some cases, it also led to the rejection of tradition altogether.

In the Fundamentalist controversy of the late nineteenth and early twentieth centuries, this claim of total authority for the Bible took a new form. The Princeton Theology, developed by Archibald Alexander, Charles Hodge, A. H. Hodge, B. B. Warfield, and J. Gresham Machen, focused on three ideas: the biblical writings were verbally inspired; the Bible is inerrant; and the inerrancy applies to the autographs, the original writings of the biblical books. It appears to be significant that this development coincided with the era in which the Roman Church announced its 1870 claim of papal infallibility. The Fundamentalist controversy, and the contemporary version of its continuation, reduced the question of authority to a theory of the inspiration of the Bible. The solution has not been satisfying.

The subject of authority in faith and theology is a matter of encounter with God. We are not speaking of a coercive power even if it be that of evidence over rational objection; rather, we speak of the impact of God's revelation in Jesus Christ to beget faith and obedience. This encounter with God, like encounters with human persons, is complex; it cannot be reduced to a single "cause."

Assume that you and I believe in Jesus Christ and seek to obey him. How did we come to believe in him in the first place? Was it because we had studied the Bible thoroughly and became convinced that it was the Word of God? Was it because we trusted the church so much that we accepted its teachings as authoritative? Was it because of a sense of the Holy Spirit's presence? Was it because of the living witness of other believers? Or was it a combination of these factors?

In Christian faith, Jesus Christ as the revelation of God has authority over all others. The Bible is the trustworthy record about him; we would be impoverished without it. We go to the Bible to learn information about Jesus Christ and his disclosure of God. Christians, however, knew and witnessed about him before they had the New Testament records. That Word had authority before it was written, and the witnesses of that message were the living presence of the church. So there is authority related to the church and the tradition. Then and now, the Word of Christ has authority because the Spirit of God illumines the minds of the hearers and enables them to hear God's Word. The Bible is the Word of God because the Holy Spirit who led in its writing and canonization continues his work in the present with the hearers. Consequently, it seems to follow that the Bible is not alone and should not be considered "the only authority" for Christian faith and thought.

To be sure, it is the primary authority among the sources of information available to us. We have reason to be hesitant about the persons who claim to have the Spirit to support their views unless those views are consistent with the Scripture. We also have reason to distrust the ecclesiastical institution that claims things for itself which are not clearly taught in Scripture. The authority of Scripture, however, is ultimately the authority of Jesus Christ. And back of all other temporal authorities stands the authority of Jesus Christ as God's fullest revelation.[23]

Notes

1. Paul Tillich, *Systematic Theology*, 1 (Chicago: The University of Chicago Press, 1951), p. 108.

2. Carl F. H. Henry, *God, Revelation and Authority*, 2 (Waco: Word Books, 1976), pp. 150, 263.

3. John Baillie, *The Idea of Revelation in Recent Thought* (New York: Columbia University Press, 1956), p. 5.

4. Ibid., pp. 18 *ff.*

5. Gordon Kaufman, *Systematic Theology: A Historicist Perspective* (New York: Charles Scribner's Sons, 1968), p. 15.

6. Otto Weber, *Foundations of Dogmatics*, 1 (Grand Rapids: William B. Eerdmans Publishing Company, 1955), pp. 171 *ff.*

7. Dale Moody, *The Word of Truth* (Grand Rapids: William B. Eerdmans Publishing Company, 1981), p. 38.

8. Hendrikus Berkhof, *Christian Faith: An Introduction to the Study of the Faith,* trans. Sierd Woudstra (Grand Rapids: William B. Eerdmans Publishing Company, 1979), p.75.

9. Weber, 1, p. 177.

10. Emil Brunner, *The Christian Doctrine of God: Dogmatics I,* trans. Olive Wyon (Philadelphia: The Westminster Press, 1950), pp. 14-21.

11. See Gerhard Kittel, ed., "The Hearing of Man," *Theological Dictionary of the New Testament,* 1, trans. Geoffrey W. Bromiley (Grand Rapids: William B. Eerdmans Publishing Company, 1964), pp. 216-220. Hereafter referred to as TDNT.

12. Baillie, p. 85.

13. Berkhof, p. 57.

14. Tillich, pp. 157-159.

15. Hans von Campenhausen, *The Formation of the Christian Bible,* trans. J. A. Baker (Philadelphia: Fortress Press, 1972), pp. 327-328.

16. Ibid., p. 328.

17. John Calvin, "Institutes of the Christian Religion," *The Library of Christian Classics,* 20, trans. Ford L. Battles (Philadelphia: The Westminster Press, 1960), Book I, ch. VII, section 4, p. 78.

18. Ibid., p. 78.

19. Ibid., p. 79.

20. Weber, p. 230. Weber cites Augustine, *The Harmony of the Gospels,* 1, chs. 35, 34 and Gregory, *Migne,* PL, 75, 517.

21. See a splendid collection of essays in Frederick J. Adelmann, S. J., ed., *Authority* (The Hague: Martinus Nijhoff, 1974) on the various aspects of authority.

22. See John Marsh, "Authority," *IDB,* 1, pp. 319 *ff.;* Foerster, "The New Testament Concept *exousia," TDNT,* 2, pp. 566 *ff.*

23. Morris Ashcraft, "The Issue of Biblical Authority," *Faith and Mission,* 1 (Spring 1984), pp. 25-35.

4

The Holy Spirit

In one of the greatest books in modern times on the subject of the Holy Spirit, H. Wheeler Robinson spoke of the Bible as the "book of the Spirit." On the first page of the Bible, "the Spirit of God was moving over the face of the waters" (Gen. 1:2). On the last page of the Bible, "the Spirit and the Bride say, 'Come' " (Rev. 22:17).[1] In between are hundreds of references to the Holy Spirit. In the Bible, the Spirit is the life-giving principle in creation and designates four realities: vitality, fellowship, personality, and service.[2]

The Hebrew word for "spirit" is *ruach* which means breath, air, or wind. As breath, it came to designate the inner life principle. The Greek word which translates it is *pneuma,* which means the same, as does the Latin *spiritus.* The Hebrew and Christian religious experience added deeper meaning to the idea of spirit.

Spirit is not peculiar to biblical faith. In fact, the concept appears to be present in most, if not all, cultures and religions. Primitive peoples of ancient (and modern) times appear to have been aware of a mysterious invisible presence of the divine or supernatural. Often this meant no more than the "great spirit," but unless we have read our views into their beliefs, they believed in the reality of spirits.

A case can be built for a uniqueness in the way the Hebrews spoke of the *ruach* of God. Other nations did not speak of God having a spirit as did the Hebrews. The Israelites apparently believed that God related himself to his creation and people through his Spirit.[3]

To be consistent with our Christological approach in which we maintain that our clearest revelation of God is in Jesus Christ, we must begin our discussion of the Holy Spirit with Jesus Christ. The Holy Spirit is God, and it follows that Jesus Christ will give us our clearest disclosure of his nature and work. We shall look at the Old Testament understanding of the Holy Spirit later.

The advantages of speaking primarily of the Holy Spirit in his relationship to Jesus Christ are that there is definite content in understanding the Spirit, the Spirit can be understood only as personal, Jesus Christ provides the criteria by which we may test the spirits and thereby avoid being deceived, and this will keep us from separating the Spirit from the *logos*.[4]

Holy Spirit as Spirit of Christ

Paul seemed to have regarded the Spirit of God and the Spirit of Christ as the same. He understood the life of faith as being related to the Spirit of God dwelling in us (Rom. 8:9). In the following verse, he stated that we do not belong to God unless the Spirit of Christ is in us. Then he said, "But if Christ is in you, . . ." (Rom. 8:10), evidently meaning that Christ and the Spirit are not different.

John, in the Fourth Gospel, made the closest link between Jesus' earthly life and the coming of the Holy Spirit. He reported that Jesus promised the disciples: "And I will pray the Father, and he will give you another Counselor, to be with you for ever, even the Spirit of truth" (John 14:16). Further, the "Counselor, the Holy Spirit, whom the Father will send in my name, he will teach you all things, and bring to your remembrance all that I have said to you" (v. 26). Jesus continued, "But when the Counselor comes, whom I shall send to you from the Father, even the Spirit of truth, who proceeds from the Father, he will bear witness to me" (John 15:26). "When the Spirit of truth comes, he will guide you into all the truth" (John 16:13).

Jesus had been recognized as Immanuel, God with us; in his going away, he promised that the Holy Spirit would be with the disciples as he had been. The Holy Spirit is God in his immanence. Those who are inclined to believe in God long for his presence. The Holy Spirit is revealed by Christ and is the *presence of God* as an *"immediate* and *active* presence."[5]

Holy Spirit as the presence of God means that God is present with his creatures whether they feel it or not. His presence gives confidence to them as they seek to do his will. The Spirit as Comforter is "called to be with" and is with us, teaches us, convinces, and comforts us. Gordon Kaufman interprets this to mean that he is our friend and companion.[6]

We should not understand Christ's revelation of the Holy Spirit in the modalistic sense that God has appeared in a chronological succession. The Spirit was present and active previously, just as God always has been. Christ, however, revealed God in a special and fuller way; so Christ revealed the Holy Spirit in such a way that we can know him intimately. The Holy Spirit is inseparably related to Jesus Christ.

Belief in the Holy Spirit is not only based on the coming of Jesus Christ but the content of that belief also is determined by Jesus Christ.

Jesus and the Holy Spirit

Both Matthew and Luke related the Holy Spirit to Jesus' birth (Matt. 1:18; Luke 1:35). Mark joined Matthew and Luke in reporting that at the baptism of Jesus, the Holy Spirit came out of heaven and descended upon Jesus in the form of a dove (Mark 1:10; Matt. 3:16; Luke 3:22). Mark reported that the Spirit drove Jesus into the wilderness at the time of the temptation (Mark 1:12), whereas Luke reported that Jesus was "full of the Holy Spirit" and "was led by the Spirit" into the wilderness (4:1).

In the Gospels, Jesus rarely spoke of the Spirit of God, but the Gospel writers reported a vital connection between the Spirit and Jesus' life in the major events of his life. Luke quoted

Jesus as saying that the Father will "give the Holy Spirit to those who ask him" (Luke 11:13), but Matthew promised not the Holy Spirit but good gifts (Matt. 7:11). Jesus' power to cast out demons was seen as the power of the Spirit of God (Matt. 12:28). All three Synoptic Gospels reported that the disciples were promised the assistance of the Spirit in their proclamation (Matt: 10:20; Luke 12:12; and Mark 13:11). The Synoptic writers also reported the teaching concerning the blasphemy against the Holy Spirit (Mark 3:29; Matt. 12:31; Luke 12:10).[7]

The Holy Spirit announced the coming of Jesus, confirmed his Sonship by coming like the dove at the baptism, led him into the wilderness for the temptation, and sustained him. Jesus promised the Spirit to his disciples.

There is a double relation between Christ and the Holy Spirit in the New Testament. In the letters of Paul and in the Fourth Gospel, however, Christ sent the Spirit. Paul spoke of the "Spirit of Christ" or the Spirit of the Son (Rom. 8:2; 2 Cor. 3:17; Gal. 4:6; Phil. 1:19). John clearly reported that Jesus promised to send the Spirit upon the disciples after his departure. These two emphases are complementary rather than contradictory since Jesus Christ is the disclosure of God in history.[8]

Spirit of God in the Old Testament

The Spirit of God was the creative power (Gen. 1:2), perhaps the creative principle of life, which God placed in his creation (Gen. 2:7). Job repeated, "The spirit of God has made me,/and the breath of the Almighty gives me life" (33:4). The prophets spoke by the power of the Spirit (Mic. 2:7). God's Spirit brought power and confidence (Hag. 2:5), and God's Spirit guarantees God's faithfulness (Isa. 59:21).[9] The psalmist could sing, "Cast me not away from thy presence,/and take not thy holy Spirit from me" (51:11).

Speaking of the Spirit of God did not appear to raise the question of plurality. God is one and the Spirit of God is not another.

Holy Spirit in Revelation and Reconciliation

When God reveals himself to his creatures, it is for one purpose only—to reconcile them to himself. Consequently, not only is reconciliation the purpose of revelation but is also the response to and, therefore, the completion of revelation. Therefore, it is necessary to consider the role of the Holy Spirit in revelation and reconciliation. If Jesus Christ is the central revelation of God, then how is the Holy Spirit involved?

The Holy Spirit is the agent of regeneration. Human beings in sin are estranged from God; they do not "hear" his word. The Holy Spirit awakens human beings to their true nature.[10] The image of God in humanity involves *spirituality* and *personality*. The Holy Spirit communicates with our spirits and awakens us to our true personalities. This awakening is spoken of as a new birth or as a new creation.

When Jesus spoke to Nicodemus, he spoke of being born again. Nicodemus was startled by the analogy. Jesus responded that one must be "born of water and the Spirit" if he is ever to enter the "kingdom of God" (John 3:5). The Word of God, or the gospel, is the "power of God" for saving persons (Rom. 1:16). The Holy Spirit is God awakening our spirits to "hear" the Word so we can respond.

Paul did not use the term "new birth" but used the terms "new creation" and "sonship" with the same meaning. "Therefore, if any one is in Christ, he is a new creation" (2 Cor. 5:17), and this new creation is a child of God. He spoke of sinful humanity as dead in sin. "By the Spirit" is how we "put to death the deeds of the body." . . . "For all who are led by the Spirit of God are sons of God. . . ." because they "received the spirit of sonship." Thus "when we cry, 'Abba! Father!' it is the Spirit himself bearing witness with our spirit that we are children of God" (Rom. 8:13-16). The same idea is expressed in Galatians (4:5-6), and the agent is the Spirit of his Son.

The Holy Spirit is God working within us at the point of our entry into the Christian life. The Holy Spirit enables the believer to appropriate the saving work of Christ into his or her own life. There are four stages or aspects of this "unitary experience": conviction of sin, repentance, election, and justification.[11]

Conviction of sin is generally acknowledged to be the work of the Holy Spirit. John wrote about the Counselor's coming, "When he comes, he will convince the world concerning sin and righteousness and judgment: concerning sin, because they do not believe in me" (John 16:8). The conviction of sin is the awareness of sin's presence and seriousness in one's own life. Only the Holy Spirit can awaken me to the depth of my own sinfulness in the context of Christ's love which points my awareness from despair to hope.

Repentance is turning to God from self-centeredness and sin. One cannot be repentant in one's own power. Repentance is a response to God in which the believer receives more than condemnation; the believer receives God's invitation to forgiveness. The awareness of sin is simultaneously the awareness of grace. Regret or "worldly grief" can indeed lead to despair and death, but godly grief evoked by the Holy Spirit "produces a repentance that leads to salvation" (2 Cor. 7:10).

The term *election* was once a beautiful word designating the conviction that God took the initiative in drawing us to himself. Unfortunately, the term fell among prosaic thieves who robbed it and laid it waste. The word designates the activity of God in calling us to himself for forgiveness. Jesus, while speaking of calling his disciples, said, "You did not choose me, but I chose you" (John 15:16). Paul wrote to the Roman Christians that he had been "called to be an apostle," and they, too, had been "called to belong to Jesus Christ" (Rom. 1:1,6). Calling does not suggest coercion or irresistible grace. The word is a precious term; it means that God's Holy Spirit makes conversation with us as we hear the Word of God and calls us to be children of God. The idea in focus is our election—not other's rejection.

The term *justification* designates the transformation in which we are made right with God through faith in Christ. Prior to this event, we were all under condemnation for our sin. God who loved us and sent his Son to reconcile us to himself proclaims us forgiven, acquitted, no longer guilty. The Holy Spirit is the personal agent who brings this inner transformation into reality.

As a part of reconciliation, the Holy Spirit brings *freedom.* We have already noted that forgiveness comes to those who in repentance believe in God. Paul regarded life in sin as a life in bondage; sinners are slaves under the tyranny of sin.

Christ, however, sets us free from this bondage, and the Holy Spirit is involved in our liberation. "There is therefore now no condemnation for those who are in Christ Jesus. For the law of the Spirit of life in Christ Jesus has set me free from the law of sin and death" (Rom. 8:1-2).

The Christian is no longer under the law but has freedom in the Spirit. The believer is no longer subject to unjustified religious requirements but is free to do right according to the Spirit. Paul wrote the Galatians who were about to return to former religious rules, "For freedom Christ has set us free; stand fast therefore, and do not submit again to a yoke of slavery" (Gal. 5:1). He admonished them not to use their "freedom as an opportunity for the flesh" (v. 13) but rather to "walk by the Spirit" (v. 16) because if they were "led by the Spirit" they were not "under the law" (v. 18). The Christian is not antinomian; rather, the Christian lives by the Spirit. Love is the motivation for ethics; the Holy Spirit is the guide and teacher.

The Holy Spirit gives *assurance* that the believer is in the right relationship with God. To be sure, this is an inward or subjective assurance. The "Spirit himself" bears "witness with our spirit that we are children of God" (Rom. 8:16).

The theme of assurance by the Holy Spirit appears also in Ephesians. The gift of the Holy Spirit is like the seal which guarantees a document or contract. It identifies one as belonging and guarantees the fulfillment of promises. The idea is that the Holy Spirit has so imprinted the lives of believers that they are secure. The giving of the Spirit is this "seal" or guarantee (2 Cor. 1:22).

Holy Spirit as Companion in Authentic Human Life

Without careful reflection, many think of Christian faith as something one believes or intellectual concepts which one holds. Then the Holy Spirit is understood as something extra to be experienced by certain types of very religious people. Christian faith, however, is a way of life which involves a basic trust in God through Christ, a commitment. The one who believes in Christ holds to Christian concepts. The Holy Spirit, however, is not some special gift or experience of the few; the Holy Spirit is God's presence in the daily lives of believers. A case can also be made for the belief that the Holy Spirit is not totally absent from the existence of the unbeliever.

God is present as the "Spirit who dwells within." Religious language can often sound strange in today's cultural environment. Many persons have a reluctance to use language related to the Spirit of God. For one thing, they believe others may think they are claiming too much if they talk about God's presence. For another, they have all heard excessive claims about the Spirit and overly emotional reports about the Spirit's workings; but we cannot speak of God at all unless we speak of the Spirit of God. If God revealed his presence in Jesus Christ in order to call his creatures into a continuing relationship with God and other persons, then he maintains his side of that covenant by being present within the lives of persons as the Holy Spirit.

Numerous statements in the New Testament speak of the Spirit as dwelling within the lives of believers. The Spirit within is the same as being "in Christ" or Christ being "within" believers. The most striking example is Paul's question, "Do you not know that your body is a temple of the Holy Spirit within you, which you have from God? You are not your own; you were bought with a price. So glorify God in your body" (1 Cor. 6:19-20). This statement, while it can be misunderstood

and presented in a way that would be showy, is really a re-
markably helpful analogy of the authentic human life. God's
Spirit dwells within us.

Human beings are creatures of God, incomplete apart from
God. Body is not merely the physical body; it is the whole
person. The statement indicates that God's Spirit takes up
residence in the lives of persons who trust God. This Companion does not deprive the person of individual existence or any
of the freedoms or responsibilities which attend human life;
rather, the Holy Spirit brings freedom from the false control-
lers of life so that a person can be genuinely human.

The presence of the Holy Spirit is known as fellowship with
God and leads to community with other persons. Christian life
does not consist entirely of remembering what God has done
in the past; it claims to be an immediate fellowship with God.
Christ has made this possible; the Holy Spirit makes this mystical relationship a reality. The human personality is in communion with God. God's Spirit dwells within us.[12]

Rudolf Bultmann understood Paul's entire theology of
human existence as an explication of the contrast expressed in
the words "life according to the flesh" and "life according to
the Spirit" (Rom. 8:5). Bultmann saw all human life without
faith as inauthentic existence—a subhuman existence. He believed that faith in God restored the dimension lost in sin and
resulted in authentic human existence. Authentic existence is
"life according to the Spirit."[13]

To live "according to the flesh" is to live without faith in
God. This life lacks a vertical dimension regardless of one's
morality. Life "according to the Spirit" is the life of faith—life
with the vertical dimension. This vertical dimension is brought
about by the indwelling Spirit.

The Holy Spirit as presence gives guidance and power to the
believer. The power to achieve certain acts is often spoken of
as resulting from a "filling" by the Spirit (Acts 2:4; 4:8,31; 6:3,5;
7:55; 9:17).

The Holy Spirit endows persons with certain abilities to

serve God and others. These are the "gifts" of the Spirit and should be distinguished from the "gift" which is the Spirit himself. The gifts, *charismata,* are endowments for ministry in the church. Paul spoke of varieties of spiritual gifts (1 Cor. 12:4) and listed among them wisdom, faith, healing, working of miracles, prophecy, distinguishing spirits, tongues, and interpretation of tongues (vv. 9-10).

The Holy Spirit endows life with its genuinely Christian and human endowments. Otto Weber saw these as peace, sonship, and freedom.[14] Peace with God is not "peace of mind"; rather, it is a deep sense of belonging and being rightly related to God and others even in a world without peace. Peace is not limited to life within; it also extends outward to others. Being *children of God* is a term of relationship with God that sets the character of life. Freedom, in the true sense, is the experience of those who have been liberated from false masters by the presence of the Holy Spirit.

The distinctive qualities of the Christian life are the result of the indwelling Spirit and are sometimes spoken of as the "fruit of the Spirit." Paul enumerated, "But the fruit of the Spirit is love, joy, peace, patience, kindness, goodness, faithfulness, gentleness, self-control" (Gal. 5:22-23).

The Holy Spirit and the Church

The Holy Spirit is known in the community of the church as well as individually. It may be that the Holy Spirit is not known even individually except through the life of the church. Traditionally, the church has been understood as the people of God, the body of Christ, and the fellowship of the Holy Spirit.

The term "fellowship of the Spirit" is actually found only twice in the New Testament (2 Cor. 13:14; Phil. 2:1). Numerous other emphases point to this basic characteristic of the church as a community in fellowship with the Spirit, guided and empowered by the Spirit. Every participant in the church entered by the experience of repentance and faith, or new birth, which was prompted by the Spirit. Each believer has received the gift of the Spirit and gifts of the Spirit which are shared in the community. The Spirit gives unity to the church (Eph. 4:4).

The Acts of the Apostles narrates how the Holy Spirit led the early church in its mission. When Jesus was crucified, his followers were limited to the small land in Palestine and to those of Jewish nationality. The Spirit led the church from Jews to Gentiles and from Jerusalem to Rome. The Spirit led the disciples beyond the boundary which existed when Jesus was crucified.

The mission of the church is directly related to the continuing presence and leadership of the Holy Spirit within the church. Failure to recognize this fact, or settling for some view of the Holy Spirit less than that of the New Testament, may well account for the weakness of many churches of the present.

To believe in the presence of the Holy Spirit as daily companion and leader of the community of faith is no different from believing in God. It is not presumptuous if persons realize that God has done the choosing and they have responded. Nor is any charge justifiable if those who believe share with love and without price of any kind their knowledge of the Spirit.

Gordon Kaufman discussed the doctrine of God under three major headings: God the Father, the Lord; God the Son, the Servant; and God the Holy Spirit, the Companion. He concluded his discussion of God the Father by listing four qualities or "perfections" of divine freedom: the unity and simplicity of God; the power of God; the holiness and righteousness of God; and the glory of God. He concluded his discussion of God the Son by listing four "perfections of divine love": the relativity of God as he relates to his creatures; the grace of God; the mercy of God; and the nonresistance of God which means that God does not compel but wins through suffering. He concluded his discussion of the Holy Spirit, "The Presence of God," with four "perfections of the divine communing: faithfulness, responsiveness, understanding, and forgiveness."[15]

God's revelation in Jesus Christ discloses God as living with and within believers as Holy Spirit. The Holy Spirit is God.

Christians are convinced that God is with us today. When asked, "How do you know it is God's Spirit and not some 'other' spirit?" we answer, "Jesus Christ has disclosed God and what he is like. The Holy Spirit is God. The Holy Spirit is like Christ."

Notes

1. H. Wheeler Robinson, *The Christian Experience of the Holy Spirit* (Oxford: James Nisbet and Co., Ltd., 1928), p. 5.

2. Ibid., p. 8.

3. Lloyd Neve, *The Spirit of God in the Old Testament* (Tokyo: Seibunsha, 1972), p. 2.

4. John Macquarrie, *Principles of Christian Theology,* 2nd. ed. (New York: Charles Scribner's Sons, 1977), p. 331.

5. Gustav Aulen, *The Faith of the Christian Church* (Philadelphia: The Muhlenberg Press, 1948), p. 252.

6. Gordon D. Kaufman, *Systematic Theology: A Historicist Perspective* (New York: Charles Scribner's Sons, 1968), p. 228.

7. Henry P. Van Dusen, *Spirit, Son and Father* (New York: Charles Scribner's Sons, 1958), p. 54-55.

8. Hendrikus Berkhof, *The Doctrine of the Holy Spirit* (Richmond: John Knox Press, 1964), p. 17-18.

9. Eduard Schweizer, "Spirit of God," Gerhard Kittel, *Theologisches Worterbuch zum Neuen Testament* (London: Adam & Charles Black, 1960), pp. 1-6.

10. E. F. Scott, *I Believe in the Holy Spirit* (New York and Nashville: Abingdon Press, 1958), p. 62.

11. Hendrikus Berkhof, *Christian Faith: An Introduction to the Study of the Faith,* trans. Sierd Woudstra (Grand Rapids: William B. Eerdmans Publishing Company, 1979), p. 327; see also Berkhof, pp. 68 *ff.*

12. Macquarrie, pp. 328-337.

13. Rudolf Bultmann, *Theology of the New Testament,* trans. Kendrick Grobel (New York: Charles Scribner's Sons, 1955), 2.

14. Otto Weber, *Foundations of Dogmatics,* 2, trans. Darrell L. Guder (Grand Rapids: William B. Eerdmans Publishing Company, 1983), pp. 249-254.

15. Kaufman, p. 235 *ff.*

5

God the Father

When speaking about God's love, grace, mercy, faithfulness, and all of the New Testament terms used to identify God, Otto Weber stated that all of these could be summarized in the single term, *Father*.[1] This was Jesus' favorite designation for God. He did not mean it only to designate his unique relationship to the Father, but he also taught his disciples to think of God in this way and to pray to "our Father who art in heaven."

The term *Father* is an analogy with great meaning and potential for speaking of the nature of God and his relationship to us. There are dangers involved. The first danger is that we may objectify God and reduce him to an idol. The second is that the term may evoke unfavorable responses from those whose human fathers were not loving or that the term will be understood as sexist language. No term would be satisfactory to all. We certainly cannot surrender this beautiful term because of its connotation to those whose human families are less than ideal. Whatever else may be implied, the biblical language, while speaking of God as Father, certainly implies nothing remotely similar to the sexist language and thought of today.

The danger of objectifying God is always a possibility. Ludwig Feuerbach, in his *Essence of Christianity*, argued that Christian faith and theology are merely a projection of human wishing.[2] For Feuerbach, God is but our objectified dream which we have constructed because we need God. There is no proof that he was wrong, but we have a very strong case for believing that he was wrong. Since we have no language but human language

102

with which to speak of God, and because analogy is a very important part of that language, we shall have to make our case in spite of the danger.

God as Father of Our Lord Jesus Christ

Belief in God as Heavenly Father is the first statement about God in Christian theology. This confession declares two basic convictions: what knowledge we have of God has come to us through the incarnation of God in the Son Jesus Christ; God, in his very nature, is revealed in Jesus Christ. There are numerous implications of this statement which are important for our understanding. Our knowledge of God is based on this disclosure.

Jesus Christ is "the image of the invisible God. . . . in him all the fulness of God was pleased to dwell" (Col. 1:15, 19). He is "the likeness of God," and the very glory of God is "in the face of Christ" (2 Cor. 4:4,6). Christ bears "the very stamp of [God's] nature" (Heb. 1:3).

When we confess our faith that Jesus Christ has revealed God to us as "our Heavenly Father," we mean that we know of God now because of Jesus Christ; we would not have known God on the basis of our own searching; and we know God, not merely about God. We also mean by this confession that God is like Jesus Christ. Jesus revealed God's nature as God really is.

If Jesus Christ the Son reveals God most fully, then what is God like? God is like Jesus Christ who is the very portrait of God; God is like the father in the parables of Luke 15; God is personal; God is loving, caring, and responding; God is free; God is *our* father and not just *my* father.

God Is Like Jesus Christ

In Jesus Christ, we see a portrait of God. Since "God was in Christ" and Christ is the "very image" of God, we must take the risk and say, "this is what God is like." God, therefore, is first of all our Heavenly Father who cares for us, loves us, and seeks us to enter a family relationship with him and live therein. In Jesus, we see that picture of infinite love even for the unlovely. We see God as one who grieves over our lostness, one who maintains a constant vigil for our return. We see God who "listens" for and to our prayers because he is our Heavenly Father.

God Is the Lord

We see God not only as Father but also as Lord. The disciples acknowledged the lordship of Christ. They did more than pay him respect; they gave him their allegiance. They called him the Lord. As we shall see later, lordship stresses transcendence. In Christ, God was immanent; he was also transcendent. The term *Father* does not reduce God to the level of the familiar; the closeness of the family tie stands in contrast to the awesome holiness of God in whose presence we bow.

The four parables of Luke 15 portray most vividly that God is Father. When Jesus kept company with tax collectors and sinners, his opponents accused him of receiving these outcasts and eating with them. The accusation was correct in that he did, but it was inaccurate in that they were no longer outcasts when they had eaten with Jesus. Jesus told four parables to illustrate what God is like.

God is like a shepherd who owned a hundred sheep and lost one. He left the ninety-nine, at some risk, and searched diligently for the lost one. When he had found it, he called in his neighbors and rejoiced. God is like this. Shepherds take risks to find a lost sheep; they rejoice when they find it. This is the nature of shepherds; it has nothing to do with the value of the sheep. The risk to the ninety-nine would nullify any concern for the value of one. The shepherd acted the way he did because it was his nature. This is the way God is.

God is like the woman who had ten silver coins and lost one. She searched until she found it and then she rejoiced. The parable teaches the same idea about the Father.

God is like the father who had two sons. They were as

different as could be but God loved them both. The younger one demanded his part of the inheritance before he was entitled to it, squandered it, but returned in desperation motivated by the memory of his father. The father forgave him, reinstated him in the family, endowed him with the symbols of sonship, and gave a feast for rejoicing. God is like that. There was no mention of restitution, probation, or conditions. God was waiting for this occasion.

The parable of the older brother was evidently told for the benefit of religious people who think their negative morality should restrict God's behavior and that God owes them something because of their religious practices. A good case could be built for the business judgment of the older brother; the younger son was a risk. But God is not a business executive; God is Father, and what father, worthy of the title, would not give it all for another chance to see his wayward son become a man?

The four parables tell first of all about the Father; then they tell us something about our lostness. The older brother was also lost. They tell us that when we are lost from God, the first thing to recall is that God our Father is searching.

God Is Personal

The revelation that God is Father means that God is personal. This may seem so obvious that its mention is unnecessary. That is not the case however. Some theologians think it dangerous to speak of God as a person since that would limit God; he would be one of a category called persons. Others think that the term *person* is a purely human term and, if applied to God, would be a crass anthropomorphism. But all terms we use are human terms. We must use them if we are to speak of God at all.

On the basis of the disclosure of God in Jesus Christ, we have no choice but to speak of God as personal. The characteristics of personality are self-consciousness and self-determination. A person is conscious of self as a self; a person has the freedom and ability to determine his or her own direction. To our knowledge, the other creatures do not have these characteristics. Human existence is personal existence. We know of no higher existence among the creatures, so we could not speak of God in less than personal terms. This means that we share with God the characteristics of complex self-experience, self-consciousness, transcendence, freedom in self-determination, awareness, free response, and privacy of consciousness.[3]

Numerous biblical teachings require the belief that God is personal. There is nothing in the Bible suggesting that God is a principle that permeates creation. Pantheism is foreign to the biblical idea of God. Deism, which would allow God to be personal but would remove him from any real connection with reality after creation, has always been unacceptable to most Christians who see God as personal Creator who continues a relationship with his creatures. Every aspect of such a relationship is possible only if God is personal.

The belief that God is known through Jesus Christ as Heavenly Father requires us to think of God in the most personal terms, and on this basis we pray.

God Is Responsive

Since God is Heavenly Father, he listens and responds. We shall note later that for human creatures to be in the image of God means, among other things, that we are capable of hearing God and responding to him. Such response is the highest endowment of personality. Often, seeking to guard the holiness and transcendence of God, we come to think of God as so remote that we cannot reach him. Indeed, we cannot reach him; but he has reached us through Christ. His purpose is to restore us to relationship with himself. This means that God listens and responds.

God is not a static but a dynamic, personal being. He has chosen to enter relationship with us. God is not available—at our disposal. He is God. He calls us. But when he calls us, he bids us call on him and promises to hear us. "Ask, and it will be given you. . . . how much more will your Father who is in heaven give good things to those who ask him!" (Matt. 7:7,11).

Early in our discussion of God it is important to note this characteristic of responsiveness. In the past, theologians spoke of God as immutable, unchangeable; the original idea was God's faithfulness. People change but God who made the covenant does not change. The idea of unchangeability or immutability became rigid, however, and God was seen as static. The belief in God as Father will not permit this notion. God took the initiative in establishing a relationship with his human creatures. In that relationship, he speaks; he also invites his creatures to speak, and he listens. Responsiveness is one of the highest qualities of human existence;[4] this characteristic of personality is even more a part of God's nature.

God Is Free

The God and Father of our Lord Jesus Christ is free. The idea is difficult to clarify. Some theologies have so stressed certain attributes of God that God has appeared to be in bondage to them. For instance, an inordinate emphasis on God's sovereignty and purpose leads to a view of predestination that leaves no room for human freedom and makes God appear as a tyrant. This is inconceivable if God is the Father who comes in Christ to reconcile us to himself. Freedom is not the contemporary misunderstanding voiced in the terms "do as I please"; rather, freedom is a personal characteristic of one who is not in bondage but is free enough to choose and act according to one's own understanding. Jesus Christ did not wear the shackles of slavery to sin, greed, fear, ambition, or pride; he was free to be himself. Brunner liked to point out that God's highest expression of his freedom as the Lord is that he can forgive sinners and set them free.[5] All human lords have power designated; the judge rules within the limits as prescribed by law. But God is free; he is not enforcing the laws made by another. He is Father dealing with his children in terms of love and freedom.

God Is Our Father

God is "our" Father and not merely "my" Father. The address in the Lord's Prayer designates not only God as Father but also that, in praying to him, we acknowledge the others who are our brothers and sisters. He is our Father; we are his children. Christian faith is very personal, but it is not individualistic. Some forms of existentialist theology, Rudolf Bultmann's for instance, are so individualistic that one speaks of God only in the first person singular. Bultmann described human existence as "mine," since all one can say is what existence means for me. We can't even speak of "ours." Since he thought we can speak of God only in terms of human existence, we can speak only of God as he is to "me."[6] Faith as known in the New Testament in response to Christ, however, is more characteristically corporate and sees God as our Father in heaven.

God Who Reveals Himself

God, as known in Christian faith, is God who reveals himself. Positively, this means that he desires to make himself known and to receive the response of faith and glory from his creatures. Negatively, it means that he is not known at all except as he reveals himself.

God reveals himself through word, act, and inspiration. In word, God speaks to give his name to his creatures; in acts, God works to disclose himself and to save his creatures; through the inbreathing of his Holy Spirit, he enables his creatures to perceive his revelation in word and deed.

God Gives His Name

God revealed himself by giving his name. When God called Moses (Ex. 3:1-15), Moses inquired as to what answer he could give if the people asked him God's name. God's reply was, "I am who I am." In other places, God introduced his word to humanity by stating, "I am the Lord. . . ." When God gave his name, he indicated at least three theological ideas: God is known only in giving his name; God is a person, not an object; and in giving his name, he established a personal relationship between persons and God.[7]

Knowing a person's name was important in biblical times. To know God's name is to know God. Also note that prayers are addressed to God in the name of Jesus and that the apostles used the phrase, "in the name of Jesus" in baptism and when speaking about the forgiveness of sin (Acts 2:38).

God revealed himself in historical events, such as the Exodus and the incarnation. In every event, God acted to redeem. In connection with the revelatory events, God as Spirit illumined the minds of the witnesses so that they could perceive and respond. Revelation is complete only when the hearer of the word or the witness of the event responds by faith. According to Jesus, the confession of faith was not accomplished by customary human ways of learning, but God was at work to make this revelation (Matt. 16:16).

God Is Holy

When God appears in the human setting, the persons involved have a strange awareness that evokes wonder, awe, and a sense of creatureliness. Moses at the burning bush removed his shoes because he stood on holy ground (Ex. 3:5), holy because God had appeared. Isaiah, in the presence of God, heard the seraphim chanting "Holy, Holy, Holy is the Lord of hosts" and cried out, confessing his sin (6:3). Saul on the way to Damascus was blinded by the light and cried out, "Who are you, Lord?" (Acts 9:5).

The unique quality in God, known nowhere else, is this holiness. To say God is holy is to say that God only is God; there is no other. Rudolf Otto has done the most definitive study on this subject in *The Idea of the Holy*.[8] The primary idea is separation; God is separate, distinct, other than. Otto used the word, *numinous,* to designate this uniquely Godlike quality.

The term means that God only is God; it is not a moral term

at all in the primary sense. Holiness stresses the majesty of God, his transcendence. The term stresses the belief that God is infinite, unsearchable, unfathomable, beyond the reach of reason. The term means that there is a permanent difference between God and creatures. This otherness of God prevents all attempts to equate God and humanity whether through idealism, mysticism, or pantheism.

We the creatures of God recognize his holiness in the sense of awe, wonder, overpoweringness, and mystery when in his presence. We rightly sense our unworthiness in the presence of his majesty. We correctly sense our creatureliness in the presence of the Creator.

Since holiness is the distinctive essence of God, no term is adequate to clarify. Holiness is associated with fire and jealousy (Deut. 4:24). God will tolerate no rivals, no idolatry. God's holiness may be compared to a devastating light shining from God's majestic holiness. If we stand in the right relationship with God, trusting him, we reflect his holiness back to him as a mirror reflects an image; this is the glory of God. If we stand in the presence of his holiness in unbelief, with our backs to him, we encounter his holiness as a devastating consuming fire; this is the wrath of God.[9]

The holiness of God points to his remoteness and his incomprehensibleness. God, however, has chosen to reach from his remoteness and hiddenness to his creatures through revelation. He is not only holy but also love. In holy love, we encounter God who both discloses himself and remains hidden, God who is at once withdrawn from us and reaching to us, and God who is both revealed and concealed.

God Is Love

In keeping with the belief that God is the Father of our Lord Jesus Christ, we can say nothing more distinctive nor significant than the affirmation that God is love. The word *love* has been overworked and misused, but there is no other word in the English language that will substitute for it.

The Greek word is *agapē* and designates that peculiar kind of love whose only source is God and whose character is determined by God who gave his Son to die on the cross. There are other Greek words for love, but they designate the kind of human love that is motivated by the worth or desirability of the beloved. The most common word is *eros* which is a beautiful word in its own right, despite some cognates in English. *Eros* can designate the love a man has for a woman or the love a mother has for her child. It can be a very desirable kind of love. In all cases, however, *eros* points to a kind of love that is motivated by the object or person loved in terms of worth, response, anticipated response or value.

Agapē is entirely different. It is the God kind of love that is unmotivated by any value or potential; it grows out of the very nature of God. God loves because it is his nature to love. He loves us because of who he is and not because of who or what we are.

The distinction between *agapē* and *eros* has been most clearly defined by Anders Nygren in *Agape and Eros*.[10] God's love is self-giving love, unmotivated love, and love that exhibits its character in the cross of Christ.

While the self-giving nature of God's love is most clearly disclosed in Jesus Christ, it is also evident in the Old Testament in many places. The author of Deuteronomy, while trying to present the idea of God's election of Israel, pointed out, "It was not because you were more in number than other people, . . . for you were the fewest of all peoples; but it is because the Lord loves you" (7:7-8). Herein is the secret of God's love: God loved Israel because of who he was and not because of Israel's value.

Hosea, in terms of love for the unfaithful wife, compared the prophet's love for Gomer to God's love for Israel. Even the unfaithfulness of Israel did not turn away God's love. God loves out of his nature and is not turned away even by human unfaithfulness.

Jesus taught this self-giving love in his statement, "But I say to you, Love your enemies and pray for those who persecute you, so that you may be sons of your Father who is in heaven" (Matt. 5:44). John understood the nature of God to be love. He stated that we love one another because "love is of God, and he who loves is born of God and knows God. . . . for God is love" (1 John 4:7). Paul gave the classic statement on the priority of love over the other Christian graces (1 Cor. 13). But the definition of love and the eternal demonstration of God's nature as love appears in Romans: "But God shows his love for us in that while we were yet sinners Christ died for us" (Rom. 5:8).

In every instance, God's love is the spontaneous and free self-giving of God to his creatures. He gives himself not because of the creatures' worth but because of his love.

Theologians sometimes include a number of other terms (attributes) about God under the heading of love. Dale Moody, for instance, sees the properties of God's love as mercy, grace, patience, kindness, faithfulness, goodness, and knowledge.[11]

In Christian revelation, God is by nature love. Jesus Christ revealed the eternal and infinite well of God's self-giving love to undeserving creatures. When we tell people about God, we should speak of this chief characteristic very early in our conversations about God.

God as Holy Love

Some theologians discuss *holiness* and *love* separately, only for the sake of definition. Then they speak of holy love because these two characteristics of God must be held together to avoid confusion. God as love is God in his coming down to humanity seeking and saving; God as holy is God in his otherness and distance. God as love is immanent; God as holy is transcendent. God as love gives himself to us; God in his holiness forever remains God. God as love wants us in relationship with him; God as holy is jealous if we do not trust him.[12]

Emil Brunner followed Martin Luther in making much of the wrath of God as God's holiness when thwarted or rejected.

Brunner then discussed the unity of God's love and holiness as seen in our giving glory to God by faithful obedience. That is God's proper work of redeeming and reconciling through Christ. But God does a strange work in that the sinful resistance to God's proper work brings guilt, condemnation, and the wrath of God. So God's holiness and love are known as one in our faithful response to Christ.[13]

Holiness and love must be seen together. The approach to the doctrine of God through discussing the attributes tends to produce a fragmentary view. Approaching through revelation produces a unitary view. God is at once holy and loving—Holy Love.

The Trinity

The doctrine of the Trinity is the most difficult of all doctrines, yet no study of Christian theology is complete without this doctrine. The limitation of space will forbid the present discussion from going into all of the historical details and philosophical problems. Numerous sources are available for those studies. The purpose here is to state the doctrine, give a brief summary of why and how it developed, and indicate its meaning.

Neither the doctrine nor the Trinitarian formula is explicitly stated in the New Testament. The formula, as later developed, stated that God is known as Father, Son, and Holy Spirit and these three are one. The King James Version popularized a Trinitarian statement which was not found in any of the early manuscripts. Later texts and translations do not include it. It reads, "For there are three that bear record in heaven, the Father, the Word, and the Holy Ghost: and these three are one. And there are three that bear witness in earth, the Spirit, and the water, and the blood: and these three agree in one" (1 John 5:7,8). The Revised Standard Version based on more reliable manuscripts reads, "And the Spirit is the witness, because the Spirit is the truth. There are three witnesses, the Spirit, the water, and the blood; and these three agree" (1 John 5:7,8).

Erasmus had placed the former statement in his edition of the Greek New Testament which became the Received Text, influencing translations for three hundred years. He omitted the statement from his later editions of the Greek New Testament because he had no reliable textual evidence for it.

While there is no specific text in the New Testament which explicitly states the formula of three-in-oneness, there are numerous passages which mention Father, Son, and Holy Spirit in such a relationship that later Trinitarian discussion was necessary or at least inevitable.

Several statements show the early references in Christian writings which would lead to the question of the oneness of God. "Yet for us there is one God, the Father, from whom are all things and for whom we exist, and one Lord, Jesus Christ, through whom are all things and through whom we exist" (1 Cor. 8:6). Second Corinthians ends with a triadic benediction, "The grace of the Lord Jesus Christ and the love of God and the fellowship of the Holy Spirit be with you all" (13:14). The Gospel of Matthew ends with a baptismal formula, "baptizing them in the name of the Father and of the Son and of the Holy Spirit" (28:19).

The early Christians were in perfect harmony with the Hebrew view of the one God as stated in, "Hear, O Israel: The Lord our God is one Lord" (Deut. 6:4). Paul, when discussing Jews and Gentiles, reasoned that "since God is one" (Rom. 3:30) he will deal with both. Jesus responded on one occasion, "Why do you call me good? No one is good but God alone" (Mark 10:18), indicating the oneness of God. Note, "For there is one God, and there is one mediator between God and men, the man Christ Jesus" (1 Tim. 2:5).

The greatest unity passage in Christian literature is in Ephesians 4:4-6: "There is one body and one Spirit, just as you were called to the one hope that belongs to your call, one Lord, one faith, one baptism, one God and Father of us all, who is above all and through all and in all."

The oneness of God in the Old Testament was not threatened by references to the Spirit of God, the Word of God, or the Wisdom of God. For reasons that we cannot understand, speaking of God as Father and as Spirit does not raise the specter of plurality. But to attribute deity to the Incarnate Son of God raised the question, "How is God one if Jesus Christ is the Son of God?"

The whole doctrine of the Trinity is an attempt to answer that question. God has revealed himself as Father, Son, and Holy Spirit. We are bound by our theological understanding to maintain the idea that God is One; and we cannot surrender the deity of Christ because he has revealed God to us.

Christian theology always sails through dangerous waters when the discussion of Trinity is raised. On one side is the threat of three gods (tritheism) instead of the One God; on the other is the threat of a unitarianism (whether a unitarianism of the Father, a unitarianism of the Son, or a unitarianism of the Spirit) which would exalt one at the expense of the others.

The development of the doctrine of the Trinity is a long and involved history and will only be sketched here.[14]

Most of the crucial controversial words used in the development of the doctrine were nonbiblical terms: Trinity, person, subsistence, substance, and essence. To our knowledge the first use of the word *trinity* (*trinitas*) was by Tertullian about AD 200, who also used the terms *substance* (*substantia*) and "person" (*persona*).[15]

While discussing the person of Christ, we noted that one of the heresies was Modalism which would make Jesus Christ one of the successive "modes" of revelation. There were also several attempts at relating Father, Son, and Spirit in one or another kind of Subordinationism.

Augustine argued for the Trinity in God by analogy with human characteristics. He saw human intellectual existence consisting of memory, intellect, and will. He also saw the human soul as having spirit, self-knowledge, and self-love.

The Greek word *ousia* came to be used with philosophical content to express ideas of essence, nature, or substance. The

phrases such as "substance of the Father" and later "like substance" (*homoousios*) figured in the controversies and creedal
statements. The intent was to establish the true nature of
Christ—that he was truly of the same nature as God. The term
"hypostases" (*hypostasis*) was added to indicate one essence in
three hypostases. This was not a clarification but perhaps a
confusion. The Latin word *persona* translated "person," while it
is common in English, is not very helpful since in our time
psychological and philosophical usage understands person in
terms of self-consciousness and self-determination connoting
individual life.

In keeping with our approach to theology along the line of
God's revelation, we are obliged to speak of Father, Son, and
Holy Spirit as some kind of unity because the revelation always involves God, Christ, and Spirit in some order. Since God
discloses himself in these modes of being and is God, the same
God, in each manifestation, then we must make some statement of triuneness.

All analogies at three-in-oneness create more confusion than
clarification. Perhaps, we should live with the remaining mystery; God is mystery. God and Spirit appear to be one; there
is no reason to think of plurality. Could God, manifested as
Father, Spirit, and Son, be one? Does unity require identity?
Not in the case of God and Spirit. Does unity require singulari-
ty? Not in Ephesians 4.

In the context of revelation, the doctrine of the Trinity is
necessary and embraceable. In the context of reason, it remains
a mystery.

The Christian faith in God comes to focus on God the Father
of our Lord Jesus Christ who is also continuing with us as the
living Christ and Spirit of Christ. We know God only through
his revelation of himself; and with the help of the Spirit, we
respond in faith. In his disclosure, he remains holy even
though he comes to us with intimate love. We love him, but
our love is always aware of his majestic holiness which re-

minds us that we are creatures and he only is God. We love
him, but we bow or kneel in his presence.

Notes

1. Otto Weber, *Foundations of Dogmatics,* 1, trans. Darrell L. Guder (Grand
Rapids: William B. Eerdmans Publishing Company, 1981), p. 423.
2. Ludwig Feuerbach, *The Essence of Christianity,* trans. George Eliot (New
York: Harper & Row, Publishers, Inc., 1957).
3. Edgar Sheffield Brightman, *A Philosophy of Religion* (Englewood Cliffs, N.J.:
Prentice-Hall, Inc., 1940), p. 363.
4. Hendrikus Berkhof, *Christian Faith: An Introduction to the Study of the Faith,*
trans. Sierd Woudstra (Grand Rapids: William B. Eerdmans Publishing Company, 1979), p. 181.
5. Emil Brunner, *The Christian Doctrine of God, Dogmatics I,* trans. Olive Wyon
(Philadelphia: The Westminster Press, 1950), p. 148.
6. Morris Ashcraft, *Rudolf Bultmann* (Waco: Word Books, Publisher, 1972),
p. 33.
7. Brunner, pp. 120 *ff.*
8. Rudolf Otto, *The Idea of the Holy,* trans. John W. Harvey (London: Oxford
University Press, 1958).
9. See Brunner, p. 160, citing Martin Luther's view of holiness.
10. Anders Nygren, *Agape and Eros,* trans. Philip S. Watson (London: SPCK,
1957).
11. Dale Moody, *The Word of Truth* (Grand Rapids: William B. Eerdmans
Publishing Company, 1981), pp. 104-111.
12. Berkhof, pp. 118-133.
13. Brunner, pp. 163-174.
14. Walter Russell Bowie, *Jesus and the Trinity* (New York and Nashville:
Abingdon Press, 1960); Henry P. Van Dusen, *Spirit, Son and Father* (New York:
Charles Scribner's Sons, 1958); R. S. Franks, *The Doctrine of the Trinity* (London:
Gerald Duckworth and Co., Ltd., 1953); George S. Hendry, *The Holy Spirit in
Christian Theology* (Philadelphia: The Westminster Press, 1956); Cyril C. Richardson, *The Doctrine of the Trinity* (New York and Nashville: Abingdon Press,
1958).
15. Weber, p. 365 citing the book against Praxeas.

PART II

Belief in Creation

The heavens are telling the glory of God;
   and the firmament proclaims his handiwork.
Day to day pours forth speech,
   and night to night declares knowledge.
There is no speech, nor are there words;
   their voice is not heard;
yet their voice goes out through all the earth,
   and their words to the end of the world.
                —Psalm 19:1-4

In the beginning God created the heavens and the earth. And God
saw everything that he had made, and behold, it was very good.
                —Genesis 1:1,31

6

Creator and Creation

The Apostles' Creed begins, "I believe in God the Father Almighty, Maker of heaven and earth." This affirmation of belief in God as the Creator is essential to Christian faith; it was recognized in the early stages of the development of Christian thought. Most, if not all, of the major beliefs hold together only if God is understood as the Creator of all.

During recent history, we have abruptly become aware of the limitations of earth. Until recently, most persons apparently thought that the earth's resources were unlimited. Now, we are reminded often that the natural resources are limited; some are almost depleted. Our lives on the planet are compared to those of passengers on a spaceship with limited food, water, and fuel and with time running out.

It is regrettable that the Christian faith has failed the world so dismally in understanding the nature of creation. Not only have we failed to teach a proper view of the material universe but we have also joined in the rape of the good land which God gave us. Our faith provides a corrective. Christians believe that God not only created the world but also entrusted it to his human creatures to manage wisely for their good and his glory. Biblical faith, both Hebrew and Christian, has much to offer in terms of understanding our role on the earth.

The belief that God is Creator leads to the belief that the world is really "creation." God, the Creator, brought into existence everything that is. Before creation, there was only God. God created all that is for reasons which he has not explained.

Within that creation, however, he has revealed himself in such a way that we can make some very positive statements about the nature of his creation.

A Theological Belief[1]

The assertion that God is the Creator of the universe should not be understood as a scientific or historical conclusion. This certainly does not mean that our theological affirmation is less important, or less true, than a scientific or historical conclusion. It may be that assertions about God are of much more value than any conclusions from other sources. As necessary and as important as scientific and historical statements are, they deal with the finite and temporal. If our statements about God are true, then, since they deal with the ultimate and with meaning, they surpass all other expressions of truth in terms of human value.

Scientific statements are made on the basis of investigation of a specific objective reality employing the method of science. Historical conclusions are made on the basis of evaluating historical sources, witnesses, historical records, and archaeological artifacts, employing a historical method. The statement that God is Creator is made on the basis of a prior belief in God known in human experience through God's disclosure of himself.

Scientific investigations of the universe, or parts thereof, are limited by the data and the method to specific aspects of the universe; science has no method for dealing with the "beginning," only with the prior stage or state. Historical research has no witnesses of an event called creation. Our statements are statements of faith based on God's revelation.

Biblical Teachings

At first glance one might think the biblical study of creation should begin with Genesis. Since, however, we believe God's fullest revelation of himself came in Jesus the Christ, it would be more logical to begin in the New Testament.

In the prologue to the Fourth Gospel, John spoke of Jesus Christ the Word who "was with God, . . . and . . . was God. . . . He was in the beginning with God." Then John affirmed, "all things were made through him, and without him was not anything made that was made" (1:1-3). The author of Colossians spoke of Jesus the Christ as

the image of the invisible God, the first-born of all creation; for in him all things were created in heaven and on earth, visible and invisible, whether thrones or dominions or principalities or authorities—all things were created through him and for him. . . . and in him all things hold together (1:15-17).

The anonymous author of the Epistle to the Hebrews wrote of Jesus Christ as reflecting the glory of God and bearing the "very stamp of" God's nature, "upholding the universe by his word of power" (1:1-3). Also he wrote that "the builder of all things is God" (3:4) and "by faith we understand that the world was created by the word of God, so that what is seen was made out of things which do not appear" (11:3).

Luke reported that, when Peter and John had been threatened and released by the council, they returned to their Christian friends and reported what the chief priests and elders had said to them. These early believers voiced their faith, inherited from ancient times but reaffirmed by Christ that God is "Sovereign Lord, who didst make the heaven and the earth and the sea and everything in them" (Acts 4:24).

Paul spoke of God's "new" creative act in Jesus Christ in terms of the Genesis account of creation when he wrote, "For it is the God who said, 'Let light shine out of darkness,' who has shone in our hearts to give the light of the knowledge of the glory of God in the face of Christ" (2 Cor. 4:6).

The writers of the New Testament were, of course, acquainted with and indebted to the Old Testament's teaching on creation. Jeremiah had written of God's word in the terms, "It is I who by my great power and my outstretched arm have made the earth, with the men and animals that are on the earth" (Jer. 27:5).

Numerous Old Testament writers speak naturally of their faith in God as Creator. Isaiah's witness was, "For thus says the Lord,/who created the heavens (he is God!),/who formed the earth and made it (he established it;/he did not create it a chaos, he formed it to be inhabited!):/'I am the Lord, and there is no other' " (45:18). The psalmist often sang of God's creation in such terms as, "The heavens are thine, the earth also is thine;/the world and all that is in it, thou hast founded them" (89:11). The Old Testament historian reported that Hezekiah in his prayer addressed God, "O Lord the God of Israel, . . . thou has made heaven and earth" (2 Kings 19:15).

The Book of Genesis preserves lengthy passages on creation. The magnificent beginning reads, "In the beginning God created the heavens and the earth" (1:1). After creating certain parts of creation, God saw or declared that they were good. The greatest misunderstanding of this passage has resulted when interpreters have tried to make it a scientific account of creation or have used it to refute scientific accounts. It should be understood for what it is, a theological statement. It should be read, "In the beginning GOD. . . ." It is about God. It maintains that everything which exists does so because God is Creator. It maintains that the things of creation are good. After creating man and woman, God "saw everything that he had made, and behold, it was very good" (1:31).

God the Creator

The belief in God as Creator affirms a number of faith convictions which clarify the expression that God is Maker of heaven and earth.

God is the *maker of all things.* Some views of creation, such as the Babylonian creation story and others, view creation as the shaping of preexisting matter or bringing order out of chaos.[2] Such views naturally assume that matter is also eternal or had some other origin. While biblical teachings do not discuss this subject per se, they leave no doubt that only God is eternal. All else owes its very existence to God. This view is vitally important to other theological considerations. It may appear to be embarrassing when we consider the fact and problem of evil, but the view of God in the Bible leaves no doubt about the oneness of God and that he is the author of all that exists.

God the Creator is *ruler of all*. Since all creation owes its existence to God, we must also assume that he remains in control of what he has made. It would be quite inconceivable for God to create a world and turn it loose or lose control of it. Either act would question his original purpose for creation or his power after creation.

The sovereignty of God hardly needs explaining. Even the term *God* implies continued rule and power. Creation and continued rule are companion concepts. Sovereignty can be misunderstood as tyranny by those who seek to revolt against God. Sovereignty can be developed in theology as the first or dominant doctrine and lead to distortion. God is much more than sovereign; we need to say other things about God along with mentioning sovereignty. It is important however. It is one basis of our assurance that we can depend on God.

To be Creator, God must be *free*. Freedom is a positive concept even though we often define it in negative terms, such as operating without restraint or need or necessity. To say that creation was a free act of God means that God chose to bring about creation for reasons or purposes of his own but not out of any necessity. In other words, before creation, only God was. There was no reason for any other existence until God chose to create. When speaking of God's purpose in creation, we need to be careful lest we try to project ourselves into God's position before creation and predict. Our statements about God's purpose in creation are derived from his later revelation to us in restoring us to relationship with God and each other.

The freedom of God is not merely the basis of our freedom. It is also the basis of our dependence on God and confidence in Creation. God was not only free in the beginning of creation but is also free in terms of his continuing relationship with creation.

Insisting on God's freedom avoids certain errors that have been attractive in some ages. Deism, for instance, which grew out of eighteenth-century Rationalism, recognized a God who created an orderly universe which seemingly operates according to its own laws. But the Deists saw no evidence or need for God's continuing relationship with Creation. Therefore, in this intellectual outlook, God was not really free to enter or relate to creation directly. In a sense, God would be excluded, or at least withdrawn, from creation.

Those who understood creation as an emanation from God thought to do respect to the universe but unintentionally denied God's freedom. In other words, creation reflects God's nature, but God is not free to act. Pantheism is similar in that God is somehow intertwined with all reality so that God and creation are inseparable, if not identical. Biblical faith maintains that the Creator acted in freedom and remains free to act within his creation as he wills.

God Remains Separate from Creation

Earlier we noted that the holiness of God indicates his otherness, his separateness, or distinctive being apart from creation. We also noted how views of emanation and pantheism blur the distinction between God and Creation.

The affirmation that God is Creator draws an indelible line between God and the universe. Only he is God. He remains God. Creation has its importance in terms of God's purpose for it and relationship to it.

The transcendence of God as implied in the concept of God the Creator does not nullify the belief that God may also act within creation. Transcendence and immanence are polar concepts which appear to state a reality. Pantheism would express immanence to an extreme degree but would deny transcendence. Since God is Creator and since God is free, then as holy and transcendent God, he may act within or relate to his crea-

tures as he wills without surrendering or jeopardizing transcendence. The continuing relationship of God with creation
would seem to require, as well as justify, the concept of God's
immanence.

Creation

Since God, as revealed in Jesus Christ, is the Creator of all
that exists, there are certain affirmations which we may assert
as our beliefs. It is more appropriate to speak of creation than
world. If God is Creator then creation is good, dependent,
dependable, unfinished, and finds its purpose in God the Creator.

The term *creation* speaks more accurately in theology than the
term *world.* For one thing, the world in the New Testament is
not always a single idea. It is the "world" which God so loved
that he gave his Son to redeem (John 3:16); it is also used for
the fallen world from which the disciples were to separate
themselves (John 15:18-19). The same word (*kosmos*) is used in
both senses. In contemporary usage, world is often used in the
sense of the material universe. It is also used in the sense of
fallenness; a certain act is "worldly."

The term *creation* reminds us of the Creator and guides us into
thinking of the universe in terms of its origin in the creative
act of God. Since God is, and is Creator, then it is all important
for us the creatures to speak and think of the universe in its
relationship to and purpose in God.

Creation Is Good

Since God is Creator, creation is good. Not only does the
Genesis narrative declare it so but the nature of God requires
it to be so. Its goodness, however defined, derives directly from
God who created it.

This means that God's creatures should enjoy creation with
all of its gifts. It also means that their joyful disposition is made
so because of their gratitude. Because of their misunderstanding, many believers have missed the joy God intended for

them. For one thing, they misinterpreted the term *world* when it designated human culture in its fallenness to mean all that God had made. To be sure, human culture displays many characteristics which are not good but are dreadfully evil. They also have taken other religious teachings in the wrong way and have labeled some of God's good creation as evil to be avoided.

The greatest challenge to our belief that creation is good is the fact of evil in God's good creation. The challenge, the problem of theodicy, is often stated in the question, If God is both good and powerful, why this evil? If he is good he would hate evil, and if he is all powerful he could and would remove it. It should be obvious that this question assumes that God is the author of evil or that some outside power has invaded his creation. Another assumption may be nearer the truth: what we call evil may be our creation in God's good universe made possible because of our freedom and power. If this be so, the question of theodicy needs to be considered alongside the responsibility of human beings.

In spite of the seriousness of evil both as a theoretical and practical problem, a mystery and a fact, we cannot surrender the idea of the goodness of creation without surrendering the belief in the goodness of God.

Creation Is Dependent

Creation is always dependent on God. Createdness means distinct existence but an existence that depends on another. The theologies of the recent past usually included a section on the "Preservation" of creation along with the doctrine of "Providence." The point was that creation is never self-existent; it exists because God created and preserves it and sustains it. Some theologians speak of the continuing creation and seem to blend creation and preservation. Emil Brunner, for instance, thought this was dangerous since creation and preservation are not the same.[3]

Augustine saw God's relationship to creation as preservation by claiming that in every moment God holds up the creation or it would fall into the abyss of nothingness.

The idea of creation implies dependence. We can maintain the distinctive existence and nature of the creation as "over against" God, but we cannot maintain its independence from God. This idea leads to a further clarification in humanity's relationship with God. It is easy to see the relationship God maintains with those who are faithful to him. But God maintains a relationship even with those who are alienated from him; he sustains and preserves them precisely during their unbelief. Saul of Tarsus, after his reconciliation to God on the road to Damascus, could look back and recognize that God was preserving him even while he engaged in the persecution of the church.

Creation Is Dependable

Creation is also dependable. While Christians cannot accept the Deists' view of natural law, we can cheerfully applaud the dependability and orderliness of God's creation. God "makes his sun rise on the evil and on the good, and sends rain on the just and on the unjust" (Matt. 5:45). One of the earliest books I read on prayer was George A. Buttrick's volume on that subject. He stated that Jesus' presuppositions when he prayed were: man is free, God is personal, and the universe is both faithful and flexible for both God and humanity.[4] This faithfulness or dependability grows out of the idea that God is the Creator.

Creation Is Flexible and Responsive

The idea that the universe is flexible is stated in several ways. The creation of God is open or unfinished. God is still at work. God trusted his creation into the hands of humanity who now have dominion to add to creation and to change it. God retains his ultimate sovereignty and can, as he wills, enter into his creation. The incarnation is the classic example of God's coming to his creation in redemption. All miracles of whatever nature testify to the fact that creation remains open to God. This brings us to the purpose of God in creation.

The Purpose of Creation

To believe that this is God's creation leads one to see a purpose or meaning in createdness in keeping with God's will. We cannot speak of God's purpose in creation if it means that we, in retrospect, speak of what God had in mind the day before he created the universe. But it has great meaning if we speak of the purpose of God for human beings in this world on the basis of his revelation to us.

Amid the bewildering perplexity and complexity of our lives, one may wonder if creation really has meaning. The literature of an age just past focused on the motif of the absurd. The threat of meaninglessness is known by all reflective persons. But faith in God endows life with a meaning. God works with us in all of life's experiences to bring them into a pattern or whole which does have purpose.

Creation Out of Nothing

Creation "out of nothing" is a strange statement which does not appear in the Bible at all. The earliest known written reference to the explicit idea of creation out of nothing appears in the apocryphal writing of 2 Maccabees. "Child, I beseech thee, lift thine eyes to heaven and earth, look at all that is therein, and know that God did not make them out of the things that existed."[5]

There are biblical passages which may imply the idea of creation out of nothing, but one cannot be certain. Hebrews speaks of the world being created "out of things which do not appear" (11:3). Paul spoke of God calling "into existence the things that do not exist" (Rom. 4:17).

Biblical faith, however, requires some statement similar to, if not identical with, the "creation out of nothing" because it is clear that God is perceived as being the Creator in the sense of bringing into existence, and not in the sense of merely shaping or fashioning a preexistent chaos. Dualism is out of place in biblical faith.

The Importance of the Belief in Creation

The belief or doctrine of creation is important for several reasons. Langdon Gilkey believes the concept of God as Creator may be the most fundamental conception we have of God and the foundation on which we make other affirmations about God.[6] The Christian concept of life is that human beings live in obedience to God, trusting, praying, serving, responding to God, and knowing God's response to them. These beliefs endure only so long as God is the Creator who continues to sustain his creation.

World as Createdness

Hendrikus Berkhof has understood the meaning and importance of seeing the world as createdness.[7] Createdness means that the world and everything in it is good and important. While nothing is absolute, createdness leads us to recognize that there is a fundamental unity in creation. The parts and variety in creation, however, have their distinctive existence. The world is dependable in that its orderliness derives from God its Creator, but it is open to change and miracles. Since God is Creator, we see a purpose in creation including us the creatures. Belief in the createdness of our universe is foundational to the Christian understanding of salvation.

The essential goodness of creation is a belief Christians cannot surrender. Faith in God leads to the belief that life has meaning and purpose. In spite of the fact and seriousness of evil, faith in God leads to the understanding of evil as an intruder or distortion subject to being overcome by the work of Christ as appropriated by faith. Even death is robbed of some of its tragedy by the belief that the Creator has a purpose for this life and beyond this life. This faith leads to the expectation that our lives can be reborn in terms of the original purpose and potential.[8]

The Christian faith rejects the notion that the world is evil and should be escaped or hurried through. This world is God's creation, and it is good. Here we come to know God, others, and the meaning of the adventure of life. Even if there were no world to come, this is a good world in spite of the evil we have introduced into it.

We believe in God the Father Almighty, Maker of heaven and earth. We believe in his creation. Furthermore, we have been entrusted with a measure of dominion over a part of it. In that role, between God and nature, we have our freedom and responsibility. We also participate in the further creation of this universe—or its dissolution. Although we are creatures, we have creative powers and inclinations, because we were created in the image of God. If one sees "world" as human culture imposed upon creation, then one may regret "that world," but one must love creation. "God so loved the world. . . ."

Notes

1. Langdon Gilkey, *Maker of Heaven and Earth* (Garden City, N.Y.: Doubleday & Company, Inc., 1959), p. 24-25.

2. James B. Pritchard, ed., *Ancient Near Eastern Texts,* 3rd. ed. (Princeton: Princeton University Press, 1969).

3. Emil Brunner, *The Christian Doctrine of Creation and Redemption, Dogmatics II,* trans. Olive Wyon (Philadelphia: The Westminster Press, 1952), p. 149.

4. George A. Buttrick, *Prayer* (New York and Nashville: Abingdon-Cokesbury, 1942), pp. 54 *ff.*

5. R. H. Charles, ed., *The Apocrypha and Pseudepigrapha of the Old Testament,* 1 (Oxford: Clarendon Press, 1963), II Macc. 7:28.

6. Gilkey, p. 79.

7. Hendrikus Berkhof, *Christian Faith: An Introduction to the Study of the Faith,* trans. Sierd Woudstra (Grand Rapids: William B. Eerdmans Publishing Company, 1979), pp. 160-178.

8. Gilkey, p. 109.

7

The Human Creatures

Faith in God leads to a kind of belief in human beings who are the creatures of God. The discussion about men and women is not a departure from theology, which is the study about God, but a vital part of it. We know God as he has disclosed himself in the human life of Jesus Christ and in our own lives.

The discussion of God always involves the discussion of humanity. Some definitions of theology simply state that theology is the study of God and humanity and their relationship. Otto Weber, for instance, following John Calvin, affirmed the interrelatedness of our knowledge of God and our knowledge of ourselves.[1]

If we human beings speak of God at all, we must speak of him in human language and analogies. In Christian theology, this is especially true because we understand human beings as the creatures of God, and our knowledge of God is revealed in the person of Jesus Christ.

The discussion of the belief in men and women naturally falls into three basic divisions: human beings as God created them; human beings in their sinful estrangement from God; and human beings as they are, or can be, restored to God.

The discussion of humanity as creatures of God will sound somewhat idealistic, if not naive, unless we continually remind ourselves of the forthcoming discussion of human beings as sinners.

Biblical faith sees human life as a perversion of basic human nature. Biblical faith also portrays an equally radical change of sinful persons back into the image of Jesus Christ the Son (Rom. 8:29).

This change is like a new birth. Any discussion of human life that is faithful to biblical teachings must always deal with the intent of God for humans, the fact of human fallenness, and the potential for change.

An on-the-spot survey or analysis will hardly be adequate for an understanding of the complex human personality. Human beings are in process, on the way. Their dreams and hopes play important roles in their growth as does their past experience. Jacob of the Old Testament was a despicable deceiver in his early life. He plotted with his mother to rob his older brother of the birthright. He displayed characteristics approaching respectability when, as an old patriarch, he stood in the presence of the rulers of Egypt. Every human being is at once a person with a past, a present, and a future—on the way. A true understanding of the person requires this multiple view.

A human being is never fully created in the sense that each one is always on the way.[2] Each person through responsibility and freedom contributes to what he or she will be. While we are affected by our environment and heredity, we add an important part to the "mix" of what we will be.

The first two chapters of the Bible speak of the creation of the world, including man and woman. The third chapter speaks of their fall into sin. The rest of the Bible speaks of God's work of bringing his human creatures back to himself.

Two Views of Human Creatures

There are two views of humanity: the classical view and the biblical view. These two views usually appear mixed either with other modern views or with each other.[3]

The Classical View of Humanity

The classical view of human life began and developed in the philosophies of Plato, Aristotle, and Stoicism. This view dwells upon *human reason* as the distinctive human characteristic. Human reason—whether related to the soul, the spirit, or the mind—sets human beings apart from all other creatures.

The exaltation of reason, mind, or soul led to a *dualistic view* of human beings. Eventually a dualism developed: a person has two parts, a body and a soul. In this view, the soul is what really matters. The idea is that the body is a prison which houses the soul. Death releases the soul which returns to its origin in some great oversoul or reality above. The soul is really understood as divine.

Since reason is sublime, we have cause for an optimistic view of our own existence. Evil is understood as related to the body and all things material. Real humanity, however, is related to the divine principle in the soul. At death, the physical and material cease to be; the soul escapes. It should be obvious that this view is radically different from the biblical view.

The Biblical View of Human Creatures

The biblical view of humanity may also be seen as having three parts: the creatures of God, creatures in rebellion against God, and creatures with the potential for fellowship with God.

As *creatures of God* in biblical faith, people are finite and created in every respect. They are understood in terms of God who created them, but they are not divine; no part of them is divine. They are finite creatures, but they are creatures of God. As such, they are good; they have purpose. They are dependent on God and derive their true identity and character from their relationship with God. Apart from God, they are subhuman.

Human beings, in biblical understanding, are all fugitives from God, *fallen and distorted creatures.* We are mindful of our origin in God's good creation, and we are aware of the tragic fact of our distance from him. This is the pessimistic part in the biblical view of humanity; we do not hold to any built-in human guarantee like reason in the classical view. We may employ reason to our own ruin and to the ruin of others when we are estranged from God, but the very awareness of our distance from God raises the possibility of hope.

Biblical faith understands human existence as open to the *possibility of salvation.* The potential for salvation means that every person is redeemable.

Contemporary Illustrations

Many interpretations of Christian faith mix the classical view with biblical teachings. Reflection, however, will reveal remarkable differences. The Christian theologian who is tempted to follow the body-soul divisions will be unable to view the body as evil. It is God's good creation. The theologian also will find that each individual is always a physical-spiritual unit; these are not separable. Every person can be called a body; each can be called a soul. The terms are inclusive. In the creation narrative, God did not give Adam a soul which he added to a body. God formed Adam from the dust of the ground "and breathed into his nostrils the breath of life; and man became a living being" (Gen. 2:7). The King James Version translated, "and man became a living soul." The Hebrew *nephesh* (soul) implies unity.

Anthropologies, the studies of humanity, influence history. It is strange, however, that even in Christian lands, biblical anthropology seems to have been mixed with modifications of the classical view. Emil Brunner cited the biological view of Darwin, the philosophical view of Nietzsche, the political-economic view of Karl Marx, and the psychological view of Sigmund Freud.[4] These views have prevailed in the modern world; even confessing Christians do not seem to know or hold to the biblical view. The views cited above are human-centered; the Christian view is theocentric—persons are seen from the standpoint of God's creation.

Creatures of God

The belief that God is Creator requires that we understand human beings as the creatures of God. The assertion that we are creatures of God implies at least two major themes: creatureliness is our basic nature, and we are truly human only when we are in the right relationship with God.

Creatureliness

Creatureliness is not unique to human beings; we share this trait with all other creatures, but there is a difference. The existentialist theologians, like Bultmann, speak of existence only for human beings. Animals, for instance, do not exist; they merely "are." We human creatures have a distinctive existence. Perhaps the most distinctive phrase is that human beings are created "in the image of God."

Creatureliness stresses many facts. (1) We have our origin and reason for existence in God's act. (2) We are dependent on God not only for our beginning but also for our continuation. (3) We are finite and must accept that limitation in all aspects of existence. (4) We are good because God created us so. (5) We are free and responsible subjects. (6) We are most truly human when we are open and responsive to God who created us.

As creatures, we have not only our origin but also our reason for being in the creative act of God. This is based on theological premises; it is, therefore, a theological assertion rather than a scientific or philosophical statement. However, it need not be in conflict with scientific or philosophical theories of origins.

Origin speaks about nature and purpose. When we ask about our identity, we look to our origin in God's purposive act. Who we are and what we are supposed to be and do must be considered in light of the belief that God created us. We must look for our purpose in theology—what God wills for us.

As creatures, we are always dependent on God. This dependency stresses more than our origin; it speaks also of our dependency on God for our continuation. Human understanding often conveys the notion of reality always being the same or of unchangeable laws of development or evolution. Biblical faith certainly appreciates continuity but grounds continuity in the faithfulness of God and God's continuing work.

We are dependent on God (and also on others) as the earth is dependent on the sun for life, light, and energy. This belief states that our lives are not only temporary but also uncertain. We are not completely in control of our destinies; we are dependent creatures.

Creatureliness is the foundation for worship and faith. Isaiah responded to being in the presence of God with a sense of awe, wonder, and reverence—creatureliness. He was in the presence of the Almighty God. At the burning bush, Moses responded in worship. He was a creature in the presence of the Creator. Rudolf Otto's use of numinous points to this awesome presence of God;[5] the human response is worship motivated by the awareness of creatureliness. This may be the beginning of all worship.

Creaturely dependence can be illustrated in everyday human life. The human infant is helpless for a relatively long time. He or she depends on parents and others for survival. The human adult is no less dependent on others for the support which makes existence human. In families, we depend on other members. In the larger human family, we depend on others. Contemporary life in a modern city is possible only because we depend on a complex system in which others provide food, shelter, and all the necessities of life. We also depend on others for the intangible elements so necessary for living.

The human quest to be independent may be an admirable example of human responsibility expressed in freedom, but the unusual desire for independence may be the human sin of pride. The quest for independence can be expressed by rejecting dependence on God. It may become antisocial and reject a wholesome dependence on others. It may even become an attempt to control others and what belongs to them. In biblical thought and Christian theology, we are dependent not only on God but also on other human beings.

Our continuation in the human family involves a healthy dependence and interdependence with others. This dependency involves more than contemporaries. We certainly are dependent on past generations. We are also dependent on future generations. The meaning of human existence includes the continuity of past and future. It is not only nearsighted and ungrateful to be unaware and unappreciative of this dependency in continuity but is also a denial of humanity—a lapse into subhuman existence.

Finitude is a permanent part of creaturely existence. We are finite in an infinite number of ways. We had a beginning, and we shall die. We are here and not there at this moment. We live in this generation and century and in no other. We are subject to powers and events beyond our control, but we are not totally at their mercy. Sometimes they threaten us with nonexistence.

Our finitude remains even in eternity. We believe that after death we shall live forever with God. We will still be limited, dependent creatures. Even though being in heaven with God involves eternity, or life forevermore, *we* will still have had a beginning in time. We will be there as God's creatures with our distinctive human existence. Only God is infinite. The human desire to violate the boundaries of finitude is close to the source of sin; the human acceptance of creaturely finitude is a part of faith and salvation.

As creatures of God, we must affirm the basic or essential goodness of human existence. God created us good. Sin against God changed us. In our sins, we don't appear to be good at all; but again, there is more to us than appearance. Human beings even in sin retain a basic humanity which is capable of good, even great good.

Theologians aware of the seriousness of sin and guilt are prone to forget the goodness of human life. Individual human beings often stand out in their own right as good. Within the human relationships, family and friends, there is love, loyalty, and respect. In daily life, despite the contradictions, there is an essential goodness which cannot be totally destroyed.

Even if we deny the goodness in human life when it has fallen into sin, we must affirm the goodness of God's creation and the possibility of human goodness in the transformed person.

The human creatures of God are responsible and free. God is free. God's greatest expression of freedom is his ability to forgive the sinner—he is not bound by any law to punish. He is free to deal with his creatures on a personal basis. Human beings are human only insofar as they are free. Freedom does not mean the absence of restraints; rather, it means the ability to decide and act in accordance with one's own purpose and intent. Determinism, whether from without or within, above or below, is an insult to personality, whether divine or human. Biblical doctrines of election and predestination deal with God's calling and guiding. They do not coerce the human will into compliance with God's law.

In biblical faith, there are many kinds of slavery: slavery to other persons, economic slavery, slavery to greed or ambition, and slavery to sin. There is even religious slavery in which persons have lost their freedom to a legalistic religious system.

Freedom in the New Testament (Gal. 5:1) is liberation from the tyranny of sin, even false religion. Christian faith frees us to be the servants of God we were created to be. Creatures of God can respond to God only if they have freedom. God does not coerce people.

Responsibility has meaning only in the context of freedom. Human creatures are *responsible* to God. They are called upon to respond to God. They are expected to respond on the basis of their own understanding and will. They are accountable to God and all others. Human existence is genuinely human only when it is open to and responsive to God the Creator. This is the meaning of dependence, freedom, and responsibility.[6]

As creatures of God, we look to God as the source of all, the purpose for our existence, the sustenance of our lives. We are genuinely human only in our responses to God and others. God speaks and we become human by responding.

Creatures in the Image of God

The Christian belief that human beings are made in the image of God is distinctive. This belief immediately raises two questions: (1) What is God like, the God in whose image we are? and, (2) What is the human form or nature of that image of God?

God in Whose Image

Christians believe that Jesus Christ is the fullest disclosure of God. Therefore, we must look to him to find our portrait of God.

It is not incidental that Jesus Christ appears in the New Testament as the very image of God. Jesus Christ is "the image of the invisible God," the agent of creation, in whom "all the fulness of God was pleased to dwell" (Col. 1:15,19). Jesus Christ was the "likeness of God" and the glory of God shone in the "face of Christ" (2 Cor. 4:4,6). Jesus Christ "reflects the glory of God and bears the very stamp of his nature, upholding the universe by his word of power" (Heb. 1:3). Jesus Christ existed in the beginning with God. But he came to earth as man and died on the cross for us, after which he was exalted to his prior place with God (Phil. 2:5-11). Jesus Christ was the Word of God who dwelt in flesh among us (John 1:14; Heb. 1:1-4) and "in Christ God was reconciling the world to himself" (2 Cor. 5:19).

Jesus Christ not only reveals to us the nature of God but also reveals to us the true nature of human life. Paul compared Adam to Christ. Adam was natural humanity of the former age; Christ is the new human, the new humanity of the new age. Christ revealed human existence as God intended us to be. When human beings are reconciled to God by faith in Christ, they are transformed into "the image of his Son" (Rom. 8:29).

God as revealed in Jesus Christ is the God who reveals himself. God, for reasons known only to him, chooses to be known and chooses to enter into relationship with others. God is the

Father of our Lord Jesus Christ who exhibits infinite love, concern, and self-giving for his creatures. He is faithful in his relationship with creatures and retains his own holiness and freedom both in terms of being and action. God is the Lord. Persons in his presence respond with awe and obedience. He is also loving Father. He listens to us and responds to us when we pray and often when we don't.

God who revealed himself in Christ also concealed himself in Christ. God permits us to know him adequately for our salvation, but he remains in holiness and mystery. Many who saw Christ did not perceive God; an inner working of God within persons enabled them to receive God. God remains concealed from us until he discloses himself.

The Image of God in Humanity

Since God is the Creator, we are able to detect his fingerprints in human beings. Since we are in the image of God, and Christ was the very image of God, then again we go to Christ to understand human nature.

The phrase "image of God" appears in three ways in the New Testament. (1) It is the singular and unique relationship of Jesus Christ to the Father. (2) It describes the likeness to God into which sinful persons are transformed when they come to faith in Christ. (3) It describes mankind's humanity as the term is used in the Old Testament.[7]

New Testament Teachings on the Image of God

Four New Testament passages clearly teach that by faith human beings are transformed into the image of God or the image of Christ. The best known statement is in Romans. "We know that in everything God works for good with those who love him, . . . predestined to be conformed to the image of his Son" (Rom. 8:28-29). By faith in Christ, people receive the Holy Spirit into their hearts and thereby are able to address God as Father. Being changed into the image of Christ is the ultimate description of salvation. Redeemed persons then become Christlike. That is the true image of God in men and women. The primary theme of the chapter is God's eternal love to humanity in Christ. Then the image of God in men and women would be recognized in their responding, trusting, and grateful love.

The *eikōn* (image) appears in two passages in 2 Corinthians. Paul wrote about Moses who put a veil over his face so that he could conceal the reflected glory of God after God appeared to him on Sinai. Then he charged that the Israelites read the Old Covenant with their minds veiled, but the veil is removed when one turns to Christ. Paul reasoned that we who believe in Christ "are being changed into his likeness from one degree of glory to another" (2 Cor. 3:12-18). Paul continued by speaking about "the light of the gospel of the glory of Christ, who is the likeness of God" (2 Cor. 4:4).

Paul spoke of the image again in connection with what he taught about the resurrection. He reasoned that Adam was the first human and is representative of physical mankind who die. Christ is the second Adam, the true humanity. We are like Adam. We are in sin, and we shall die; but in Christ, we are new creatures and will share his life. We "have borne the image of the man of dust, we shall also bear the image of the man of heaven" (1 Cor. 15:49). True human life is to be like Christ.

A fourth passage illuminates the theme of being transformed into the image of Christ. Paul reasoned that in Christ our old sinful nature is replaced by a new nature (Col. 3:1-17). Those who "have been raised with Christ" set their minds on things above. They put to death the old sins of anger, malice, slander, and the like. They have "put off the old nature with its practices and have put on the new nature, which is being renewed in knowledge after the image of its creator" (Col. 3:9-10). Paul immediately stated that human distinctions, such as "circumcised and uncircumcised," could no longer stand. The distinctive human nature is the image of God in Christ. This basic nature applies to all human beings.

Old Testament Teachings on the Image of God

There are three Old Testament passages on the image of God (Gen. 1:26-27; Gen. 9:6; Ps. 8), although the term *image* does not appear in the last one.

In Genesis 1, God made humans in his own "image" after his "likeness" and gave them dominion over the nonhuman creation. A specific distinction is made between the rest of creation and men and women who are created in the image of God. "So God created man in his own image, in the image of God he created him; male and female he created them" (Gen. 1:27).

The other passage in Genesis announces the death penalty upon the person who kills another person because "God made man in his own image" (Gen. 9:6).

The phrase "image of God" does not appear in Psalm 8, but the idea is clearly in the background. After describing the wonders of creation, the psalmist declared, "When I look at thy heavens, the work of thy fingers,/the moon and the stars which thou hast established;/what is man that thou art mindful of him,/and the son of man that thou dost care for him?/Yet thou hast made him little less than God" (vv. 3-5).

Summary of New Testament Teachings

By far the most important idea in the New Testament on the image of God is that Jesus Christ is the true image, likeness, and very stamp of God's nature. This points us to God's image as that of a loving, caring, forgiving Heavenly Father who reveals himself manifesting the will to be known by his creatures. He is self-giving and self-sacrificing. He spares no effort in establishing a relationship with his human creatures. He responds to them, speaks to them, and guides them in their purpose in life.

The next most important idea is that, through the reconciling work of Christ, human beings can be changed into the image

of Christ. This change happens when they come to faith in
him.

Christian faith brings changes in human beings. There is a
new relationship with God. This results in a new relationship
with other persons. The new attitude toward God is one of
answering love and gratitude. It expresses itself in worship, a
new way of life, and love to others. It appears as a new human
desire to respond to God. It is also an alert, sensitive responsiveness to the life situation of persons and concerns of other
persons. It especially reflects a new condition of freedom (freedom from the tyranny of false gods, even false religion) out of
which one is able to respond to God. The new person in the
image of Christ or God begins to show Christlike attitudes,
actions, and graces as the former characteristics of pride, malice, greed, and envy diminish.

Summary of Old Testament Teachings

It is not quite so easy to focus on the precise meaning of the
image of God in the Old Testament. We can be certain, however, that the phrase stresses the uniqueness of human creatures. In many ways, they are different from all other creatures.
This likeness or image of God forever sets them apart. One
may kill animals for food, but people are forbidden to kill other
human beings precisely because "God made man in his own
image" (Gen. 9:6).

The phrase "image of God" certainly points to humanity's
dominion over other creatures. This is clearly stated, "So God
created man in his own image, . . . male and female he created
them. . . . God said to them . . . have dominion . . . over every
living thing" (Gen. 1:27-28). This dominion over nonhuman
creatures endows us with power, dignity, a kind of sovereignty, a measure of transcendence, and certainly a heavy responsibility under God. We must exercise this sovereignty in keeping
with the will of the Creator to whom we are responsible.

The idea of dominion can, of course, be twisted into domina-
tion and exploitation of nature and other persons, but it need

not be so. This God-given dominion may be compared in one sense with the dominion of earthly rulers. They exert authority and sometimes power over their subordinates. Dominion as related to the image of God is not a license for tyranny or exploitation; rather, it is a challenge to responsibility and the duty to seek what is right and to cause right to prevail.

The phrase means that we are creatures with *extraordinary dignity*. As Bruce Vawter interpreted, God not only placed us in a universe which he had created with purpose and declared good but also placed us here not as the playthings or targets of demonic forces and unpredictable deities. He placed us here bearing his own likeness with the ability and responsibility of ruling, improving, and developing creation.[8]

Human beings are *personal beings*. Personality is identified by self-consciousness and self-determination. This involves more than just consciousness; it designates our consciousness of God and our possible relationship to him. In self-determination, we have one insight into the meaning of freedom. Freedom means, among other things, the ability to evaluate, decide, and so move as to change one's basic direction and personal development in life. This, of course, means that we can become better persons than we now are.

Responsibility is one aspect of the image of God. It is common in the popular sense to think of responsibility as a synonym for accountability. To be sure, accountability is a characteristic of responsibility, but only one of the several traits. H. Richard Niebuhr said responsibility includes several traits: response, understanding or evaluation, accountability to God and to others and to future generations.[9]

To be a human being means to have the *potential for response*. It means to be intelligent, alert, sensitive, and pointed outward to God and others. It is inhuman, or subhuman, to be unable or unwilling to respond to others. That is why it is sinful to fail or refuse to respond to God. Why is our salvation by faith? Is not faith simply a trusting response to God? The New Testament indicates that persons cannot know God's forgiveness unless they will forgive their fellow human beings. Those who do not respond cannot claim to love God. We love God by loving our neighbors and responding. Is it possible that the rich man clothed in purple went to hell because he did not respond to the man begging at his gate (Luke 16)? The failure to respond to human beings suggests the incapacity of responding to God. A basic self-centeredness appears to have blinded the rich man to the meaning of human life. Suppose he did not know about the beggar? Does not human responsibility oblige us to know and to make an effort to respond? Does not responsibility also mean "respond-ability"?

The responsible person responds in light of his or her *own understanding and evaluation.* Hence, legalistic religion or ethics will always be inadequate. We are not responsible if we behave merely because the law requires it or because religious tradition demands a course of action. Human beings are at once free and responsible; therefore, we must consider both laws and religious traditions and understand them so that our responses can be genuine obedience from within. There is a better reason for not killing a person than that the law forbids it, although that is an adequate reason for unreflective persons.

Accountability is a basic human trait. Clearly, we are accountable to God. The biblical theme of judgment, often misunderstood and misrepresented, nevertheless stresses that we all stand under God and shall stand before God. We are also accountable to our fellow human beings, not in the sense that we must have a conference or survey before every decision. Rather, it is in the sense that most, if not all, human decisions and actions do affect others. We live with the awareness of this accountability. Persons who charge ahead with what they want regardless of the effect on others are often successful, but they are irresponsible. The attitude of indifference to others and the preoccupation with one's own desires is what the Bible calls sin—self-centeredness.

If God had not required accountability of us, we would have invented it ourselves. Often, when in a bind, legally or otherwise, people are heard to say, "I was drunk and so I was not responsible," or "He is just a boy; he didn't think; he isn't responsible." If, however, you ask those persons to sign a legal document that the said person is irresponsible or incompetent, they will almost always refuse. To admit being irresponsible (unaccountable) is to say that one is not fully a human being.

God, in whose image we were created, is responsible. The biblical term is usually *faithful*. It means that God always acts in keeping with his own true nature and the covenants he has made. Men and women should not cringe at the requirements of responsibility; they signal the high honor we have for being the creatures of God in his image.

To be in the image of God means to be *free*. Miracles illustrate this freedom. God sometimes does the unpredictable; that is, he acts in what appears to be a way contrary to nature. We are prone to think of nature as an unchangeable complex web; God moves with freedom. His creation, however, is dependable. God is not capricious. God is free within his own creation.

To be in the image of God means to be *capable of faith*. Some interpreters see the image of God as focused in the idea of relationship with God. This is very close to what it means. In an age like ours, many persons have a low estimate of religious faith. They have this view because they do not understand what faith is.

God, in creation, trusted human beings with his creation. Our destiny is tied up in his trust in us; we cannot be human beings apart from that trust any more than a child can grow up into a responsible adult unless people trust the child with freedom and responsibility. God trusts us. Would it be an overstatement to say that faith is the foundation of all human life? As finite creatures, we have no guarantees about even tomorrow; we trust. We cannot guarantee the fidelity of those upon whom we depend; we trust. We put our money in the bank, go to the doctor, and drive down the highway only because we trust.

A basic characteristic of human existence is trust, or *faith*.

One cannot be human apart from trusting; one cannot be fully human without trusting God. This is a part of our being in the image of God. God took the greatest risk and showed the greatest trust when he created human beings and trusted us with his creation. We measure up to that image of God in us to the degree in which we trust God.

Historical Illustrations of the Image of God

Theologians have struggled to provide a rational explanation of what happened to the image of God in men and women when they sinned against God. It is obvious that we are quite different from the picture of humanity as created in the image of God.

If the image of God is lost, how can human beings hear the Word of God and respond? If the image of God is lost or destroyed, how do we speak of human beings as human? If there is any image of God in us, why are we so ungodly?

Since something is lost and something is retained, how do we speak of it? Irenaeus distinguished between the "image" and the "likeness" found in Genesis. He thought the likeness referred to the original righteousness which characterized human life and that it was lost in the fall. He taught that the image remained in human beings even when they were in sin. Then the image would be characteristic human nature. The view has not been widely accepted because there is no biblical basis for the distinction between the two Hebrew words. They are almost certainly a Hebrew parallelism, words meaning essentially the same thing and used for the sake of variety.

Thomas Aquinas stressed reason as this basic image of God or universal humanity. Of course, it involves knowing and loving God. The emphasis on reason as the distinctive human characteristic is most often found among the theologians who have been influenced greatly by Greek philosopohy. This idea appears to have truth in it. Martin Luther, however, in his characteristic way, dismissed it on the ground that the devil would thereby qualify!

Luther rejected the idea that the image of God in man is reason which all persons have even while in sin. He appeared at times to be thinking of original righteousness which had been lost. He believed that sin defaced the image but left a relic in human beings capable of responding to God. This view preserved the unity of the image (image and likeness are the same) and retained a way whereby the sinful person remains human and able to respond to God.

Emil Brunner distinguished between the formal image and the material image. The formal is identical with human existence and cannot be lost; the material image can be lost. Brunner saw the image in terms of our relationship with God. Relationship means responsibility, responding to God in freedom. The formal structure of our responsibility to God remains intact even when we are in sin. Our relationship with God, which is our destiny to live in God's love, is lost.[10]

To be creatures in the image of God means that we are the special creatures of God created with a *relationship* with him which consists of *responsibility and freedom*. We hear his word and respond. We have a destiny of growth and purpose beyond what we already are. We are always under God and over nature and among other persons who also are in the image of God.

Human Existence as Responsibility in Freedom

What does it mean to say we are free? The issue has been clouded by several factors: freedom has been defined as freedom of the will; freedom has been contrasted with determinism; it has been defined as the power to do what one pleases; some assume that freedom means the absence of all inward and outward constraints.

Freedom

Freedom certainly involves choice, but it is a much deeper and richer term which involves the whole of one's being. Bishop William Temple has persuasively argued that freedom is behind all choices and acts; it is a continuing state of mind and spirit.[11] The person is free; freedom is a divine and human characteristic made real in choices but not fully disclosed in them.

Freedom is not the opposite of determinism. Any determinism, whether from above or below, is an affront to the human spirit. No one can deny the influences, motivations, and impulses which beckon behavior. The religious belief that Allah or God is the all-determining power, if taken in the full implications, means that people are not human beings but robots on the end of strings. On the other hand, the idea that human beings live and act solely out of urges, appetites, or desires is likewise an insult to a human being who, even in his wrongdoing, insists that there is freedom in so doing.

To speak of freedom as "doing what one pleases" is to speak in childish terms. Such a statement implies that one has not yet become acquainted with the community of persons in which all decisions and actions take place.

To assume that freedom means the absence of all restraints is to deny any existence at all. Every human life is finite; finitude assumes restraints. Freedom, however, does not exist at the mercy of restraints. Freedom is a positive God-given quality of existence. Elton Trueblood liked to say that the real heart of human freedom is the "twin experience of *deliberation* and *decision.*"[12] The power of deliberation is marvelous indeed. It is part of human nature; animals do not engage in it.

In biblical faith, *freedom is a gift from God.* The creation story indicates that Adam and Eve were given the Garden and all within it with one exception. Human freedom like every other human quality is limited. No one would deny that we have knowledge; but, our knowledge is limited. We are not omniscient. Our freedom is limited because we are creatures, but it is genuine freedom.

The Word of God addressed to us calls us to an *awareness* of him and his will and calls us to respond to him in *repentance* and *faith.* Such an address would have no meaning unless we have the freedom to consider God's Word and respond accordingly.

Human sin is often compared to slavery. Individuals apart from God lose their freedom and become slaves to their greed, fear, ambition, pride, or sensuality. The covenant people who turned against God found themselves in slavery. Returning to God meant liberation from slavery.

Jesus came to liberate people from their bondage to sin. He spoke of "release to the captives" (Luke 4:18). John reported that Jesus said, "You will know the truth, and the truth will make you free" (John 8:32). His listeners were indignant because they regarded themselves as already free, but Jesus indicated that they were slaves to their sins.

Paul understood all human life away from God as a bondage to sin; faith in Christ sets one *free from sin* and makes that person a servant of God (Rom. 6:12-23). True freedom is known only by those who trust in God; others think they are free, but they are slaves to a thousand tyrants. Paul urged the Galatians to remain in the freedom Christ had given. His readers were in danger of submitting again to the yoke of tyranny from religious sources. True *freedom,* then, is liberation from the slavery of sin so that we can be servants of God, which is the reason for our creation.

When Luther and Erasmus debated the freedom or bondage of the human will, Luther was in keeping with biblical teaching. There is no neutral third ground labeled human freedom in which we can stand to decide whether we want to serve God or some other master. When we become aware of the choice, we are already in bondage to sin. Our choice is twofold: we can remain in sin, or we can trust in God. True freedom, then, is a new bondage—to God.

There are some difficult passages in the Bible which speak on God's purpose for human life and which appear to deny our freedom. God is like a potter, and we are like clay (Rom. 9:10-24). God chose some and not others (Rom. 11:7-8). He chose us from before the foundation of the world (Eph. 1:6).

There are also numerous passages which stress human freedom and responsibility. Even in the difficult passages of Romans 9—11, Paul suggested that the Gentiles who have believed may provoke the rejected Jews into being elect again. God desires all persons to be saved (1 Tim. 2:4). The invitation to salvation is universal, not limited to an elect number (Rev. 22:17). Even in the figure of the clay and the potter, we have something to say about the kind of vessels we become (2 Tim. 2:20-22).

The underlying presupposition of both Old and New Testaments is that human beings have the freedom to decide whether they will repent. The strongest adherents to the notion that God calls us—Paul and Jeremiah—never suggested that they were passive captives; rather, they responded to God with the full resolve of their own faith.

Freedom, however, is much greater than that which is made known in mere choices of the moment. It is a quality of human existence in which reflection, understanding, and responding take place. The individual human being is finite, caught between birth and death; each one is also finite in terms of freedom. Within those human boundaries, however, we have amazing freedom. We have the freedom in which to say yes to God or no to God. God does not veto that human expression of freedom throughout all eternity. Well-meaning persons often think that ultimately every single person will be saved and enter the eternal presence with God. One of the strongest arguments against such a hope is the reality and depth of human freedom. If universal salvation were true on that basis, then a human being could never say no to God; his no would only mean not yet and not yet would eventually be yes. Biblical faith portrays human life as possessing the awesome power to say an ultimate no to God the Creator.

Responsibility

Freedom, however, does not exist apart from responsibility, nor should it. Our lives are bound to other persons and to God and to our own freedom. This bond is part of the freedom we enjoy. We belong to other persons as in the family. This belonging is a bond; in one sense it restrains freedom. One cannot come and go without reference to others. The interdependence within the family frees each one so that some coming and going are possible. Dietrich Bonhoeffer argued that this is true freedom without which there would be no responsibility.[13]

Bonhoeffer's argument is that in order to be free one has to become selfless; one has to escape the slavery of self-centeredness (which is sin) and be open to other persons. He saw life, and I think in the Christian sense, as being open and responsive to God by being a person for others. This is a large part of responsibility.

Freedom and responsibility are always corresponding concepts; neither exists without the other. Genuine freedom in the human sense is known only by those who respond to God and to other persons.[14]

H. Richard Niebuhr's volume entitled *The Responsible Self* has a chapter entitled, "The Meaning of Responsibility."[15] Niebuhr defined responsibility as including at least four elements: response, responsiveness in terms of our own interpretation, response in terms of our accountability, and response in terms of our social solidarity.

To be responsible, we must respond in the age in which we live to the issues of our time and to the persons with whom we share life. We must make our responses in the light of our own understanding—that is, we must reflect and respond in the light of our reflection. Legalism is not ethical. Accountability means we are answerable for what we decide and do. We are answerable to ourselves and, if we have integrity, to God and to others. We are members of the human family, those who have preceded and those yet unborn generations. Responsibility means that we exercise our freedom in that continuum. Understanding and gratitude should be our response to history.

Responsibility in Freedom

Our freedom is the context out of which we respond. To be in God's image we respond. *Respond-ability* is a distinctively human capacity. Many of us have stood by the bedside of a friend critically injured in an automobile accident and said, "If you hear me, squeeze my hand." Any response of life and communication is feverishly awaited; how much more must God await some response from his creatures.

The first acceptable response to God and to others is to *hear*. The Hebrew call to worship begins with the words, "Hear, O Israel: the Lord our God is one Lord; and you shall love the Lord your God with all your heart, and with all your soul, and with all your might" (Deut. 6:4). How often Jesus repeated, "He who has ears to hear, let him hear." Do you recall Paul's great discussion on the way of salvation, "So faith comes from what is heard, and what is heard comes by the preaching of Christ" (Rom. 10:17)? Counselors often hear men and women state about the alienated spouse, "He (or she) never hears a word I say." And, many times oppressed black people said when injustice prevailed, "No one will listen." In the words of Paul Tillich, "love listens." Only love can be trusted to use power to achieve justice. Love first listens, then love forgives, and then love gives.[16]

The incredible gift of hearing marks the human being as one in the image of God. God listens, is attentive to, and hears us. We are most godly when we hear or listen for the words of God and when we hear others.

After hearing, the response is *faith.* The term *faith* is rich in meaning. It designates more than believing that something is true; that is assent. Faith designates a decisive trusting of self to God; that is commitment. It involves the intellect, the evaluation of other witnesses; but it goes beyond to a personal decisive commitment. To be in the image of God means to have the capacity for responding to God in decisive trust.

Responsible freedom under God expresses itself in *obedience* to God. Today an incorrect, popular understanding of freedom has been coupled with an adolescent resentment of authority. This has left contemporary culture with a kind of "outlaw" psychology regarding freedom. The Christian word *obedience* is different, indeed. It designates the joyful response of a lost traveler who has found the way and with joy and confidence wants to travel it without anymore detours. It involves both smart thinking and a decision, "This is the right way. I want to follow it."

Responsible freedom involves alert *consciousness and awareness.* Personality has been defined as self-consciousness and self-determination. Freedom is implied. We human beings in the image of God have the potential through awareness to change our environment and to improve our lot and that of others. As such, we are creative. Only through keen sensitivity can we, however, be aware of our opportunity and hence respond appropriately in our freedom.

Responsibility in freedom means *acceptance of God and human persons.* Of course, faith includes acceptance. But the word *acceptance* has acquired a meaning of its own. In our self-centeredness, we believe that God is; but we may not accept him and his ways into our lives, which is sin. We know the other people about us; but in our pride, we think we are better than they are and do not enter into any kind of friendship with them. Acceptance means that we actively include others, respect them for who they are, and allow and encourage their growth. Persons possess considerable creativity when it comes to finding ways to reject other persons. Responsible freedom means responding in our freedom. To respond to persons means to accept them as they are and where they are.

Jesus' parable about the good Samaritan identifies the "neighbor" (Luke 10:25-37). Our neighbor may not live next door; the neighbor about whom Jesus spoke is the person whose name we don't even know. He or she is that person whose life crosses ours only once in what appears to be chance. But our eternal destiny is being written by the way we respond to these persons whom we chance to meet along a crowded road, whether we know each other or not. To be a human being is to be one who responds.

Male and Female

Sexuality is a fundamental characteristic of human existence. In the creation account, we read, "So God created man in his own image, in the image of God he created him; male and female he created them" (Gen. 1:27). This statement has led many interpreters to conclude that even the image of God is not understood apart from the bisexual nature of humanity.[17] The generic term *man*, which is causing so much grief in our time because of efforts to achieve equality for women, always included mankind in general and was not primarily a sexual term.

The modern preoccupation with sex and sexuality can easily cause one to misunderstand biblical teachings. There can be no doubt but that the Hebrew culture, in which the Old Testament language was shaped, was dominated by males. It is also obvious that some of the New Testament writers, influenced by that male-dominated language, made statements which appear to subordinate women on theological grounds (1 Cor. 11:7). But in the Corinthian passage, the confusion is increased by the rabbinic argument which is strange to modern ears. Note also that Paul continued by stating, "for as woman was made from man, so man is now born of woman. And all things are from God" (1 Cor. 11:12).

There is no basis in Scripture for any subordination of women; they are not inferior to men. Whatever "image of God" means, it applies equally to males and females.

The polarity of sex is not only a part of God's good creation but is also a part of the image of God. Human individuality is known only in community. The first and most important relationship of human beings, except with God, is the relationship between husband and wife. They may forsake all others, if necessary, for each other. We are twofold beings.

God is love. Human destiny is also one of love. The love of man and woman in marriage is not the only human love, of course, but it is foundational. Loneliness on an extended basis is not good for human beings (Gen. 2:18). People need other people. Basic human love normally includes that love which a man and a woman have for each other out of which they form a permanent bond. As such, they become coparticipants with God in the creation process.

Dale Moody is particularly helpful in showing the social nature of humanity as expressed in the man-woman relationship. The social relationship is a more enduring one than a mere sexual relationship. The New Testament teachings greatly elevate the status of women, even comparing Christ's love for the church to the love of a husband for his wife. Even Paul's choice of the single life was vocationally motivated; he spoke as an apostle living constantly in danger for his life and expecting the quick return of his Lord.[18]

We human beings exist in pairs. Many people feel incomplete apart from the marriage relationship. Those who choose the single state and others bereft of their mates find human companionship in other ways. The insistence in modern times, indeed in most historical periods, by celibate priests for the privilege to marry speaks to this basic fact of human nature.

The Unity of Humanity

As individuals we are social creatures, created for relationships. This does not in any way, however, minimize the reality of individual human existence.

In the earlier Old Testament period, there was a strong emphasis on the human community or corporate personality. This does not mean there was no regard for individuals; rather, it means that individuals existed in and for the community, tribe, or nation to the extent that individual rights were secondary and sometimes not considered. In the days of Joshua, Achan violated a military order to take no spoils in the battle at Ai. When he was apprehended, Joshua and the people took him, his sons and daughters, all of his livestock, and stoned them, burned them, and stoned them again (Josh. 7:24-26). This act appears to us both brutal and unjust, especially for the other members of the family and the livestock. But in those days, the individual was understood as part of the family and clan. If one individual were guilty, the whole was guilty.

By the time of Ezekiel and Jeremiah, however, this idea had moderated; a strong statement of individual responsibility had emerged. There was an old saying, "The fathers have eaten sour grapes, and the children's teeth are set on edge." Jeremiah said, "But every one shall die for his own sin; each man who eats sour grapes, his teeth shall be set on edge" (Jer. 31:29-30). Ezekiel referred to the same proverb and commanded that it not be used anymore but that every individual assume responsibility for his or her own sins. (Ezek. 18:1-4).

The Unity and Integrity of the Individual

A human being is a responsible and free individual under God and among other persons. The individual existence is real; integrity and unity of the individual must not be neglected. At the same time, every individual exists within a community of persons and can be an individual only in that context of others.

Each person stands alone before God in the sense of individual freedom and responsibility. The outstanding personalities of the Bible, though always involved in the life and mission of the community, were distinct individuals with integrity and character. There is no hint in biblical faith that a person should be absorbed into some mass, either now or hereafter. The prophets were never more distinctively individuals than when they were boldly taking risks for the cause of God and their people.

Each person stands before God alone in certain moments. The Word of God comes through other persons and usually in a context of other persons. However you and I hear God's call to repentance as a very personal shattering experience. While others may encourage us, we decide in the loneliness of our own inwardness whether to trust God. During our pilgrimage as believers, when God speaks to us, we are alarmingly alone in the time of reflection and decision. This is true even though we may be surrounded by a throng of sympathetic persons.

The individual is a unity and should resist every effort to be divided. A classic religious division is that of understanding the individual as a body inhabited by a soul which may be detached—like a tenant that moves in and out. This view had its origin in Greek thought, flowered in Stoicism, and has prevailed in some streams of Christianity.

To be sure, Christians think the human individual is a physical-spiritual unity. This does not require a division of body and soul. Nor are we any clearer with a division of body, soul, and spirit. No one can deny numerous New Testament passages which use the body-soul terminology. Nor can we overlook a few passages that suggest a threefold division: body, soul, and spirit. Paul wrote in the closing paragraph of his first letter to the Thessalonians, "May the God of peace himself sanctify you wholly; and may your spirit and soul and body be kept sound and blameless at the coming of our Lord Jesus Christ" (1 Thess. 5:23). Did he intend this to be a psychological analysis of a human being? Or was it a wish for their total lives to be blessed?

In the creation narrative, God made us out of the earth and breathed into our nostrils "the breath of life" and we became living souls (Gen. 2:7). The biblical narrative stresses the unity of a person; each individual is physical and spiritual.

The Greek idea distinguished between the material (body), which was evil, and the spiritual (soul), which was divine. This distinction, so attractive to common reason, became very influential in Christian thought but it brought a Trojan horse in with it. The Christian understanding of God makes all of creation, including us, distinct from God. We in our entirety are created; we have no element of divine in our nature. The assertion of a divine element in human nature would be blasphemy. We are creatures. Now the Spirit of God may communicate with our spirits and may live within us as if we were temples, but that is quite different from having souls which are divine.

The body-soul division led, albeit unwittingly, to other interpretations which appear to do less than justice to basic Christian thought. Some Christians following this division excuse their sins as not their own but sins of their bodies while their souls presumably remain pure. Biblical faith has no way of denying responsibility for sin.

The idea of human sexuality has likewise suffered from the notion that the body is evil and that sex is an act of bodily appetite. This is erroneous on two counts: the body is God's creation and as such is good; and sex is more than a bodily function because it involves the entire person.

While we shall certainly continue to use the term *soul*, we should not think of this as something separate from the body. We should think of our individual lives in their unity; we should think of ourselves as individuals with integrity. This loss of unity is a sign of the distortion of humanity.

Dale Moody has given a thorough discussion of the unity of the human individual, even though allowing for the possibility of a disembodied spirit. He would argue for saying that we are living souls who have "a created human body and a created human spirit living in unity until death separates them."[19]

G. C. Berkouwer rejected the traditional view of a body inhabited by an immortal soul and argued for the whole person as a unity. He especially rejected the idea of an immortal soul since only God is immortal. In Christian thought, one does not automatically live forever as immortal; rather, God raises the faithful from the dead and gives them life as new creations.[20]

The Unity and Community of the Species

Biblical faith throughout regards all human beings as belonging to one family, the descendants of Adam. This belief is true regardless of one's view of evolution or how men and women were created. Passages such as Romans 5:12 reflect the unquestioned assumption that all human beings have descended from a common family. Despite the bewildering complexity of the different cultural achievements and cultural patterns, the human species is one family.

There is no evidence to suggest any superiority of one racial group over another; there are only cultural differences which can be overcome quickly.

A Christian view of human existence requires the belief in the basic unity of the human race. This means equality under God and mandates equality among other persons. It also means that we must respond to the other members of the family whom we may not have known before.

The unity of the species is particularly important in the consideration of the doctrine of sin. It is not that we have inherited sin through biological transmission; rather, it is that we are all related and interrelated in a complex web of sinfulness so that our sins are both individual and collective.

Creatures of History and Destiny

In every moment, we human beings are conscious of a past, a present, and a future. We know the past as memory or history. We know the present by immediate observation and involvement. The future stands before us as something which is not yet, which we anticipate or dread.

Our history is so important that it has become the norm of reality for some. Even Christian theologians following the principle of historicism made the historical happenedness the norm of reality, just as Hegel had made the rational element the norm of all truth. Gordon Kaufman has written an entire Christian theology from this viewpoint, *Systematic Theology: A Historicist Perspective.*[21]

The existentialist theologians have tended to major on the present moment of human existence with some apparent neglect of history and the future. Bultmann, for instance, was not concerned with the historical Jesus, only the Christ of faith. He saw the eschatological hope of Christians in terms of a present reality instead of a future possibility.

To be sure, some religionists have abdicated responsibility for, if not citizenship in, this world which God made. They anticipate a future world and deny this one in their other-worldliness. Christian ethics is a part of Christian faith. On the other hand, neither must one forget the future. That is human destiny—purpose.

To understand ourselves as creatures of God, we must keep our past, present, and future in focus simultaneously. To ignore our history would not only consign us to ignorance and illiteracy but would also convict us of ingratitude, a most sinful response. To be unaware of and uninvolved in our present is irresponsibility. This is God's world. It is in our hands for a time. Now is our opportunity to live. But tomorrow! Only we creatures in the image of God have a tomorrow! And we have something to say about what goes into the making of tomorrow.

Our destiny enjoys the guidance of God and can be shaped by the responses we make. God's creation is unfinished; he still works. We work with him. We have neither the idea nor the imagination adequate to grasp what God has in store for his creatures (1 Cor. 2:9; Rom. 8).

Human destiny has not been charted, let alone explored. God has made us for himself. Our future can be as bright as we will permit or make it.

To put it another way, we are creatures of faith. We were created by a loving God to love. We were created with hope. This hope is grounded in God whose promises in the past have been faithfully kept.

Our destiny may be more important than our history. Our individual and corporate lives may be influenced more by our dreams, hopes, plans, and expectations than we know. Reason is a great endowment which God has given us; no one should neglect it. Destiny belongs to those creatures of God who bear his image. Destiny goes beyond the threescore years and ten. Through destiny, we creatures also become creators.

Creatures in Between: Anxiety

According to Psalm 8, God has made us a little lower than himself and given us great dominion and destiny. The "little lower" than God, however, is a vast chasm.

We are creatures "in between." We are very much creatures of the world. We are a part of nature. We participate in its uncertainties, sufferings, frustrations, and limitations. We are also aware of God and the infinite. We must respond to God above and to nature below and to other persons who are "in between" with us. This creates an anxiety which is unbearable unless we are in the right relationship with God and other persons.

This anxiety, which originates in our finitude and awareness of the infinite, is the Achilles heel of our existence. The temptation is to deny our creatureliness and try to usurp the prerogatives of God or to deny our relationship with God and lose ourselves in one of the changing gods of nature. This leads us into the discussion of sin or unbelief.

Notes

1. Otto Weber, *Foundations of Dogmatics,* 1, trans. Darrell L. Guder (Grand Rapids: William B. Eerdmans Publishing Company, 1981), pp. 529-530.

2. John Macquarrie, *Principles of Christian Theology* (New York: Charles Scribner's Sons, 1977), pp. 59 *ff.*

3. Reinhold Niebuhr, *The Nature and Destiny of Man* (New York: Charles Scribner's Sons, 1949), pp. 4 *ff.*

4. Emil Brunner, *Man in Revolt* (Philadelphia: The Westminster Press, 1947), pp. 34-39.

5. Rudolf Otto, *The Idea of the Holy,* trans. John W. Harvey (New York: Oxford University Press, 1958).

6. E. Frank Tupper, *The Theology of Wolfhart Pannenberg* (Philadelphia: The Westminster Press, 1973), pp. 70 *ff.*

7. David Cairns, *The Image of God in Man* (London: SCM Press, 1953, rev. 1973), p. 40.

8. Bruce Vawter, *On Genesis: A New Reading* (Garden City, N.Y.: Doubleday and Company, Inc., 1977), pp. 52 *ff.*

9. H. Richard Niebuhr, "The Meaning of Responsibility," *On Being Responsible*, ed. James M. Gustafson and James T. Laney, (New York, Evanston, and London: Harper & Row, Publishers, 1968), p. 35.

10. Emil Brunner, *The Christian Doctrine of Creation and Redemption, Dogmatics* II, trans. Olive Wyon (Philadelphia: The Westminster Press, 1952), p. 61.

11. William Temple, *Nature, Man and God* (London: Macmillan & Co. Ltd, 1st ed., 1934 1956), p. 223.

12. Elton Trueblood, *Philosophy of Religion* (New York: Harper & Row, Publishers, Inc., 1957). p. 278.

13. Dietrich Bonhoeffer, "The Structure of Responsible Life," ed. Gustafson and Laney, p. 39.

14. Ibid., p. 61.

15. H. Richard Niebuhr, "The Meaning of Responsibility," *The Responsible Self* (New York: Harper & Row, 1963).

16. Paul Tillich, *Love, Power, and Justice* (New York: Oxford University Press, 1960), p. 84.

17. Brunner, *Dogmatics II*, pp. 63-64.

18. Dale Moody. *The Word of Truth* (Grand Rapids: William B. Eerdmans Publishing Company, 1981), pp. 212-238.

19. Ibid., p. 181.

20. G. C. Berkouwer, *Man, The Image of God*, trans. Dirk W. Jellema (Grand Rapids: William B. Eerdmans Publishing Company, 1962), pp. 194-233.

21. Gordon Kaufman, *Systematic Theology: A Historicist Perspective* (New York: Charles Scribner's Sons, 1968).

PART III
Unbelief and God

For the wrath of God is revealed from heaven against all ungodliness and wickedness of men who by their wickedness suppress the truth. For what can be known about God is plain to them, because God has shown it to them. Ever since the creation of the world his invisible nature, namely, his eternal power and deity, has been clearly perceived in the things that have been made. So they are without excuse; for although they knew God they did not honor him as God or give thanks to him, but they became futile in their thinking and their senseless minds were darkened. Claiming to be wise, they became fools, and exchanged the glory of the immortal God for images resembling mortal man or birds or animals or reptiles.
—Romans 1:18-23

All we like sheep have gone astray;
   we have turned every one to his own way;
and the Lord has laid on him
   the iniquity of us all.
                    —Isaiah 53:6

But God . . .   *Rom 5:8*

8

Human Creatures in Unbelief

Many publications on unbelief will entitle their discussions "the doctrine of sin," or merely "human sin." Rather than trying to focus on the nature of sin as such, in keeping with the methodology of this volume, this chapter will focus on the human creature in sin. A number of subjects will be discussed. These include our knowledge of our sin; the fact that we are the sinners; the identifying marks of our lives as sinners; the consequences of this sin in our lives; the origin of this sin in our lives; and the fact of our continued relationship with God, even though we are sinners.

There is a rich variety of terms both in Scripture and theological writings on the subject of human sin. Certain key terms seem so important that they tend to include the others. The rich terminology, however, is too important in its variety to permit us to stop using any of the terms. If we would understand theology when we listen and read, we need to retain and understand these terms about human sinfulness.

Introduction

The definitions which appear in standard dictionaries are quite inadequate for the understanding of sin. *Webster's New Collegiate Dictionary*, for instance, defines *sin* as a "transgression of the law of God." Other uses stress such things as offenses in general, even misdemeanors. The emphasis is upon breaking divine law by certain actions or neglect. The word is used in a secondary sense to indicate a violation of human rights or

law. The definition confuses sin with crime. While the violation of a human law is a crime, it may or may not be a sin.
The Oxford Universal Dictionary has a better definition even
though it focuses primarily on a transgression of God's law. It
recognizes that sin is an offense against God or a violation of
some standard or command of God. While this definition does
include the observation that sin is against God, it tends to focus
more on sin as a transgression of the law or the command of
God. In biblical faith, *sin* is a term that always includes a
personal element and is a reality only in terms of a severed
relationship between the human person and God.

Preliminary Definitions

John Macquarrie has argued with considerable persuasive-
ness that the basic sin is *idolatry*. He does this because of his
belief that human beings are the creatures of God and derive
whatever meaning and life they have from God. Sin, therefore,
is humanity's fall into disorder and alienation from God.
Human beings, who were created in the image of God and for
God, seek to live their lives as if God were not. When they do
this, they establish their lives upon other beings, upon idols,
upon other persons, excluding God for finite entities. To forget
God, to take God out of the center of one's life, is to fall into
idolatry, whatever the idolatry is. That is precisely the perversion of human life by sin about which Paul was speaking in
Romans when he said, "Because they exchanged the truth
about God for a lie and worshiped and served the creature
rather than the Creator" (Rom. 1:25).

Some people think of sin as a given action or even an attitude
of the human being. This view is so shallow that it almost
makes the concept of sinfulness of little worth. To see our sin
as idolatry, however, reminds us that sin is a complete and
terrifying reorientation of our whole lives away from the true
God to some lifeless idol. The terrifying nature of sin is more
nearly recognized when we see it as this basic idolatry of the
human person.[1]

Sin may be defined as *estrangement from God.* Paul Tillich understood and discussed sin under this basic concept. To be a sinner is to be estranged from God. Tillich used the term *Ground of Being* as synonymous with God. Estrangement, of course, means not only alienation from God but also estrangement from one's own self and from other beings. He understood this estrangement as related to certain key concepts: unbelief, hubris, concupiscence, as both fact and act, and, as both individual and collective.[2]

Unbelief is not a momentary shaking of the faith; rather, it is an act and attitude of the entire person who turns away from God to live in this world as if God were not, in defiance of God. Unbelief, so understood, is a dreadful estrangement.

Hubris is a word most often defined as *pride.* Popular usage of the word *pride* has made the word nearly useless. The word can be used with reference to the attitude of an individual toward his or her clothing; it can also be used with reference to the athletes' attitudes toward their competing performance. Needless to say, the theological word *pride,* which we will have to use anyway, is a very serious term.

Pride, in the theological sense, designates the self-elevation or self-exaltation which the human being does at the expense of his or her faith in God. Human beings as created have God at the center of their lives. The sin of pride is the exaltation of self to the throne. This self-exaltation, or pride, is a classic portrait of unbelief. If one can speak chronologically, before we human beings sinned we recognized that God was the center of our being; after we sinned, we think of ourselves as the center of our own being.

Sin may be defined as *concupiscence.* This word is often translated as *sensuality.* Both words are hard to understand in theology, so I shall define them and hereafter use the term *sensuality.*

Thomas Aquinas understood the original sin as concupiscence which he saw as an expression of self-love. He thought that all of our sinful acts grow out of some inordinate desire or love for something which in itself is good. If a person loved some temporal good thing inordinately, that person did so because of his or her inordinate self-love.

Reinhold Niebuhr defined *sensuality* as "the inordinate love for all creaturely and mutable values which results from the primal love of self, rather than love of God."[3] This is a very good definition. It recognizes that the creation of God is good, and creaturely values of themselves are good. It also acknowledges the validity of love for things. The sin is the "inordinate love" motivated by the prior self-love at the expense of love for God.

The liability of the word *sensuality* is due partly to the fact that in contemporary culture we have a preoccupation with sexuality. We tend to understand sensuality as sexuality. Sex as the creation of God is regarded as good. The improper expression of sex or the inordinate love for it would certainly be sensuality. There are many sins of sensuality which may not appear at first to be evil at all. One's inordinate love for career, fame or fortune, family, success, doing good works, or even religion, could be a form of sensuality which could keep one from God.

Our estrangement from God is both fact and individual act. We cannot avoid our responsibility for sin by alluding to a doctrine of original sin. We do know, however, that sin is a universal reality, and all of us individualize it in our own lives.

However else sin may be defined, it has to include both an individual and a collective component. We are sinners individually, and we are members of communities in which we are sinful to a degree beyond that of individuals' sinning.

Sin is a *comprehensive and personal disorder.* Sin should not be seen as a "something" or even as an act. *Sin* is in reality the term that designates our personal estrangement from God, from self, and from others. In a previous discussion we noted that all human beings are created in the "image of God." This affirmation that all human beings are sinners is just as basic and as comprehensive as the affirmation that we are creatures in the image of God.[4]

Methodology

The methodology of this volume is theological; it is based upon the belief that God revealed himself personally in Jesus Christ. Therefore, all that is said in this chapter about human sinfulness will be directly related to what has been said about God and humanity.

Jesus Christ is the foundation of Christian theology and the norm by which we construct all of our beliefs and doctrines. The primary witness is always the Bible, and the secondary witnesses are the experience of the church throughout the ages. These include human reason, historical experience, and, we hope, the guidance of the Holy Spirit in formulating statements of beliefs. Consequently, the discussion of human creatures in unbelief follows that methodology.

Humanity in Terms of God's Revelation

Creatures of God

This affirmation, which requires us to see ourselves primarily as the creatures of God, will require us to understand our sin primarily in terms of its direct relationship to God. The previous chapter dealt rather idealistically with human existence; it now becomes necessary to deal more realistically with the fact that, although we are the creatures of God, we are the sinful creatures of God in revolt against him. We shall not understand our sinfulness unless we understand it in relationship to God.

Christ as True God and True Man

Through Christ, we learn that God the Father is by nature the Heavenly Father who loves his creatures with a self-giving love. Jesus Christ was in the very image of God, and therefore, our concept of God must be shaped largely by the person of Jesus Christ. In light of those divine characteristics, our sins will likely appear to be much more serious than we would have otherwise imagined.

In Jesus Christ, we have revealed to us the true nature of human existence. In other words, Jesus Christ was a true human being who did not suffer the ravages of sin in his own personal life. We human beings should be characterized by those virtues which he embodied. Therefore, when we deal with our sin against God, we shall not be dealing with the violation of a law however good it may be; rather, we shall be dealing with our own lives as they are mirrored back to us from looking at the life of Jesus Christ, who was at once truly human and truly God.

Christ as the Image of God

The awareness of what it means to be human, in the image of God, will point up the great gulf between what we are and what we were destined to be. Consequently, as we deal with our own distorted lives, we shall have to come to terms with sin which has robbed us or distorted us so that the image of God is not often apparent. This is likely to lead us into the understanding of our sinfulness as fallenness, degradation, perversion, and subhuman existence.[5]

Humanity as Dependent

Dependency is a characteristic of creatureliness. We are dependent upon God for everything, and we are very dependent upon other persons for the essentials of living. Since they too are dependent upon us, we can speak of our interdependency with persons. In any event, however, the basic stance of a human being is to look upward and outward. Too much introspection may be very dangerous. An inordinate concern for one's self can be very close to the root sin.

A human being can actually live in sin by being inordinately dependent upon God and unaware or unconcerned about other persons. It is just possible that certain religious people who concentrate upon looking upward become blind to the horizonal dimension. Walter Rauschenbusch noted with perceptive insight that Jesus avoided the great temptations which so often beset those of religious genius. Particularly sensitive religious spirits were prone to the temptations of mysticism, pessimism, and asceticism.[6]

Great mystics are tempted to pursue the secret inner way of life to God and look with disdain upon the smaller, mundane duties which bind human beings to their world. Other great religious spirits are tempted to pessimism. Because of their own religious insight and commitment, they tend to view the evils of others in such a way that they consider their situation hopeless. This pessimism is a negative expression of the sin of pride.

Some religious spirits fall to the temptation of asceticism which is a form of other-worldliness. They tend to withdraw from the world as it is and seek to live in the other world before it arrives. Jesus withstood these temptations, but all of his followers have not been so successful.

By the same token, it is possible for persons to become so concerned with persons around them that they lose sight of God above who is the primary reason for being able to love one's neighbors and to look outward to them.

In the theological setting, sin turns out to be our departure from faith in God and our denying or forgetting the implications of that relationship.

Human Existence as Responsibility in Freedom

Human beings live in *freedom with responsibility*. The characteristic of freedom means that human beings have an openness within themselves out of which they partially determine their present and future. They possess the ability to deliberate and to decide. This marvelous freedom is one of the ways in which they resemble God their Creator.

If freedom is this much a part of basic human nature, then sin which distorts human nature is inevitably pointed in the direction of bondage.

Responsibility always means the ability to respond in the light of one's understanding and carries with it accountability for that response. If basic human nature is responsibility in freedom, then sin is the failure to respond or to respond inadequately or to respond in the wrong way or for the wrong reason or to respond to God and fellow human beings without accountability. In short, sin will take on the characteristic of irresponsibility.

Human existence is, therefore, a relationship, and sin will be the disruption of that relationship. We noted that some theologians would define the image of God in humanity as simply that of relationship. However one defines the image of God, a relationship between human beings and God is an inevitable part of being human. I have defined this relationship in terms of response. Sin will, therefore, be understood as a breaking of that relationship. This suggests words like *estrangement, alienation, unbelief, flight from God,* or *indifference.*

Since creaturely life is a life of faith, then sin will be understood as *unbelief.* The only single word capable of expressing the entire appropriate response of human beings to God is the word *faith.* Faith is a trusting commitment which establishes and maintains the relationship. Loss of faith, eclipse of faith, or temporary abandonment of faith disrupts the relationship with God and introduces the fact of sin into human existence.

The Integrity of Human Existence

Since each individual is a unity with integrity, sin is understood as that which divides the person or destroys the integrity. This idea is closely related to the idea of responsibility. Quite often persons are heard to blame their sins upon the flesh or upon the body. Consciously or unconsciously, they are seeking to say that a part of them is not sinful. In biblical faith and the theology derived from it, such an explanation is not possible. Each individual is a unity and as an individual stands before God and with one's fellow human beings.

This integrity of character is a basic human characteristic derived from being in the image of God. One would not think of dividing the unity of God in such a manner. By the same token, human integrity and character are measured by the degree to which the individual has integrated all of his or her life into a unity. The lack of integrity may be illustrated by the person who thinks correctly religiously but makes decisions toward and treats fellow persons in a lesser way. Biblical faith calls this the sin of hypocrisy.

Another example is the person who holds to religious opinions that have not been thought out and integrated into one's overall understanding of life. Frequently, one encounters a religious individual who is well informed in one of the scientific disciplines, for instance, but has refused to integrate the truth acknowledged in that area with the larger area of truth which includes one's faith in God. Obviously, such lack of integrity results not only in hypocrisy but also in prejudice, bigotry, dishonesty, and a host of other ills.

Since humanity itself is also a unity with its own integrity, sin cannot be discussed adequately without taking into account the fact of our collective sin. This usually brings us to the doctrine of original sin, which is frequently misunderstood to mean biological or genetic transmission of sin from one generation to the next. In fact, that doctrine intends to stress not only the universality of sin as being a part of the lives of every individual but also seeks to stress the fact that the entire human family is tied up together in a solidarity in sin.

When the prophet Isaiah stood in the presence of Almighty God, his awareness of the holy God prompted several responses: a sense of awe overcame him; he became aware of his individual sin and cried out, "Woe is me! For I am lost; for I am a man of unclean lips"; then he went on to confess, "and I dwell in the midst of a people of unclean lips" (Isa. 6:5). Isaiah did not intend to diminish his own personal responsibility by blaming society; rather, the awareness of individual sin brought with it the awareness that he was part of a community of sinners. We draw from and add to the sinfulness of society. Our collective sinning guarantees that the coming generation will be faced with a sinful situation out of which it will be inevitable that they too will be sinners. Consequently, the understanding of the unity of the human race requires a consideration of our solidarity in sin.

Anxiety in Human Existence

Anxiety is the lot of creatures who are finite and who are aware of the infinite. Since God created us a little lower than himself and placed us over the rest of creation, we are in an "in-between" position which becomes the occasion through which temptation attacks. To be creatures aware of the infinite God and related to the world of nature with all of its limitations subjects us to tremendous tension. The anxiety makes us vulnerable to the temptation of pride in that the tempter suggests to us that we usurp the prerogatives of God; our relationship to nature with all of the good things of God's creation makes us vulnerable to the temptation of sensuality—to lose ourselves in some of the mutable goods of God's creation.

Anxiety is, therefore, a part of creaturely existence. To recognize our creatureliness is to accept both the awareness of and relationship to the infinite as well as our relationship to and obligation for the finite. It is not surprising, therefore, that many theologians see the origin of our sin as originating in this tension within us.

Biblical Ideas About Sin

There are several special terms in the Old Testament which describe sin. These words designate missing the mark or failing, transgression or rebellion, twistedness, and going astray. Some terms stress direct transgression or defiance against God; others mean merely straying away from God. Some words imply that sinfulness changes persons and describe persons not only as guilty but also wicked.

In the Old Testament, sin creates a condition of serious estrangement from God, a personal alienation from God. There is a suggestion of demonic influence in Genesis 3 when the serpent tempted Adam and Eve, but demonology is not important in the Old Testament, and there was never any suggestion that human sin was caused by demons.

Sin is usually related to a corrupt heart in human beings in the Old Testament. It speaks with deep pathos about the seriousness of this evil within the heart (Gen. 6:5; 8:21). Throughout the Old Testament, human beings were responsible for their sin even though their sins may have grown out of a perverted freedom. In fact, responsibility for sin is not limited to the people in the covenant but also extends to all persons outside the covenant.

Within the Old Testament, there is both individual and corporate responsibility for sin, but this issue is not as sharply drawn as it is in the New Testament. In the earlier stages of the Old Testament, the emphasis seemed to be upon the community. By the time of Jeremiah and Ezekiel, however, we find a very strong statement regarding individual responsibility for sin. That statement focused in the old proverb about the fathers' having eaten sour grapes and the children's teeth having been set on edge. Both prophets insisted that every individual is responsible for his or her own sin (Jer. 31:29; Ezek. 18:2).

The New Testament repeats the Old Testament themes and adds other terms to clarify the meaning of sin. Sin is missing the mark or deviating from that which is right. Sin is a trespass or a violation of the accepted norm of behavior. Sin is described as lawlessness, disobedience, ungodliness, injustice, unrighteousness, and impiety.

Jesus did not discuss the subject of sin but showed concern for sinners. The apostle Paul understood sin as an evil power or principality which worked against human beings (Rom. 5:12 to 8:10). In the writings of John, there are hostile forces in the world, a realm of darkness (John 1:5; 3:19-21; 1 John 2:11).

Certain ideas about sin in the Bible are inescapable and will be discussed in great detail later. Sin is always regarded as a very serious matter in the sight of God. It is either estrangement, rebellion, or ungodliness. It results in injustice and unrighteousness. It is so serious that "the wages of sin is death."

Biblical faith stresses that, despite temptation and demonic powers, human beings are responsible for their own sins. There is no suggestion of permitting some outside power to be blamed for our sin.

The universality of sin is echoed in many places in Scripture. All individuals are sinners and all humanity is somehow caught up in a complex scheme of sin.

Biblical faith, in both Old Testament and New Testament, always takes sin seriously but knows of a victory over sin. God's forgiveness will remove sin from the life of the person. Repentance and faith toward God reestablishes the human relationship with God after which sin loses its power. While the greatest saints are never entirely free from sin, and Paul expressed a fear that after having preached to others he might himself be disqualified, there is the promise of the forgiveness of sins. Through faith and repentance, a new relationship is established which brings people back to God, and the sin problem is within reach of the grace of God.

The Consciousness that We Are Sinners

The awareness of sinfulness is a very personal knowledge and is possible only in a context of the knowledge of God. This is due to the fact that sin has no existence apart from the sinner and also that sin is always against God. Consequently, we become aware of our sinfulness only in the presence of God.

Such awareness is not a strange or unusual experience inasmuch as all persons are created in the image of God and their basic nature is to be related to God. It is quite reasonable to assume that they would at least on occasion be conscious of their sinfulness. The biblical writers did not make any distinction between a religious and a reasonable concept because they understood reason itself to be a part of God's creation of man.

A good example of this is found in the prophecy of Isaiah. This great book begins with the call of God for heaven and earth to hear God's word which calls them to the awareness of their rebellion. Isaiah stated, "The ox knows its owner,/and the ass its master's crib;/but Israel does not know,/my people does not understand" (1:3). This is a strong appeal to human reason, but the appeal is stated even more strongly in the words that follow: "Come now, let us reason together,/says the Lord:/though your sins are like scarlet,/they shall be as white as snow;/though they are red like crimson they shall become like wool./If you are willing and obedient,/you shall eat the good of the land" (18-19).

Awareness of Sin Comes in the Presence of God

A uniform confession of worshipers is that, in the presence of God, they are keenly aware of their own sinfulness. The prayers and liturgies which constitute our worship are constant reminders that we have not worshiped God until we have confessed our sins. The beginning of worship is the awareness of the presence of God, as Rudolph Otto has so clearly demonstrated in his discussion of *The Idea of the Holy*. Along with or immediately after this awareness of God's presence, there comes the personal awareness of one's own sinfulness.

In Isaiah's vision, he became aware of his sin. In the presence of God, he cried out, "Woe is me! For I am lost; for I am a man of unclean lips, and I dwell in the midst of a people of unclean lips, for my eyes have seen the King, the Lord of hosts!" (Isa. 6:5).

The psalmist understood this awareness of sin as well as any writer of the Old Testament. In the beautiful penitential psalm, he stood in the presence of God praying, "Have mercy on me, O God, according to thy steadfast love;/according to thy abundant mercy blot out my transgressions./Wash me thoroughly from my iniquity,/and cleanse me from my sin!/For I know my transgressions,/and my sin is ever before me./Against thee, thee only, have I sinned,/and done that which is evil in thy sight" (Ps. 51:1-4a).

This awareness is clearly in the background of the very unusual story of Elijah and the widow of Zarephath. After God had accomplished a miracle by replenishing the jar of meal and cruse of oil, the son of the woman became ill. She said to Elijah, "What have you against me, O man of God? You have come to me to bring my sin to remembrance, and to cause the death of my son!" (1 Kings 17:18). Despite the miraculous gift which God had provided, she associated even the presence of the man of God with the awareness of her own sins.

When we become aware of our sin, we often cringe in guilt and fear. Without adequate reasons, we seek to get rid of our guilt by explaining it away or having someone else to help us rid ourselves of it. There is a sense in which the consciousness of our sin is a very wholesome awareness which extends to us two avenues of hope: it reminds us that we are creatures destined for better things than the sin which at the moment haunts us; and it reminds us that God's presence has not completely abandoned us so that our reconciliation is still possible.

It is quite natural to assume that in Jesus' presence persons would respond with the same awareness of God. One example is the criminal who was crucified alongside Jesus Christ. One criminal railed at Christ, just as the crowd did. The other, however, rebuked the criminal saying, "Do you not fear God, since you are under the same sentence of condemnation? And we indeed justly; for we are receiving the due reward of our deeds; but this man has done nothing wrong." And then he said, "Jesus, remember me when you come into your kingdom" (Luke 23:39-42).

When Paul was met by the risen Lord on the road to Damascus, he immediately asked the Lord, "What wilt thou have me to do?" (Acts 9:6, KJV). There is no declared confession of sin, but when he heard Jesus' question, "Saul, Saul, why do you persecute me?" (Acts 9:3) and learned it was Jesus, Paul's response was obedience. When Paul retold the story in Acts 22, he repeated the charge that he was persecuting the Lord. And, when he repeated the story before Agrippa (Acts 26:9-11), he confessed in detail to the sin of which he was guilty.

When Jesus told the disciples to make another effort in their fishing, they took a very large catch of fish. Simon Peter recognizing that in Jesus Christ he was in the presence of God's revelation "fell down at Jesus' knees, saying, 'Depart from me, for I am a sinful man, O Lord' " (Luke 5:8).

There are numerous stories in the Gospels in which persons who knew they were sinners sought out Jesus for forgiveness. Hearing the Word of God produces a consciousness of sin.

The prophets of the Old Testament addressed Israel with a call to repentance. The proclaimed word of God not only held out the offer of forgiveness but also called the Hebrews to the awareness of their sins against God. This is not a difficult concept because in the Old Testament the word of God is in a real sense the presence of God.

Both the awareness of sin and the awareness of God's will are made known through hearing. The Hebrew call to worship begins, "Hear, O Israel: The Lord our God is one Lord; and you shall love the Lord your God with all your heart, and with all your soul, and with all your might" (Deut. 6:4). This statement is followed by instructions for doing the will of God and warning the people against sin.

Jesus often used the expression, "He who has ears to hear, let him hear." A part of his bringing people to the awareness of God and God's claim upon their lives was to get them to listen to the Word of God. His own call to repentance was clearly stated with reference to questions brought to him about Pilate's massacre of the Galileans and the victims upon whom the tower of Siloam fell. In each instance, he strongly admonished people to repent.

The Law of God and Awareness of Sin

In the first three chapters of Romans, Paul argued that all persons are under condemnation for their sin. He condemned his countrymen because they had sinned knowingly against the will of God stated in their covenant. He argued that those outside the covenant were condemned because God had made plain to them his own invisible nature and they had turned to idolatry (1:18-23). Paul appears to have been arguing that Gentiles outside the covenant have a natural knowledge of the law written in their hearts (2:15). Paul concluded that all humanity is under the condemnation of God for sin, but his logic was based upon the fact that the law of God revealed to us the fact of our sins. He stated this clearly "for no human being will be justified in his sight by works of the law, since through the law comes knowledge of sin" (3:20). He concluded his argument by saying that the righteousness of God has come through faith in Christ (v. 22) but that all are under condemnation because all have sinned.

The significant statement is that the law of God brings a knowledge of sin. Paul had a high estimate of the law of God and saw it in a positive way. His long and involved discussion of the law in the Book of Romans does not clarify all questions we would like to have answered, but he appeared to believe that the law of God brought an awareness of sin and thereby served the purpose of God. Paul stated it rather clearly in the letter to the Galatians, "Now before faith came, we were confined under the law, kept under restraint until faith should be revealed. So that the law was our custodian until Christ came that we might be justified by faith" (3:23-24). This appears to mean that the law of God produces an awareness of our sins and thereby makes a positive contribution toward our repentance.

The Awareness of Sin Comes in Forgiveness

While human beings are in sin, they are estranged from God and are not often conscious of God's presence. Hence, they are not actually conscious that their lives are ones of sinfulness. The Reformers so believed in the utter depravity of all persons that they thought they were incapable of being aware of their sin until after their forgiveness. This may be an overstatement, but there is an element of truth that we only recognize the seriousness of our sin in or after we have come to faith in Jesus Christ. Only after being reconciled to God do we see the real meaning of our previous sinful estrangement.

Albrecht Ritschl argued that we can only comprehend sin from the standpoint of the Christian community. He believed that it was necessary for us to recognize our own individual sin for ourselves before we could recognize that we are also sinners as individuals in the community with all others. Ritschl believed that we could be familiar with the fact of sin even apart from Christianity; but we could never understand its nature, its compass, or its seriousness apart from the revelation of God in Christ. In fact, he believed that we could only grasp the consciousness of our own sin from membership within the Christian community because "the Gospel of the forgiveness of sins is actually the ground of our knowledge of our sinfulness."[7] It should be clear that the fuller consciousness of our sinfulness comes only with reflection after one has entered the Christian faith. Paul would be a clear example.

We certainly could be aware that something is wrong with us and with our society, but the consciousness that sin is a malady expressing our disrupted relationship with God appears to come along with or after our reconciliation to God through forgiveness. It is as if we remember that we once lived in Eden. Within our own experience, we seem to recall the image of God and that God expected more of us than we are. Faith brings a full awareness of the actuality and seriousness of our sin.

Our Sin Is Personal and Theological

Our study thus far has indicated two guidelines for the understanding of sin: *sin* is a word which has no meaning except in terms of personal relationship; and, it is a theological subject in that sin is against God and must be understood in that relationship.

The predominant understanding of sin in the Bible is that of personal estrangement from God. When sin is spoken of as something we do, it is something we do against God out of an attitude of alienation from God. Consequently, sin is a purely personal term. The expression "forgiveness of sins" in the creeds and the expression in the Lord's Prayer "and forgive us our debts, as we also have forgiven our debtors" (Matt. 6:12) are very personal. The tax collector who stood far off with his eyes to the ground, beat upon his breast, and said, "God, be merciful to me a sinner!" (Luke 18:13) was expressing a true understanding of the nature of ourselves as sinners.

Berkhof, while speaking of the nature of human sin, points out that we cannot discover any origin for sin except in human beings. It is not something that exists outside of us and is introduced from someplace else; rather, it originates in human beings in terms of severing a relationship with God.[8]

When we say that the subject of sin is purely theological, we mean that sin is against God and understood only when we think of God. When the psalmist prayed, "Against thee, thee only, have I sinned" (Ps. 51:4), he was not denying any wrongdoing against other persons; rather, he was stating his conviction that sin is against God. If tradition is correct that this is a psalm of David when Nathan the prophet came to accuse him of his sin against Bathsheba, he could hardly have been claiming to have done no wrong to other persons, particularly when we think of the husband of Bathsheba. But the point is that sin is against God. Crimes are committed against persons and are so regarded as crimes in the sight of the law; sin, however, is an offense against God.

When we think of our own sinning, we need to remember that it is against God. Consequently, we can hardly think in terms of making up for it or paying back whatever seems to us to be the sum total of our wrongdoing. When we speak of sin against God as estrangement, we are certainly stressing the personal and theological nature of our subject.

Our Identity as Sinners

It is customary for those writing on this subject to entitle the section before us "The Nature of Sin." That terminology tends to make sin a something which can be defined; I have chosen to deal with the personal nature of sinners for the sake of clarity.

There will be considerable overlapping of terms. Many of the terms are partly inclusive of elements in the other terms. Many of our terms have only slight distinctions from the other terms. There seems to be, however, an advantage to listing the terms in spite of an obvious repetition.

We recognize ourselves as sinners in the context of God's revelation and our awareness of him. Consequently, the identifying marks of sinners will appear as confessions.

We Are Unbelievers

Unbelief should be distinguished from doubt and the temptation to turn away from God. Doubt is in a neutral zone from which one may go in either direction. One may either go deeper into doubt and ultimately into despair. One may go through doubt to a stronger faith. Unbelief, though negative in form, is a positive turning away from God even though it may appear to be an almost innocent drifting.

Unbelief is not nearly as innocent as refusing to believe the doctrines of the church or the moral rules laid down by religious groups. It is rather an act or state describing a human being who turns away from God and seeks to realize his or her own meaning in life without God. Unbelief is the first human step into estrangement.

When Adam and Eve were tempted in the Garden of Eden, the serpent introduced a question about God's dealing with them. The serpent then implied that God was holding out on them by denying them access to the tree so that they would know what God knew. When they entertained the question of God's trustworthiness and surrendered to the temptation as presented, they declared in undeniable terms that at the moment they did not trust God. All of the reasons at their disposal suggested that they should have trusted God; but without reasons, they turned away in unbelief.

As sinners, we are primarily those who do not believe in

God. We may affirm that we do because the culture in which we live has so educated us. We may say we believe there is a God because of logical arguments which others have made or the conclusions to which we ourselves have come, but such general affirmations are radically different from believing in God—trusting God.

Unbelief is a basic violation of God's creation and the nature of human existence. In biblical faith, we are the creatures of God, dependent upon God, and capable of knowing our destiny only by faith in God. Our unbelief is not a benign attitude of disinterest; rather, it is the deliberate direction of our lives. We are unbelievers in spite of all of the evidence which would point us to trust in God. We have numerous reasons for believing in God; the Bible which we trust as authoritative has numerous reminders of our unfaith and calls to us to believe; we even know that we cannot trust ourselves or others. In spite of our better judgment, however, we have turned away from God and find ourselves lost in unbelief.

Some theologians would see unbelief as the basic sin. All theologians see unbelief as near to the origin of sin. Gordon Kaufman, for instance, says that "separation from God" was the root sin from which all others sprang.[9] Unless I am mistaken, separation from God is identical to unbelief. Faith is the only bond we have to God.

We Are Self-Centered

The sin of pride may well be the basic sin, even a rival to unbelief. In the history of the church, two terms have been most often used to describe the nature of our sinfulness, *pride* and *sensuality*. It is almost certain that pride is a sin prior to sensuality. It is certain that theology following Augustine has always favored pride as the basic sin.

In reading again the story of Adam and Eve, one can see included in the response of the parents of the race to the temptation of the serpent not only unbelief but also a strong element of self-centeredness. Prior to this act they appeared to

trust God and live in joyful dependence upon him. The temptation somehow placed their own selves as rivals of God. Then,
when they agreed to do the sin which had been suggested to
them, they asserted themselves against God in a manifestation
of pride.

Perhaps the classic definition of pride in the New Testament
is to be found in Paul's Letter to the Romans. He described how
both Jew and Gentile had refused to obey God who had revealed himself to them in different ways. Paul argued,

> For what can be known about God is plain to them, because
> God has shown it to them. Ever since the creation of the world
> his invisible nature, namely, his eternal power in deity, has
> been clearly perceived in the things that have been made.
> . . . Claiming to be wise, they became fools, and exchanged the
> glory of the immortal God for images resembling mortal man
> or birds or animals or reptiles (Rom. 1:19-23).

This attitude of human beings, who claimed to be wise and still
chose other gods which are obviously not gods at all, is the
expression of both pride and idolatry.

Pride is self-assertion or self-exaltation; it is certainly not
ignorance. Reinhold Niebuhr, in his superb work on anthropology, has given a thorough discussion of sin as pride. He
distinguished three types of pride: pride for power, pride of
knowledge, and pride of virtue. The pride of virtue easily
becomes self-righteousness and spiritual pride.[10]

Our pride is a deep reservoir of sin which generates and
nourishes many other sins, such as the will to power over
others, greed, cruelty, hypocrisy, self-righteousness, dishonesty, and pretension.

It is probable that our pride is one of the essential elements
in all of our other sins. If we analyze the specific things we do
wrong toward God and others, we will usually find a very large
element of self-centeredness.

The biblical admonitions dealing with the remedy for sin
frequently point to the necessity for an awareness of this self-

centeredness. The confession in Isaiah stated, "All we like sheep have gone astray; we have turned everyone to his own way" (Isa. 53:6). When Jesus invited others to follow him, his statement, "If any man would come after me, let him deny himself and take us his cross and follow me" (Matt. 16:24), did not mean that persons could deny themselves by doing without some particular food or drink which they enjoy; rather, Jesus meant that anyone seeking to be his disciple would have to make a basic rejection of self-centeredness in order to follow him.

Weber has recognized *pride, unbelief,* and *disobedience* as the three essential elements in our sinfulness. It was pride that accepted the offer of the serpent to attempt to usurp the prerogatives of God; unbelief which expressed this pride meant that we simply don't trust God; the disobedience which followed is essentially the same as unbelief.[11]

We Are Idolaters

The biblical charge of idolatry sounds a bit strange on modern ears. The sophisticated people of our time would hardly think of themselves as being idolaters. They would think it rather foolish to create a god of wood or stone or precious metal and then bow down before it. The prophets of the Old Testament would probably charge us moderns with the same practice of idolatry as they charged their contemporaries.

In addition to the literal worship of custom-made idols, the idolatry was synonymous with unfaithfulness. The prophets of the Old Testament charged the people with harlotry when they worshiped gods other than Yahweh.

Paul made the basic charge that both Jews and Gentiles who rejected the true God had, in fact, become idolaters (Rom. 1:22-23). Paul's accusation is intelligible in light of the theological concepts which stand back of his writing. Paul believed that God was the Creator and that human beings were the creatures. He believed that human beings were dependent upon God and should acknowledge him as God. For that reason, he could correctly charge all of them and us with idolatry.

There seems to be good evidence for believing that human beings are dependent upon someone or something beyond themselves. Religion is an almost universal phenomenon, as if there is something innate in human beings which expresses our nature as creaturely. Apart from the revelation of God, religion often degenerates into mere superstition. It seems to indicate that we creatures must look to a power beyond ourselves.

At least one contemporary theologian considered idolatry the basic sin. Working out of his understanding that human existence is incomplete and inauthentic apart from a commitment to God, John Macquarrie saw every example of the creatures' forgetting God as idolatry. It is idolatry because we attempt to build our lives upon ourselves and to understand the depth and importance of human existence in terms of only finite entities at the exclusion of God. Macquarrie saw Romans chapter 3 as a classic expression of exchanging the truth about God for a lie and worshiping something else. He also recognized the profound truth which placed as number one of the Ten Commandments, "You shall have no other gods before me!"[12]

If a person accepts Paul Tillich's rather general definition that God might be defined as "that which ultimately concerns us," then the question of our idolatry is no longer in doubt. One need but ask the questions, Is God my ultimate concern; who takes precedence over all other concerns? or Does my life have its ultimate concern in some other reality or value?

We Are Ungodly

The term *ungodly* is used rather generally in the ethical sense to describe those whose ways are contrary to God. Paul, however, used the term in his classic statement about the wrath of God in such a way as to make it comprehensive. Not only is the wrath of God revealed against all ungodliness (Rom. 1:18) but a number of other assertions were also made which seem to describe ungodliness. The ungodly suppress the truth. The truth of God has been revealed to them in creation; in spite of the evidence, they do not honor God but rather exalt themselves in pride, and resort to idolatry. Having abandoned God, their degradation sinks even lower. Having exchanged God's truth for a lie, they degenerate into dishonorable passions, a base mind, and improper conduct. Then Paul listed a number of terms which characterized the ungodly: wickedness, evil, covetousness, malice, envy, murder, strife, deceit, malignity, gossip, slander, insolence, haughtiness, boastfulness, etc. (Rom. 1:18-32). As creatures in the image of God, we should be godly. Both theologically and ethically, we as sinners fall into the category of the ungodly.

We Are Sensual

In Roman Catholic and Protestant circles, pride has been most often regarded as the first or root sin. In the Eastern Church, sensuality has more often appeared to be the basic sin.

Sensuality certainly includes the lust for sexuality, but is a broader term indicating life is centered on the pleasures that appeal to the human senses. Sexual sins are always a number-one contender. In the first chapter of Romans, Paul seemed to make the sin of pride or idolatry the prior sin which led to the sin of sensuality.

Thomas Aquinas appeared to include in sensuality the love for good things also, but the sin consisted in the fact that we love certain good things inordinately. In short, one may derive great pleasure from fame or wealth or even good music, and give oneself so inordinately to that temporal good that one forgets God. But Thomas Aquinas apparently understood this kind of sensuality as itself the result of a prior love for one's self.

If sensuality is an unlimited love for temporal values and good things, it is but another expression of the sin of pride or self-love.

We are reminded of the Lord's teaching that we should love

the Lord our God and neighbors as we love ourselves. The twofold commandment appears to leave adequate room both for loving our neighbors and for loving ourselves after a prior love for God. Sensuality would reverse that combination and focus on the love of self and the love of those things which the self enjoys.

We Are Rebels

Sin has often been characterized by the term *rebellion.* The word *rebellion* certainly implies the willful aspect of our sinfulness. There are strong biblical teachings to the effect that our turning against God is a willful decisive turning and that the idolatry in which we engage is not merely a childlike mistake. The concept is so well grounded that Emil Brunner entitled his Christian doctrine about human existence *Man in Revolt,* but he did not play on the word *rebellion* itself.

There are examples of our sinfulness which may be characterized as missing the mark or straying away. When Jesus told the four parables that are in the fifteenth chapter of Luke, he included one parable which clearly stressed the willful nature of the sin. While all four parables illustrate the nature of God, the parable of the prodigal son stresses a sinfulness related to willful choice or decisiveness. In the same chapter, however, the lost coin and the lost sheep parables, while stressing the nature of the owner and the shepherd, nevertheless, in a secondary way suggest a kind of lostness not easily describable as willful. The older brother, while adhering to the religion and the property of the father, exhibits the prideful self-love that would qualify as rebellion.

We Are a Universal Conspiracy

The expression *universal conspiracy* is intended to denote at least three beliefs: every individual is a sinner; all of humanity constitutes a community in which sin is a basic characteristic;

and this situation is not an accident or inheritance, but an evil creation which we have willfully superimposed upon the original creation.

The universality of sin appears to be a well-established fact which needs no justification. Paul worded the belief without feeling any need to explain or illustrate, "since all have sinned and fall short of the glory of God" (Rom. 3:23).

There are numerous indications that the whole of humanity is related in sin. Isaiah confessed his individual sin and then the sin of his community (6:5). Paul not only taught the universality of sin as including all individuals but he also assumed that the entire race of humanity was related in sin. While contrasting Adam and Christ, he pointed out, "Therefore as sin came into the world through one man and death through sin, and so death spread to all men because all men sinned" (Rom. 5:12). He was not speaking of biological transmission but of the fact that humanity is one in its sinfulness just as it is one in its original creation. Because of our interrelatedness in the human community, some have attempted to interpret sin as being transmitted through human culture from one generation to the next and throughout the culture.

As individual sinners and as a family of sinners, we are responsible for the sin in our own departure from God and in the creation of our culture which for all practical purposes is idolatrous. We worship money and luxury.

The doctrine of original sin has been mistakenly assumed by some to mean biological transmission of sin. In fact, it stresses the universality of sin, that all of our individual lives have been tainted by sin in all aspects of our lives and that we are tied up in a community of sinfulness. The collective nature of our sin is adequately illustrated in customs and prejudices and especially in nationalisms, in which we create suffering and misery for other persons through what we rationalize as principle or patriotism.

We Are Fallen

The sin described in Genesis 3 is often referred to as the "fall of man." The phrase tends to be weaker than the narrative permits because *fall* suggests something benign like stumbling, or straying, or accidentally falling. Actually, the phrase designates the awareness that we were created to live on a high plane as God's creatures but that we are actually living on a much lower plane in estrangement from God.

Albert Camus, an atheist and an existentialist, wrote a book entitled *The Fall.* He did not believe in God nor the theological concepts in this book. The main character Jean Baptiste Clemenceau tells his life story as a successful lawyer. The whole point of the story is the progressive discovery of his fallenness. He apparently recognized his fallenness when he heard the screams of a woman drowning in the river Seine in Paris while he walked nearby. For a moment he was tempted to plunge in and save her, but he did not do so. He looked to see if anyone were watching and walked away. For a while he heard her cries in the nights that followed, but they were not so loud or frequent. He noted how he championed the causes of the widow and the orphan in court. He thought he was noble until he discovered that he did it to be seen—for his sake, not theirs. He portrayed the sense of pride as a desire for height above others. This was Augustine's view of sin as pride.

Human beings are constantly aware, even though it may be a remote awareness, of their destiny. This vague memory from the distant past reminds us all that we, indeed, were in Eden but long ago departed. We are the fallen creatures destined to live in fellowship with God, but we have settled for much less.

We Are a Mystery and a Contradiction

Our sinfulness is a contradiction. We know better, and we know that we know better. We go on, however, living in our estrangement, aware of God from whom we are estranged and who waits to reconcile us to himself. We do evil deeds knowing that, even if they bring momentary pleasure, they result in long and bitter suffering for ourselves and for others. Wars have taught us through bitter experience that we cannot solve our problems through fighting and killing, but we deplete the resources of our planet stockpiling weapons capable of destroying everything on the planet. We continue with more conventional weapons to kill and destroy. And we all know better. Our lives are a bitter contradiction.

We live our lives under a curse. The curse of sin is not an arbitrary decree of God imposed upon humanity; rather, it is that evil creation we have superimposed upon God's creation. We remember Eden, but we are fugitives. We are the hunter and the hunted. The toil and the pain and the thorns and thistles are real.

Our sinfulness is not merely a problem, for problems can be solved. Our sin is a mystery in which we participate; it is a part of us, and it is irrational. We cannot give a reason why we are sinners. In fact, there appears to be no explanation. We cannot point to the cause of our sin; we can only indicate the occasion and the context and our own mysterious involvement in it.

We cannot define sin as "something." For God is the Creator and the things which God created are good. Our sin is a denial of creation which in some mysterious way becomes very real. It is a terrifying reality and certainly not something which is just imperfect or may someday be good; as Weber says, it is "positive negation."[13]

The Consequences of Our Sin

There is a considerable amount of overlapping between the nature of our sin and the consequences of our sin. It is not always easy to distinguish between a characteristic of the thing itself and a result of that reality. The following consequences are rather generally acknowledged and will be discussed only briefly.

Estrangement

We are estranged from ourselves, from God, and from other persons. This estrangement is the direct result of our sin against God. As human individuals in the image of God, we possess an integrity and a unity within our own selves which is the creation of God. When in our sin we cease to believe in God, we introduce a contradiction within ourselves which is like a wedge driving us apart. The inward conflict is universally confessed today, acknowledged in therapy sessions, and exposed in novels and plays. Paul wrote a penetrating analysis of this estrangement in the seventh chapter of Romans.

We are estranged from God because we severed the bond of faith. Estranged from God and then from each other, Adam and Eve were cast out of the Garden. They were left with a haunting memory of what it was once like when they were right with God.

In sin we are estranged from one another. It is not incidental in the account of Adam and Eve that Adam sought to blame Eve for the sin which he had done. His own estrangement from God led to an estrangement from Eve. Human beings confess to a loneliness within their own families, to a sense of having been abandoned even in the presence of friends. When human beings have lost the vertical dimension of faith in God, they become aliens in God's world and strangers to their own households. The existentialist theologians like Tillich, Bultmann, and Macquarrie are particularly perceptive at the point of sin as estrangement.

Lostness

There is no better word in the English language to describe the consequence of sin than the word *lostness*. This word carries with it not only the idea of not knowing the way to one's destination but also the idea of danger and, worst of all, aimlessness. The figure calls to mind our having known or read about persons who were lost at sea or in the desert or in the mountains. This lostness evokes deep feeling for the lost and those who wait.

A part of the anxiety in lostness is the danger and the uncertainty. The child who is lost by having strayed away from the group while on a camping expedition is in the wilderness alone, and there are many dangers even in a friendly wilderness. People wait feverishly by their radios for news of the lost.

Worst of all, however, lostness means aimlessness or purposelessness. What could be worse for a human being created in the image of God with destiny than to be drifting aimlessly in a world such as this with all of its opportunity and challenge? What greater suffering than to live in a challenging age without a purpose? God gives purpose to his creatures. And those who are in sin are lost.

Jesus described his purpose in life by saying that he came "to seek and to save the lost" (Luke 19:10). He described what it means to be lost in the four parables of the fifteenth chapter of Luke.

Lostness is one stage worse than estrangement. Estrangement implies someone to go back to; estrangement carries with it a memory. Lostness means that one has neither the sun by day nor the moon or Polaris by night—only an endless and meaningless horizon without any point of reference.

Loss

A devastating consequence of our sin is loss. There is quite a difference between lostness and loss. Lostness may be temporary; loss has the sound of permanence. Lostness may be removed by finding and followed by rejoicing; but loss is deprivation, ruin, destruction; and there is no way to recover the years which the locusts have eaten.

A consequence of sin is the loss of precious days and years and opportunities. It is the lost love and fellowship which characterizes relationship with God. Sin results in the loss of life as a pilgrimage and bankrupts it into a vagrancy.

Bondage

Sin may be described as bondage. Bondage may be a consequence of sin. One cannot discuss the subject of sin without
discussing the bondage. The freedom in which and for which
God created human beings has been replaced by a slavery
which appears in a multitude of guises. Rightly do people
cringe at the thought of physical slavery in which one human
being is bought and sold like property; but there are numerous
forms of slavery more terrifying than the servitude of one
human being to another. Those of us who have never been in
prison are terrified at the thought of the bondage of imprisonment; but many of us are in a greater, more degrading, and
more permanent slavery than those within prisons; and some
persons in prison, Bonhoeffer for instance, have exhibited a
remarkable freedom.

Paul used the expression "sold under sin" (Rom. 7:14) and
pointed out that "our old self was crucified with him so that
the sinful body might be destroyed, and we might no longer
be enslaved to sin" (Rom. 6:6).

The whole theme of salvation can be stated in the word
redemption, which means God redeems us from our slavery and
sets us free. Paul frequently spoke of our salvation as having
"been set free from sin" (Rom. 6:18,22; 8:2) and our new estate
as Christians as one of freedom, "For freedom Christ has set
us free; stand fast therefore, and do not submit again to a yoke
of slavery" (Gal. 5:1).

Irresponsibility

Just as responsibility is a basic human characteristic, irresponsibility is a characteristic of our lives when we are in
unbelief. In each act of sin, we exhibit a noticeable tendency
to blame someone else or to deny responsibility for our actions.
Adam denied his responsibility by first blaming Eve and then
God. We blame others, our environment, our weaknesses, even
our parents. It is quite obvious when one is caught in a serious

fault. Persons guilty of serious crimes will often plead insanity as the last resort to save their lives, but they usually plead "temporary" insanity. Basic humanity is responsible; sinful humanity is irresponsible.

The first step from unbelief to faith is repentance; and, repentance is the turning to God from self with the confession, "I am the sinner." Most human judges are prone to leniency toward the accused in proportion to the accused's acknowledgment of responsibility or guilt.

Depravity

More will be said later about original sin, but one aspect of it needs to be mentioned at this point. The phrase designates a serious and continuing condition of the human being in sin. It designates the belief that sinful persons have nothing within them of a meritorious nature to commend them to God. Some see this as an inherited trait, but that is tied to the idea that original sin is transmitted biologically from parents to children. This idea is not consistent. Biological transmission would not allow a basis for individual responsibility. It would make sin a natural, not a moral, fact like the color of one's eyes.

Depravity designates a consequence of sin in which the human person is twisted. It is more than an inclination toward sin. One's basic nature is so that sins of self-centeredness are inevitable. Some use the phrase *total depravity*, but that has created considerable mischief because it led to the idea that we are totally bad or totally evil, which is not the case. As sinners we are self-centered, living in unbelief, estranged from God, the source of our life and purpose, and, therefore we are crippled, retarded, subhuman.

Depravity means that all of our lives are affected by our sin, but it does not mean that we are totally evil, incapable of any good at all. It does mean that our sin affects every area of our lives and that by ourselves we cannot remove sin from our lives and earn the favor of God.

The Curse

The strange term *curse* appeared as one of the immediate consequences of sin (Gen. 3:14). The word sounds like magic, hexes, or voodoo to us, but that is a mistake. The curse was the consequence of sin. Adam and Eve lived with the consequences of their sin. God did not decree that Cain would kill Abel as a punishment for their sin; rather, sin has consequences which inevitably follow. The "wrath of God" in Romans almost certainly means living in the fallen world with sinful individuals and humanity suffering the consequences of our sin not according to the will of God but contrary to it. God wills that we should obey him and live in peace.

In the biblical sense, the whole world today lives under the curse of our sins. We have the resources and ability to produce enough food for all people, but a large percentage of the people of the world are hungry. We have the knowledge that our weapons can destroy civilization; but because of our fear, greed, nationalistic pride, or something else, we plunge downward on a course toward annihilation. We have the ability to eradicate many diseases; but our boundary lines, fears, and prejudices consign many peoples to lives of misery and early death. To live in a world like this with the potential for such achievement, but to be unable or unwilling to do the good, is to live under a curse—another consequence of sin.

Death

"For the wages of sin is death, but the free gift of God is eternal life in Christ Jesus our Lord" (Rom. 6:23). The fact of death is the most disquieting awareness in human existence; it stalks our lives with the constant threat that we shall cease to be at all—a total negation. In the language of the Bible, death is a complex term.[14]

In the classical view of humanity from Greco-Roman thought, death is not serious at all. It may be terminal but it is not ultimate because in that understanding the soul is all that really matters and it is immortal. Only the body dies. In the naturalistic view, humanity sees death as the ultimate end of human life from which there is no escape. We, like the animals, die and are no more.

The biblical view of death is quite different, even though the distinctions are not always clear. Death is, of course, the opposite of life, but it is also about as complex. In the Old Testament, for instance, death was seen as being gathered to one's fathers (2 Kings 22:20), as going down to the dark and shadowy Sheol (Ps. 6:5). There are times, however, when death appears in a more cheerful context as if after death we shall go to be with God (Ps. 73:24).

With reference to sin, death means much more than that which the coroner certifies. It means separation from life because it is separation from God. Physical death is a separation from life, in one sense; but in the case of Jesus Christ who was raised from the dead, the separation was not ultimate. Biblical faith posits the fearful possibility of an ultimate separation from God and life which is called "the second death" (Rev. 21:8). Apparently, physical death is the first death, and this ultimate negative judgment is the second.

It is more complicated, however, than merely numbering them. In the New Testament, death is a separation from God and life even while we are still living. Paul described our sinful lives as being "dead through the trespasses and sins" (Eph. 2:1).

Paul used the terms *death* and *life* with a richer meaning than mere biology. We are already "dead in sin" while we are still alive—separated from God and life. We can die to sin and be buried and raised to a "newness of life" (Rom 6:4) right now. He spoke of our old sinful estranged personal humanity as our "old self" who has been crucified with Christ and in whose place a "new self" appears right now. Here both death and life are present realities. The resurrection, also, without losing its future hope is a present reality. Faith creates such a radical transformation of a sinful person into a new person that one can say, "our old self was crucified with him . . . no longer enslaved to sin. . . . So you also must consider yourselves dead to sin and alive to God in Christ Jesus" (Rom. 6:6-11).

To say that "the wages of sin is death" (Rom. 6:23) is much more serious than to say that at some time our earthly lives will cease. It is to say that our sin consigns us to a life of death now, each day we are separated from the source and destiny of life, and we stand in jeopardy of eternal separation from God. It does mean physical death. Jesus died. Adam did not die immediately in the physical sense when he sinned against God as a literal reading of Genesis would require.

The Christian understanding of death is not a casual one because this life is a gift and stewardship from God. This existence is as important as eternal life; it is just not as long. Christians do not want to die prematurely. For Christians, however, physical death is not the last word; we believe that Jesus Christ was raised from the dead never to die again, so we also believe that is our destiny because of our faith in him. This is the argument of 1 Corinthians 15, and here is the clue toward understanding Paul's expression that "the wages of sin is death."

Paul contrasted Adam with Christ, death with life. He reasoned, "For as by a man came death, by a man has come also the resurrection of the dead. For as in Adam all die, so also in Christ shall all be made alive" (1 Cor.15:21-22). Paul argued that the race of humanity is one. We are all the family of Adam, and we are all sinners like Adam. The result of our sin is death. In contrast, Christ is the new Adam. When we have faith in Christ, we become new persons, we are a family, our sin is overcome, and the end is life, not death. As sinners we are now living in death and estrangement from God. Our destiny as sinners is death. The ultimate destiny of sinners is the eternal second death.

The Origin of Sin

Seemingly, we deceive ourselves into believing that, if we could discover the origin of sin, we could explain it. If we could explain it, we would have reduced it to a problem; and we can solve problems. If sin is a negative reality, can we do more than describe it and point to its location? If indeed, as I believe, the discussion should focus on sinners and not sin, then the rest of this discussion may be irrelevant.

If we regard sin as an entity, then there are only two possible explanations as to its origin: either God created it or we human beings did. Its origin would have to be in God's creative act or in human freedom.

Sin exists only in personal embodiment; then, we are talking about unbelief, pride, rebellion, or disobedience. We are talking about a strained or estranged relationship. We need clarification on the terms common in the discussion of our sinfulness: original sin, Satan, and misuse of freedom.

Original Sin

On the popular level, original sin has been understood to mean that Adam's sin, the original sin, has been inherited by all other human beings. The doctrine has been founded not only on Genesis 3 but also on a statement in the Psalms (51:5) and two statements by Paul (Rom. 5:12; 1 Cor. 15:22).

When the psalmist wrote, "Behold, I was brought forth in iniquity,/and in sin did my mother conceive me" (Ps. 51:5), he was confessing his own sin, not reporting on his mother's. This passage has been used by theologians to suggest that sin is biologically transmitted, thereby not only denying our personal responsibility for our sin but also making God's creation and our procreation by means of sexual union evil in itself. This passage must not be interpreted, "as any attempt at self-justification via a concept of hereditary sin or congenital depravity." Such an idea is "foreign to the Bible."[15] Rather, the psalmist was confessing his sin and that of his entire human existence and community. He did not date his sin even with awareness of it, but rather, from the very beginning of his life.

Paul wrote, "Therefore as sin came into the world through one man and death through sin, and so death spread to all men because all men sinned" (Rom. 5:12). Many have taken this to mean that all others inherited their sin from Adam. Paul was using the rabbinic understanding of the fall based on a passage from 2 Esdras (3:21-22; 4:30). He went on, however, to contrast this fact of our solidarity in sin through Adam with our new humanity in Christ. His point was not that we automatically became sinners through inheritance; or it would be necessary to argue that all are, therefore, saved automatically through Christ. He was stressing the universality of and solidarity in sin.[16] The other passage, "For as in Adam all die, so also in Christ shall all be made alive" (1 Cor. 15:22), while speaking in the context of the resurrection, stresses the same contrast: in Adam we are all sinners destined to death; in Christ we are destined to life.

The idea of family or clan solidarity is not easy for modern people to understand. It was not difficult for the ancients. When the individual Achan violated the orders of Joshua and was convicted, not only he, but his entire family and livestock were stoned to death. The passages indicated do not stress inheritance and certainly not biological transmission of sin. They stress the universality of sin, and our solidarity in sin. Yet "in spite of this the individual does not lose his responsibility."[17]

Satan

Another way human beings have sought to avoid responsibility for their sin is to blame the devil. In the New Testament, numerous terms designate this adversary or tempter. Examples are Satan, devil, prince, enemy, dragon, Belial, etc.

In the Genesis account, there was a serpent. Only in the Book of Revelation (20:2) is the serpent identified as "the Devil and Satan." There are only three references to Satan as a proper name in the whole Old Testament (Zech. 3:1; Job 1 and 2; and 1 Chron. 21:1). In these instances, the adversary is a tempter, not the cause of human sin.

Temptation is not the same as sin. Persons often feel guilty for their temptations. This is an error; it is an injustice to oneself. Jesus was tempted. So long as one resists the temptation and maintains integrity with faith, it is not sin. We have misunderstood Jesus on his statements about hate and lust. Deep-seated hate is murder; cultivated lust is adultery. The temptation or thought of either, however, is not necessarily sin—only temptation.

The idea that the devil is the cause of sin is based on a misinterpretation of the Bible. The serpent, or the devil, is the tempter, the suggestion, the occasion. Never is the tempter the "cause" of our sin, only the occasion. We are the cause; and we are always responsible.

Misuse of Freedom

Previously we noted the marvelous freedom and responsibility of the creatures in the image of God. We noted the tension within the finite creature who is aware of the infinite. We noted that temptation is attractive to us precisely at the point of this tension. Neither finitude nor tension, however, can be charged with procreating our sin. This may be the location of its origin, but the "why" has not been explained.

Conclusion

To ascribe to Satan the power to invade God's creation and snatch us away from God would mean that God is not God, but only a god. Our faith in the one God forbids such a notion. We are left with only two who could be held responsible for our sinfulness: God or us. In our freedom, we turned from God into idolatry and unbelief. So we are responsible for our sins.

We have not explained our sin. Our sin is irrational and contradictory. One cannot explain the irrational. How could one give a rational explanation for an irrational act? Every time we are overcome by a serious sin we ask ourselves the question that has no answer, "Why did I do it?" While it has no answer or explanation, there is a victory over it, a return from it, or a deliverance. Better still, God in his grace has provided a way to restore human beings to their destined relationship as his creatures in faith and freedom. That story has to do with Jesus of Nazareth and a cross outside the north wall of Jerusalem.

If while we were fleeing from God he still sought after us, our estrangement from him was not total. His search and our memory of the image of God, however dim, maintained a relationship. Even estrangement and rebellion are kinds of relationship. God the Creator, who can create out of nothing, can create a new creation out of an estranged one.

Notes

1. John Macquarrie, *Principles of Christian Theology*, 2nd ed. (New York: Charles Scribner's Sons, 1977), pp. 260-262.

2. Paul Tillich, *Systematic Theology*, 2 (Chicago: The University of Chicago Press, 1957), pp. 44-59.

3. Reinhold Niebuhr, *The Nature and Destiny of Man*, 1 (New York: Charles Scribner's Sons, 1941), p. 232 quoting Thomas Aquinas, *Summa*, Part II (First Part), Question 77, Art. 4.

4. Ibid.

5. Otto Weber, *Foundations of Dogmatics*, 1, trans. Darrell L. Guder (Grand Rapids: William B. Eerdmans Publishing Company, 1981), p. 592.

6. Walter Rauschenbusch, *A Theology for the Social Gospel* (New York and Nashville: Abingdon Press, 1917), pp. 155 *ff.*

7. Albrecht Ritschl, *The Christian Doctrine of Justification and Reconciliation*, trans. H. R. Mackintosh and A. B. Macaulay (Edinburgh: T. & T. Clark, 1900), p. 327-328.

8. Hendrikus Berkhof, *Christian Faith: An Introduction to the Faith*, trans. Sierd Woudstra (Grand Rapids: William B. Eerdmans Publishing Company, 1979), p. 199-200.

9. Gordon Kaufman, *Systematic Theology: A Historicist Perspective* (New York: Charles Scribner's Sons, 1968), p. 363.

10. Niebuhr, p. 188-189.

11. Weber, p. 594.

12. Macquarrie, p. 260; also citing Exodus 20:3.

13. Weber, I, 594.

14. Moody, pp. 293 *ff.*; TDNT, III, 14 *ff.*

15. John I Durham, "Psalms" *The Broadman Bible Commentary,* 4 (Nashville: Broadman Press, 1971), p. 276.

16. C. H. Dodd, "The Epistle of Paul to the Romans," *The Moffatt New Testament Commentary* (New York and London: Harper and Brothers Publishers, 1932) p. 79.

17. William Sanday and Arthur C. Headlam, "Critical and Exegetical Commentary on the Epistle to the Romans," *The International Critical Commentary* (New York: Charles Scribner's Sons, n.d.), p. 136.

9

Providence and a World in Unbelief

When we speak of God, we are always speaking of God as he has revealed himself in human history. Consequently, we are speaking of God as he is related to creatures. Previous chapters have tried to speak of the nature of God. We come now to think of God in relation to a world in unbelief.

Creation speaks of origin. It also speaks of the reality which continues. Those who believe in God prefer to speak of the universe as God's creation. We want to deal now with the continuing relationship of God to the creation.

All that can really be said about God with any assurance must be said on the basis of revelation. Revelation involves personal disclosure to personal beings—not objective information. Consequently, there are many questions about the physical universe that are specifically religious questions and deserve attention. The space limitations of this volume preclude that specific investigation.[1] We shall have to concentrate primarily on the continuing relationship of God with the human creatures.

Theologians speak of this continuing relationship in several ways. They speak about continuing creation, the unfinished creation, the preservation of creation, and God's providence. I have chosen to use the term *providence* for reasons that will be obvious.

Providence

The word *providence* comes to us from the Latin *pro videre* which means "to see beforehand" from a Greek antecendent *pronoia* which means "to know before."

Providence has come to designate two ideas in belief: (1) God sustains the creation, and (2) God governs or guides the creation. G. C. Berkouwer, for instance, sees the sustenance as maintaining creation and the governance as related to the purpose or end to which God guides creation.[2] Langdon Gilkey, who has written a significant work on the subject, understood providence to designate "the rule of God over both natural and historical events."[3]

Preservation

Modern people seem to think that the universe is self-existent. However, biblical faith sees creation as dependent on God. The belief that God preserves or sustains creation is vital to the belief in God. The idea in no way ignores the orders of creation or the "laws of nature," as we say. It insists, rather, that the entire creation is dependent on God. The idea is more involved than mere continuation; it also includes the idea of coherence.

When one Old Testament writer spoke of creation, he thought about God, "Thou art the Lord, thou alone; thou has made heaven, the heaven of heavens, with all their host, the earth and all that is on it, the seas and all that is in them; and *thou preservest all of them* " (Neh. 9:6, author's italics). The universe does not exist of itself. God sustains it. The great Augustine spoke of God as upholding the creation over the abyss of nothingness into which it would fall if God at any moment did not actively hold it.

The New Testament writers also thought of God as "holding" it up and together. "He is before all things, and in him all things hold together" (Col. 1:17). Jesus Christ "reflects the glory of God and bears the very stamp of his nature, upholding the universe by his word of power" (Heb. 1:3). Jesus said the

Father keeps watch over every sparrow (Matt. 10:29). In God, "we live and move and have our being" (Acts 17:28).

Governance and Guidance

Belief in God requires believing in the sovereignty of God. If God is sovereign, then obviously he is in ultimate charge of the creation. God, however, created human beings to whom he delegated freedom and power. God gave us dominion. God entrusted to human creatures power to change themselves, others, and history—even the earth to a degree. When God created human beings and gave us such freedom, he imposed a limit upon himself at least temporarily.

We have noted the human rebellion against God and the serious effects of that estrangement. God does not govern every detail in history. People make real decisions in their freedom. The will of God is not done on earth as it is in heaven. We live in a world at war with God. In what way, then, does he sustain and govern a world in unbelief?

God guides those persons whom he calls and who trust him. This is one way, probably among other ways, in which he guides his creation toward its purpose. We need to note that God is not excluded from his universe. He could call it to judgment or to a halt at any moment of his choosing. As long, however, as he allows his creatures true freedom, he limits his own power. He does not coerce the wills of persons. He does call them, however, and guides many of them.

The call of Abraham was an act of God related to God's guiding the history of his people. The subsequent history of Israel in the covenant demonstrates God's continuing relationship, sustenance, governance, correction, and achievement of his purpose in the lives of people who are still free to respond or revolt.

The Joseph story is a beautiful saga from patriarchal times which reveals one way in which providence works. The older brothers, jealous of Joseph, sold him into slavery. That is a crime anywhere and at any time. God does not condone crime;

he is not a slave trader. God, however, does not abort his purpose every time a creature commits a crime. In this instance, God continued his sustenance and guidance over both the victim and perpetrators of the crime.

The young man had a long layover in Egypt, but his pilgrimage was filled with both adventure and purpose. His rise to high position, while it may have been aided by God's help, was not without skill and work on his part. Joseph obviously did not at the time see the meaning of the history in which he was a principal actor. During the famine in later years when his older brothers came to Egypt for grain, Joseph was the official to whom they appealed.

The amazing response of Joseph illustrates providence. He could have had them beheaded and would have been applauded for it. Joseph did not forgive his brothers out of a sentimental, familial concern. Rather, he realized that both they and he had a purpose under God which was greater than their crime or his anger. He said, "As for you, you meant evil against me; but God meant it for good" (Gen. 50:20). That abrupt turn in the sentence expressed in the words, "but God . . ." reminds us of providence. Gerhard von Rad recognized the theological importance of this long narrative. He noted that the hand of God works even through the confusion of human crime and guilt to direct everything "to a gracious goal."[4]

Jeremiah had the misfortune of living in the grim generation before the fall of Judah. God called him to be a prophet. Later Jeremiah could look back and see the hand of God in his life from the beginning of the pilgrimage. He spoke of God's call in these terms, "Before I formed thee in the belly I knew thee, and before thou camest forth out of the womb I sanctified thee" (Jer. 1:5, KJV).

Centuries later Paul, whose early career included persecuting the church, was called to be an apostle. He looked back even over the years of his rebellion aware of the unseen hand of God in his life and wrote, "But when he who had set me apart before I was born, and had called me through his grace, was pleased to reveal his Son to me" (Gal. 1:15).

Peter, who had willingly responded to Christ, did not know the purpose of God very clearly. The death of Christ seemed to be the end. He spoke on the Day of Pentecost, however, indicating that the crucifixion of Christ had been a human crime, "But God raised him up" (Acts 2:24). At this point he could see the hand of God but not before. "But God. . . ."

After Paul had reflected and understood what God had been doing throughout the centuries, he wrote, "But when the time had fully come, God sent forth his Son, born of woman, . . . to redeem" (Gal. 4:4-5). This insight is the recognition of God's providence.

A Personal Belief

All of the information cited indicates that belief in the providence of God is based on an understanding of personal experience. *Providence* is not a term that would substitute for something like natural law. We are speaking about our understanding of God's work in our lives and in the personal history of people. Most religious people can look back and see the hand of God in their lives. The belief is always one stated in retrospect however.

Providence in History

The insistence that providence is personal does not take it out of the realm of history as a whole. History is the story of persons in community. The covenant people of Israel and the Christian covenant are illustrations of our belief in God's providence on the larger screen of history. The passage cited in Galatians 4 is a sweeping view of the providence of God in history.

To speak of God's providence in the history of Israel and the Christian community is not to overlook history as a whole. We believe that both Israel's role and that of the church involves all peoples and all history. The kingdom of God is not a refuge for Christians; it is the purpose of God for all of his creatures. The Christians are the welcoming committee and that only because they are there.

There are parallels to the idea of providence in nonbiblical thought, but they are quite different. Emil Brunner cites the Stoic idea as a kindred notion. It was different, however, because it was impersonal and deterministic. The biblical idea of providence is personal and allows freedom to humanity.[5]

Augustine, in his *Confessions,* indicated in retrospect how he had recognized God's providence in his life. He had left the Manichaeans not because of his piety but so that he could study astronomy. His pious mother, Monica, would have kept him in Carthage so she could have led him to salvation. He lied to her, however, and went to Rome to enhance his teaching career. Later he went to Milan to hear the eloquent preacher Ambrose. His interest was not religious edification. He wanted to improve his own rhetoric. He later wrote, however, how God had knowingly led him to Milan as a part of the process by which Augustine became a Christian. Augustine abandoned the use of the word *fortune* and spoke of God's providence.

Augustine, however, despite his predestinarian views, did not relieve humanity of the responsibility for sin. He thought that we sin in freedom. He thought that God sustains the powers of nature and our own lives. He taught that God sustains us even when we are living in sin and estrangement.

Thomas Aquinas saw *predestination* and *providence* as terms which relate God's actions to the world. Providence is God's control. The world is mixed with good and evil. He apparently thought that God permitted evil so as to bring forth some greater good.

John Calvin, as one would expect, followed Augustine in a way and then went beyond in terms of predestination. Calvin thought of providence as God's daily operation of the universe. The sun would not come up in the mornings unless God raised it. He argued on the ground of the "long day" when Joshua fought the battle, and he also argued that God turned back the sundial for Hezekiah to prove to us that it does not operate by chance but only on the command of God.

Meaning and Destiny

The idea of providence reminds us of God's continuing relationship to the world in terms of sustaining and governing it. This gives our lives meaning in a creation with purpose.

Our destiny is pointed toward a future of God's design. This destiny will ultimately prevail for those who trust God. This conviction dignifies daily life and puts hope in life by giving it direction, destiny, and purpose. Believing in the providence of God makes life an adventure.

Providence, Not Fate

The word *fate* designates a belief that human lives and events are determined in advance by the gods or chance or material considerations or God. In some systems, fate is a kind of principle in reality which is all-determining. It should be obvious that *fate* is an alien word in the biblical vocabulary. Christians do not talk about fate; rather, they talk about the purpose of God in the lives of free and responsive persons—providence.

Providence and the Mystery of Evil

In the discussion of "Human Creatures in Unbelief," we looked briefly at the devastating effects of human sin on human life. We did not, however, really consider the larger problem of evil, nor does space allow us to do so now. Serious thinkers are always troubled by the cosmic evil that seems to prevail at present. A glance at the literature will reveal a deep concern for the evil in God's good creation.[6]

Evil as Problem and Mystery

Evil is both a problem and a mystery. In general, we think of a problem as something "there" which obstructs our progress in some way but which can be solved, or at least we think it can be solved. A mystery, however, is of a different species. A mystery does not yield to the probes of reason. After all of our research and effort, the mystery still remains. It goes without saying, however, that our diligent effort may well get irrelevant matters and superstitions out of the way. If so, we are free to deal with the mystery. It is a mystery, however, because it is a part of us and not a problem out there before us.

While discussing sin, we noted that it is irrational. We all perpetuate evil in our irrational thinking and behavior. We often reach the correct rational conclusions and still, for no reason at all, act contrary to our better judgment. Evil is both a theoretical and practical problem. That, however, though serious, is relatively mild compared to the larger fact of evil as mystery.

Biblical faith appears to acknowledge a fact of evil on a greater scale than human sin. The presence of a tempter before the sin of Adam and Eve suggests an evil presence or person in the creation before human sin. The concept of the devil, or Satan, is an attempt to acknowledge this awareness. It needs to be noted, however, that Satan does not give us an explanation of the presence of evil in God's good creation. If one takes the position that Satan, like human beings, was a good creation who fell, the person still has not "explained." It is not reasonable that God would permit such a fallen being to harass all earthly creatures. Biblical teachings never permit people to blame their sins on the devil. The devil is the tempter, the occasion, but not the cause, of sin. We are responsible.

Some interpreters make a distinction between natural and moral evil. Natural evil is that which results from natural causes like tornadoes, epidemics, or diseases. Moral evil is that which results from immoral decisions and acts of persons. The concern of this volume is exclusively about moral evil. A case could be made that natural evil is a contradiction of terms. If it is from nature, then we may control or change it or, in the case of diseases, prevent or cure by inoculation. If it can be solved technologically, it is not evil in the first place. Its results may be devastating, but the word *evil* should be used to deal with matters in the moral area.

The Problem of Theodicy

The attempt to give a rational explanation for the presence of evil in God's good creation is called *theodicy*. The word means the "justification of God" from *theos* (God) and *dikē* (just). The question is, If God is both good and powerful, how can you explain evil? It is reasonable to say that if God is good, he would oppose evil and if all-powerful, would prevent it. The problem of theodicy is the most serious argument against believing in God.

The seriousness of the problem of theodicy is marked by the regular appearance of new attempts to deal with it. In the work *Encountering Evil,* there are several helpful essays: "A Theodicy of Protest," John K. Roth; "An Irenaean Theodicy," John H. Hick; "Free Will and Evil," Stephen T. Davis; "Creation Out of Chaos and the Problem of Evil," David R. Griffin; "Anthropodicy and the Return of God," Frederick Sontag; and "The Problem of Evil and the Task of Ministry," John B. Cobb, Jr.

The attempt to "explain" evil reduces it to a small number of alternatives. It is inconceivable that God is its creator. It is hard to retain the belief in God if some "outsider" could invade and devastate God's universe. If that were so, in what sense would God be God? If Satan devastates with the permission of God to achieve some good end, what sort of God would God be? Is human sin in its accumulated and collective form adequate to account for the "ills unlimited" which fill the pages of every daily newspaper?

Human sin is the best clue we have toward understanding. While we cannot "explain" our sin, we can "understand" it. We do know the right and the wrong and that we often do the wrong. We also know the way of victory over sin and the new creation in God.

Admittedly, we have no explanation, no acceptable theodicy.[7] We live with a radical contradiction within ourselves and in our whole world. We are not, however, without any hope. Belief in God is still the most reasonable human stance.

Providence, the Basis of Hope

The discussion of providence usually appears in connection with the doctrine of creation. In the following chapters, providence will be discussed as a vital part of faith for the Christian life. Many authors deal with providence almost exclusively in relationship with the Christian life and its issues.[8]

The belief in providence appears at this point precisely for the reasons stated as follows: God continues his sustaining and guiding work on behalf of those who flee from him; God works for the reconciliation of his creatures; and the Christian hope which sustains us stands on this belief in providence.

God's Providence Includes a World in Unbelief

All of the biblical witnesses who have been cited spoke after their reconciliation with God to the effect that, in retrospect, they could see the hand of God in their lives even while they were in rebellion. This is precisely the point. God does not abandon the whole creation because the creatures turn away from him. God is the God of all creation. All of it and all therein are under his care.

Our freedom is genuine. God does not coerce us. God, however, as Heavenly Father cares for all of his creatures and probably watches over all of us in ways beyond our imagination. God is free also. If he wills to care for us even if we don't care for him, he does this in what we call providence.

Do not all Christians pray for God to watch over their loved ones who do not acknowledge God by faith? How does he do that? We don't know. We know he cares. We know that he will not coerce compliance from those who do not believe. We have strong reason to believe that he watches over unbelievers as well as believers within those bounds. He "sends rain on the just and on the unjust" (Matt. 5:45).

God Works to Reconcile Creation

The story of salvation is the story of God's providential acts within and on behalf of his human creatures. Reconciliation is a personal restoration. God could surely muster the forces to overcome those who oppose him. God sees his creatures, however, as his children and seeks to reconcile them. This continuing work of providence within the limitations God assumed (no coercion, no violation of human freedom) led to the cross.

The Christian Hope

The redeeming work of God in Christ endowed Christian faith with the hope of salvation and life everlasting. This hope is not limited to the few. God does not wish "that any should perish, but that all should reach repentance" (2 Pet. 3:9). Christians who have come to know this providence of God in their personal lives also hope for the salvation of all others.

Christian hope extends beyond this earth and threescore years and ten. The realization of this possibility depends upon the sustaining and guiding hand of God.

Belief About Unbelievers

God's care and love are not limited to those who have already responded. Like the father of the prodigal son, God cares for those who have not yet come to faith. The persons who do not believe in God should consider the possibility that he believes in them and through his providence cares for them.

Notes

1. Claude Y. Stewart, Jr., *Nature in Grace: A Study in the Theology of Nature* (Macon: Mercer University Press, 1983).

2. G. C. Berkouwer, *The Providence of God* (Grand Rapids: William B. Eerd-mans Publishing Company, 1952), p. 50.

3. Langdon Gilkey, *Reaping the Whirlwind: A Christian Interpretation of History* (New York: The Seabury Press, 1976), pp. 159-187.

4. Gerhard von Rad, *Genesis: A Commentary* (Philadelphia: The Westminster Press, 1961), p. 433.

5. Emil Brunner, *The Christian Doctrine of Creation and Redemption, Dogmatics II*, trans. Olive Wyon (Philadelphia: The Westminster Press, 1952), pp. 155 *ff.*

6. See works such as M. C. D'Arcy, *The Pain of This World and the Providence of God* (London: Longmans, Green and Company, 1935); Lindsay Dewar, *Does God Care?* (London: Hodder & Stoughton, Ltd., 1936); H. H. Farmer, *The World and God* (London: Nisbet & Company, Ltd., 1935); Austin Farrer, *Love Almighty and Ills Unlimited: An Essay on Providence and Evil* (Garden City: Doubleday & Company, Inc., 1961); Peter Geach, *Providence and Evil* (Cambridge: Cambridge University Press, 1977); David Ray Griffin, *God, Power, and Evil: A Process Theodicy* (Philadelphia: The Westminster Press, 1976); John Hick, *Evil and the God of Love* (London: Macmillan and Company, Ltd., 1966); Paul Schilling, *God and Human Anguish* (Nashville: Abingdon Press, 1977); Stephen T. Davis, ed., *Encountering Evil: Live Options in Theodicy* (Atlanta: John Knox Press, 1981).

7. P. T. Forsyth, *The Justification of God* (London: Independent Press Ltd., 1957), originally published in 1917 with a subtitle "Lectures for War-Time on a Christian Theodicy.

8. Peter R. Baelz, *Prayer and Providence* (New York: The Seabury Press, 1968); Georgia Harkness, *The Providence of God* (New York and Nashville: Abingdon Press, 1960); Roger Hazelton, *Providence* (London: SCM Press, Ltd., 1956).

PART IV
Belief in Reconciliation

But God shows his love for us in that while we were yet sinners Christ died for us.

—Romans 5:8

From now on, therefore, we regard no one from a human point of view; even though we once regarded Christ from a human point of view, we regard him thus no longer. Therefore, if any one is in Christ, he is a new creation; the old has passed away, behold, the new has come. All this is from God, who through Christ reconciled us to himself and gave us the ministry of reconciliation; that is, in Christ God was reconciling the world to himself, not counting their trespasses against them, and entrusting to us the message of reconciliation. So we are ambassadors for Christ, God making his appeal through us. We beseech you on behalf of Christ, be reconciled to God.

—2 Corinthians 5:16-20

10

The Cross of Christ

For I delivered to you as of first importance what I also received, that Christ died for our sins in accordance with the scriptures, that he was buried, that he was raised on the third day in accordance with the scriptures, and that he appeared (1 Cor. 15:3-5).

In the early preaching of the Christian disciples, no statement compares with this proclamation of Paul, "Christ died for our sins." It is not an oversimplification to assert that the entire Christian gospel is summarized in this statement.

The cross of Christ not only became the primary symbol of Christianity but is an almost universal symbol of mercy and helpfulness. The cross of Christ, while the central symbol of Christian faith, is usually mentioned in a sequence including also a reference to the resurrection of Christ. Therefore, when we speak of the cross, we mean the cross of Christ which was followed by his resurrection from the dead.

The death of Christ is spoken of in many ways in the New Testament and in Christian tradition. Terms referring to the blood of Christ, the suffering, sacrifice, and so forth, are all related to if not synonomous with, his death on the cross.

The complexity of Christian theology today is in stark contrast with the simplicity of the earliest gospel, but the essential content is not different. C. H. Dodd published a volume in 1936 in which he sought to disclose the content of the earliest Christian preaching. He analyzed the sermons in Acts and other early writings, such as the passage cited from 1 Corinthians, and concluded that there were seven major themes in that proclamation: (1) The Old Testament prophecies have been fulfilled and the new age inaugurated by the coming of Christ; (2) Christ was a descendant of David; (3) Christ died according to the Scriptures to deliver us from the present evil age; (4) Christ was buried; (5) Christ rose on the third day, "according to the scriptures"; (6) Christ was exalted to the right hand of God and is Son of God and Lord; and (7) he will come again as Judge and Savior.[1]

In the first Christian sermon after the crucifixion (that has come to us), Peter interpreted the death of Jesus as a crime of men. He told the audience at Pentecost, "you crucified and killed by the hands of lawless men. But God raised him up" (Acts 2:23-24). In the same statement, however, he interpreted the event as something that happened "according to the definite plan and foreknowledge of God."

The crucifixion and resurrection of Jesus Christ constitute the central event in the Christian tradition and preaching. Our knowledge of the person of Christ came to us precisely through his work. Christology, the study of the person of Christ, and atonement, the study of the work of Christ, are inseparable. Who he was and what he did are inseparably intertwined.

The word *atonement* is an English word literally formed by the components *at-one-ment*. Consequently, it is very close to meaning the same as reconciliation. In historical usage, however, the word *atonement* designates the work of God through Christ's death to achieve our salvation; reconciliation speaks more specifically about the new relationship between God and sinful persons established on the basis of the atonement.

The Necessity of the Cross

Christian literature reflects an unceasing interest in the cross of Christ. The hymns of the church repeat in fascinating variety the many aspects of the cross. Theologians have never been satisfied with former writings on the mystery of the cross and have added their own efforts in trying to interpret the meaning of Christ's death. This continuing attempt indicates the importance of the cross for Christian faith; the variety in the literature reflects the variety that appears in the New Testament itself, along with our own different ways of understanding in each age.

The atoning work of Christ on the cross is the basis for the Christian view of forgiveness. P. T. Forsyth, in his marvelous little book entitled *The Cruciality of the Cross,* argued persuasively that the atonement is the central theme of the Christian gospel and the Christian experience and is also a leading feature in modern thought.[2]

Apart from the cross and resurrection of Christ, the distinctiveness of Christian faith would not exist. The similarities between the moral teachings of Judaism and Christianity are so obvious that one can understand why Roman governors thought of Christianity as a Jewish sect. The cross of Christ, however, made the difference. The event and the interpretation that Christ's death provided a basis for our reconciliation with God distinguishes Christian faith from all others.

Biblical Teachings on the Atonement

Old Testament Teachings

As is the case in studying other doctrines, we can hardly grasp the meaning of the atonement without understanding some of the Old Testament antecedents. Jesus was a Jew. His first disciples were Jews. What we know as the Old Testament was their Bible. They saw Jesus as a fulfillment of the hopes in the Old Testament and the one in whom the new age had dawned.

In a general sense, we could argue that the first two chapters of the Bible deal with creation, the third with sin, and all of the others deal with God's work of reconciling sinful humanity to himself. From the outset, God was seeking his estranged creatures. The mark on Cain, the murderer, often misused and misinterpreted as ostracism, was, in fact, a mark to secure his safety. When Cain became a fugitive and wanderer, knowing the law of blood revenge, he complained that "whoever finds me will slay me." God replied, "Not so!" and put the mark on Cain to protect him (Gen. 4:14-15).

Many Old Testament teachings show God's seeking his creatures: God's deliverance of his people from Egypt and his discipline leading to repentance and forgiveness during the prophetic period. We shall look, however, at only two Old Testament themes at the moment, sacrifice and Suffering Servant.

The Old Testament Idea of Sacrifice. The practice of sacrifice in the Old Testament is almost unintelligible to moderns. Our mindset is shocked by the thought of animal sacrifice. The prophets spoke against the abuses of the system and the error of the people who tried to substitute their religious sacrifice for righteous living. Isaiah, for instance, indicated that God was offended by the practice of the people who brought a multitude of sacrifices but did not seek justice and righteousness (1:11-20). Micah contrasted the folly of sacrificing to God while living unrighteously. He indicated that God required justice, kindness, and a humble walk with God (6:8). But no prophet, not even Amos, rejected the sacrificial system. Jesus did not reject the sacrificial system even though he appeared to have a rather detached view as to its relevance in his time.

Perhaps we can view sacrifice in terms of its instructional value prior to the New Testament, as we see the law as an instructor preparing us for Christ's coming.

Imagine a family in the Old Testament period walking in solemn procession to the place of sacrifice on the appropriate day, leading the best lamb of their flock. In a ritual of worship, they "draw near" to God at the place of sacrifice. The priest, or family leader, placed his hands on the head of the lamb and spoke words of confession, dedication, and supplication. Then he cut the throat of the animal, releasing its life. Life is in the blood. The point was not killing and death; rather, it was in giving the life. The blood was sprinkled or poured on the altar, symbolic of the giving of the life for the atonement for sins. Parts of the animal were eaten. Perhaps parts were burned. The family then returned home with a sense of having been reconciled to God.[3]

In spite of its proneness to abuse, the system of sacrifice was a way of approaching God. It was meaningful to many. The placing of the hands on the animal has suggested to many the transfer of guilt, the substitution of the animal for the guilty people; it may have meant only the dedication of the animal to God.

The New Testament preachers and writers naturally saw Jesus in terms of sacrifice. He was the "Lamb of God, who takes away the sin of the world!" (John 1:29; Acts 8:32; 1 Cor. 5:7; 1 Pet. 1:19; Rev. 5:6,12). The Lord's Supper portrays the sacrificial nature of Christ's death.

The danger in interpreting the atonement as sacrifice is to think too objectively of Christ as being sacrificed by someone to God. Jesus Christ is the Son of God who came not to appease the wrath of an angry God but precisely to demonstrate the love of God. As Son of God, Christ's work was a work of God and not a sacrifice to God. "But God shows his love for us in that while we were yet sinners Christ died for us" (Rom. 5:8). We shall more likely understand Christ's sacrificial death if we think in terms of a person who, out of love for another, risks and perhaps loses his or her life for that other person. The death is sacrificial not because someone willfully sacrifices another but, rather, because one person willingly risks and gives self for another. That is what Jesus did.

The Suffering Servant. The Servant poems in Isaiah (42:1-4; 49:1-6; 50:4-9; 52:13 to 53:12) provide a clue for understanding Christ's atoning work. The Servant, whether Israel or some contemporary leader or figure yet to come, appears in a strange role of suffering, redemptive suffering. The Servant was not impressive or beautiful. "He was despised and rejected . . . /a man of sorrows . . . /we esteemed him not./Surely he has borne our griefs/and carried our sorrows;/ . . . he was wounded for our transgressions/ . . . /All we like sheep have gone astray;/we have turned every one to his own way;/and the Lord has laid on him/the iniquity of us all" (53:3-6).

The poem is marked by sudden shifts from the third to the first person—his suffering, our healing. There was a relationship between the Servant and God. At first the suffering was merely observed; later it was recognized as redemptive suffering related to us. It was vicarious and sacrificial. Some see it as substitutionary.

The writers of the New Testament saw Jesus in terms of this Suffering Servant. Jesus himself alluded to this concept (Luke 22:37). In the Gospels, Jesus' purpose was related to his forthcoming death (Mark: 8:31; 9:31; 10:33). The statement in Matthew, "He took our infirmities and bore our diseases" (8:17), sounds like Isaiah 53. Jesus was certainly interpreted in terms of the Servant by John 12:38; Acts 3:13; 4:30. Philip preached Christ to the Ethiopian eunuch on the basis of interpreting Isaiah 53 which the eunuch was reading (Acts 8:26-40). First Peter preserves a paraphrase of Isaiah 53 in which the suffering of Christ is clarified (1 Pet. 2:21-25).

New Testament Atonement Themes

In the simplest terms, the New Testament teaches that "Christ died for our sins" and "Christ died for us." His atoning work, however, appears in a great variety of terms and ideas. The rich variety gives insights without which we would be impoverished, and we should not neglect any of them. The greatest danger in the theories of the atonement is that they focus on a single theme or interpretation or image and neglect or reduce the meaning of the other ideas.

Vincent Taylor identified fourteen atonement ideas in the New Testament and charted their appearance in the various books.[4] (1) The death of Christ was related to God's purpose. (2) The death of Christ was messianic in character. (3) Christ's death was vicarious. (4) Christ's death was representative; it includes us, or in his death we die. (5) His death was related to our sin. (6) His death was sacrificial. (7) His death was interpreted in terms of the Suffering Servant. (8) His death is always related to the resurrection. (9) The atonement of Christ is appropriated by faith. (10) The death of Christ is illustrated in the Lord's Supper. (11) The idea of suffering with Christ is involved in his suffering. (12) His death is related to the love of God. (13) His death is related to moral and spiritual ends. (14) There is a universal aspect in Christ's death.

Vicarious Atonement. To say Christ "died for us" means that he died "on our behalf," "for our benefit." There is quite a difference between "on behalf of" and "instead of." One is vicarious; the other is substitutionary. "Christ died for our sins" (1 Cor. 15:3). "Christ died for us" (Rom. 5:8), and "for us all" (Rom. 8:32). He "died for all" (2 Cor. 5:14). There are scores of New Testament passages on this theme; Paul summarized the idea well when he said, "I have been crucified with Christ; it is no longer I who live, but Christ who lives in me; and the life I now live in the flesh I live by faith in the Son of God, who loved me and gave himself for me" (Gal. 2:20).

Sacrificial Atonement. The New Testament writers interpreted Christ's death in terms of the Old Testament idea of sacrifice. The redemption in Christ was described in the terms "whom God put forward as an expiation by his blood" (Rom. 3:25). This is sacrificial language; Christ's death covers or removes our sins. Christ is "our paschal lamb" who "has been sacrificed" (1 Cor. 5:7). Also, "Christ loved us and gave himself up for us, a fragrant offering and sacrifice to God" (Eph. 5:2).

Representative Atonement. Christ's death was of such a nature that he represents us by drawing us into his sacrifice for us. In other words, it is as if we had died with him. We are existentially included. While interpreting the meaning of baptism, Paul points out, "our old self was crucified with him," and "we have died with Christ" (Rom. 6:6,8). The same idea appears in Galatians (2:20). It means that since Jesus Christ "died for all; therefore all have died" (2 Cor. 5:14). Obviously, this concept assumes that we are drawn into his death and resurrection by our faith in him. This idea is very close to the idea of vicarious atonement.

Suffering Servant. Reference has already been made to the New Testament passages which reflect the Servant poems of Isaiah. The biblical writers did not explain suffering or how suffering is related to our reconciliation; they merely noted its mystery. Suffering, as such, is not redemptive; often it "is debasing and destructive."[5] Suffering may create resentment and bitterness. When the Son of God, however, identified himself with men and women and suffered with and for them, God turned the suffering into their reconciliation. The poet in Isaiah missed the point at first but later saw that we are the beneficiaries of the Servant's suffering; the disciples missed the point at the crucifixion but later saw that Christ was suffering for them and that in his suffering they were drawn to God. Love is a disquieting, disturbing presence with those in rebellion against God. We cannot bear his presence; we would crucify him again if he returned. He could destroy our rebellion—us. The mystery appears to be that love confronts evil, willing to suffer, even to be destroyed, and only in that way do sinners recognize the depth of their sins. They repeat the confession, "Christ died for me. He was willing to suffer for me."

Atonement and Forgiveness of Sins. The death of Christ focuses on reconciliation. In other cases, however, in which sin or sins are looked upon as "something," the death of Christ removes them, or covers them, preparing the way for reconciliation. When sin is regarded as slavery, then the reconciliation is redemption. The two themes are together in the statement, "In him we have redemption through his blood, the forgiveness of our trespasses" (Eph. 1:7).

Some views of the atonement regard sins in such a way that they have to be "paid for" or a penalty or sentence assessed. Views of this kind appear to overlook the fact of God's forgiveness. God forgave sins in the Old Testament period when people repented. Jesus forgave sins; no reference was made or implied regarding a payment for sin. Forgiveness is the gracious act of God who removes sin and its guilt by an act of sheer love and repairs the broken relationship.

At this point, we take note of the fact that we speak about the death of Jesus Christ, Son of God and man. He revealed God as loving Father; he went to the cross as an expression of God's love (Rom. 5:8), not as a demand for payment. He also went there at the hands of a conspiracy of human beings.

Our sinfulness sent him to the cross; his love prompted him to go that far to reveal himself so that he could reconcile us to himself. The creeds, based on the New Testament confession, are correct when they relate his atoning death to our sins.

The Cross as Expression of the Love of God. This affirmation is not intended to overlook God's judgment on sin or the "wrath of God." Both terms, *judgment* and *wrath of God,* stress an inevitable consequence of sin. Sinfulness leads to judgment because men and women are responsible; it leads to the wrath of God which is degradation of life for those who abandon God (Rom. 1:18 *ff.*) and worship their idols. The death of Christ, however, is related to God's love and purpose to redeem us.

Those who would interpret the atonement as something Christ suffered to appease God's wrath forget who Jesus Christ was. He was not working for us against the Father but, rather, was working to do the will of the Father out of the Father's love for us.

Christ's Atonement as an Once-for-All Event. "The death he died he died to sin, once for all, but the life he lives he lives to God" (Rom. 6:10). The author of Hebrews, while presenting Christ's death in the sacrificial terminology of Hebrew faith, noted, "He has no need, like those high priests, to offer sacrifices daily, first for his own sins and then for those of the people; he did this once for all when he offered up himself" (7:27). The finality of Christ's atonement is noted in 1 Peter, "For Christ also died for sins once for all, the righteous for the unrighteous, that he might bring us to God" (3:18).

In the discussion of God's revelation in Christ, we encountered a finality in Christ—a belief that God had spoken his Word in an unrepeatable way. Christ was the full disclosure. Now the atonement of Christ is presented as an event which is "once-for-all." It is a singular, unique event. It is not only unrepeatable but is also adequate, sufficient for all persons of all ages.

Historical Theories of the Atonement

A theory of the atonement is an attempt to interpret the entire doctrine in a single concept or explanation. Each theory, of course, is derived from or related to biblical teaching and, therefore, gives some insight or insights into the meaning of the belief. The sharp focus, however, tends to bend biblical teachings to fit the "theory" and, of necessity, minimizes or overlooks the rich variety of ways in which the atoning act is described.

Theories tend to fall into two different types: objective and subjective. The objective theories stress that the death of Christ did something to change the attitude of God toward the sinners, thereby leading to reconciliation. The subjective theories, however, stress that the death of Christ accomplishes a change in human attitudes toward God and sin, thereby making them forgivable. An illustration of the objective type is the Penal Substitutionary view which teaches that God's attitude toward sin requires a punishment for sin; Christ's death is the penalty which changed God's attitude. An illustration of the subjective theory is the Moral Influence theory. In this view, Christ's death brings the sinner to sorrow for sin, and then he or she is a suitable candidate for God's mercy.

Scholars list and discuss the theories in different groupings. Gustaf Aulen has reduced the interpretations to three basic views: the Latin or Objective type; the Subjective type; and the Classic view. The Latin type is illustrated by the Satisfaction theory; the Subjective type by the Moral Influence theory; the Classic view is the one most faithful to the New Testament and portrays Christ's death as a victorious struggle over the powers of sin, death, and the devil.[6]

Vincent Taylor has identified four main types which in different forms have survived through the centuries. They are these: the Ransom theory which is almost identical with Aulen's Classic view; the Satisfaction theory of Anselm; the Moral Influence theory, which he prefers to call the "Theory of Revelation"; and the Forensic theory which is the view that Christ was the substitute suffering the penalty for men and women.[7]

Robert H. Culpepper, in a very thorough discussion of the theories, has listed seven before discussing views prevalent in modern times. They are the Dominant or Ransom theory which prevailed for a millenium, the Satisfaction theory of Anselm, the Moral Influence theory of Abelard, Luther's view of Penalty and Victory, Calvin's view of Sacrifice and Penal Substitute, the Example view of Socinus, and the Governmental view of Grotius.[8] This listing has the advantage of showing a difference between Luther and Calvin.

The similarities among the views permit some combinations without distortion. While I am not convinced that Aulen has completely made his case that the Classic view is the same as the Ransom theory (Luther, for instance, does not limit his interpretation to one view), I think the similarity allows them to be discussed together. The Satisfaction theory is the most persistent of the Objective types but is quite different from the Penal Substitutionary view, so I shall list these as two. The Governmental theory is a variation of the Satisfaction theory. The Example theory is also a variation of the Moral Influence theory. So let us look at the Ransom theory, the Satisfaction theory, the Moral Influence theory, and the Penal Substitutionary theory.

The Ransom Theory

Jesus spoke of giving his life as "a ransom" (Mark 10:45). In 1 Timothy, Jesus was spoken of as the one "who gave himself as a ransom for all" (2:6). In 1 Peter, "You know that you were

ransomed from the futile ways inherited from your fathers"
(1:18). In the new song sung in Revelation, the words appear,
"Worthy art thou to take the scroll and to open its seals, for
thou wast slain and by thy blood didst ransom men for God
from every tribe and tongue and people and nation" (5:9).

There are numerous statements which speak of Christ as
redeeming persons. He is the Redeemer. This is another way
of speaking of his death as a ransom.

The Ransom theory focuses on one point primarily; humanity was enslaved to sin and Jesus Christ set us free. In the words
of Paul, "You are not your own; you were bought with a price"
(1 Cor. 6:19). This view stresses the beautiful concept of Christ
setting us free from the bondage of sin and death. When he
came, we were slaves; after his death, we are free.

The Ransom theory was particularly attractive during the
age when most peoples lived in literal dread of physical slavery. Conquering armies captured prisoners and sold them to
defray the cost of their campaigns. A person could be eman-
cipated if someone would pay the price of the slave and willed
to set the slave free.

To this day, the theory speaks meaningfully of the work of
Christ in freeing us from the bondage of sin. The doctrine,
however, fell into literalistic minds who reasoned that if a
ransom was paid, someone had to collect it. Obviously, that
was the devil. Then God was in a transaction with Satan.
Origen (c. 185-254) spoke of the ransom being paid to the
devil. Gregory of Nyssa (c. 335-395), perhaps unwittingly, introduced the element of deception. He spoke of God as making
himself accessible to Satan by veiling himself in our human
nature. He compared Christ to the bait on a fishhook which the
devil devoured, not knowing that in so doing he was losing
humanity back to God.[9]

The Ransom view spoke eloquently of God's redemption of
humanity from the enslavement to sin. To those who knew the
slave market, it was especially meaningful. It still speaks today.

Aulen's Classic view is a larger version of the Ransom theory which prevailed for a thousand years. Aulen interprets the New Testament ideas as all related to the idea that Christ engaged all the powers of darkness, sin, death, and the devil, and on the cross won the victory—*Christus Victor*—for those who believe in him. Aulen traced the history of the doctrine along with its aberrations until Anselm's Satisfaction theory overshadowed it. He maintained that Luther recovered the view for a while, but his followers lost it again.

The Satisfaction Theory

Anselm (1033-1109) introduced the Satisfaction theory in a volume entitled *Cur Deus Homo?* [10] This is the basic Latin-type or Objective atonement. Briefly, it means that God had been so dishonored by human sin that a drastic action was necessary to reconcile sinners to God. There were two alternatives: punishment and satisfaction. The just punishment was for us to die for our own sins, so Anselm took the route of satisfaction.

To understand this theory, we need to understand some of the characteristics of feudalism. In a feudal state, the lord of the manor had absolute authority. His honor was such that he would fight duels, even wars, when he was offended. The feudal lord would demand satisfaction, say in a duel. In a duel, the feudal lord might subdue the opponent, hold his sword against the disarmed and defeated opponent's chest, and either run him through or spare him by saying, "I am satisfied."

In a feudal age, Anselm's view spoke of the atonement. Obviously, men and women had sinned against God. He was due our obedience; we denied it. We offended God. Even if we were to turn from our wicked ways and obey God, we would still owe him "satisfaction" for the past offenses. If God were to forgive sin without such payment, he would be encouraging or condoning laxity. The only alternative to punishment was satisfaction. Christ died to satisfy God's offended honor.

There are no specific biblical passages which teach this view, certainly not in this form. It is based on legal argument. It correctly recognizes the honor which is due God and the seriousness of human sin. It appears, however, to do an injustice to God whose love is manifest in Jesus Christ and to separate God's work of redemption in that Christ as a man is dying toward God.

The Moral Influence Theory

Abelard (1079-1142) was a younger contemporary of Anselm. He vigorously opposed the ideas supporting a Satisfaction theory and maintained that Christ's work did not effect any change in God's attitude, which needed no change, but rather, it changed the sinner's attitude. Hence, it is the Subjective view; all of the change is in the subject—humanity. Abelard saw nothing in God that needed satisfaction or appeasement; God was always willing to forgive. Forgiveness is not dependent upon a payment or a sacrifice. Instead, when the sinners saw that Christ died for them out of love, they were moved to awareness of their guilt. Then God reconciled them.

The Example theory of Socinus (1539-1604) is very similar to the Moral Influence theory. Its point is that Christ showed us the example; our salvation is in imitating him. These Subjective views have been prevalent in the modern period. They appear in great variety.

The Penal Substitution Theory

Anselm chose the idea of satisfaction over punishment. By the time of the Reformers, feudalism was giving way to other forces. Theirs was the age of jurisprudence. In the state, crime cannot go unpunished. By analogy, God cannot allow his law to be violated; punishment is demanded. Jesus Christ suffered the judgment of God on sin in a substitutionary way. This view differs from the Ransom theory in that the ransom here was paid to God and not to the devil; it differs from the Satisfaction theory in that God demands punishment rather than satisfaction.

In the period following the Reformation under the influence of absolute monarchies and jurisprudence, this view, sometimes called the Forensic theory, was very persuasive. Sin was a violation of God's law; sinners were criminals. The atonement was a legal device by which the inviolable demands of God and justice were upheld in such a way as to spare the sinner from the death penalty. This view continues into modern times partly because it does recognize the seriousness of human sin. It does, however, miss the New Testament emphasis on God's love and forgiveness and tends to separate Christ from God. It is legalistic to such a degree that one wonders how it could be so attractive to those who follow Jesus Christ, who spent his lifetime in a struggle against legalistic religion.

The Meaning of the Cross

All of the theories listed above deal seriously with the atonement, even though they are vastly different. It may be impossible to settle on a single theory of the atonement without distorting the doctrine beyond recognition. It may be that an acceptable view of the atonement must include both an objective and a subjective element. The historical "once-for-allness" is a kind of objectivity; the personal appropriation of the cross by faith is certainly subjective.

There are several guidelines that must be noted in doing justice to the belief in the atonement.

The Cross Is Central in Reconciliation

The early Christians left the records to establish that they believed Christ's death on the cross was a focal theme of their faith. The great preachers and theologians of the church have centered their faith and proclamation on the cross of Christ.[11] The hymn writers have left a vast witness about the cross.

It was Christ's cross; its meaning is derived from who he was, divine and human. The paradox of the incarnation comes into prominence at the cross. It was as God and humanity that Christ died for us. It is only as God and human being that his death on the cross is both judgment of God and redemption for humanity. Since Christ was "truly God and truly man," we can say, "we were crucified with Christ."

The Cross Is Both Human and Divine. In taking Christology seriously, we have a clue toward understanding the cross. He was genuinely human, like us in every way except our willingness to sin. His death, therefore, was truly death at the hands of a human mob and a weak unjust government. He was Son of God. The cross, therefore, is not a sacrifice to God; rather, it is the expression of God's love toward us. He came to call sinners back to himself. He would not allow their opposition to defeat his love. Jesus Christ was faithful to his purpose even to death on the cross (Phil. 2:8). Peter spoke of this mystery in his sermon at Pentecost. The cross was the work of lawless men. It was also "according to the definite plan and foreknowledge of God" (Acts 2:23).

The Cross Expresses the Love of God. Some of the historical theories of the cross have divided God and Christ, making the cross an event of sacrifice to God. The hymn writers have seen the meaning and nature of the event more clearly than those theologians. Paul, who wrote often about the mystery of the cross, stated it clearly, "God shows his love for us in that while we were yet sinners Christ died for us" (Rom. 5:8).

The Cross Is Judgment on Sin. Christian thinkers have often asked, Was the cross necessary? If one is to discuss this question, it is necessary to ask, Why any necessity? or necessary for whom? Those holding to Objective theories of atonement have tended to see a necessity in God. The Penal Substitutionary theory, for instance, understands God in such a way as to interpret a necessity on his part. Sin has to be punished. God forgave sin before Christ. Christ forgave sins in his lifetime. To interpret his death on the cross in a retroactive way is very arbitrary and unconvincing.

To say that the cross was a necessity for human beings requires some clarification. Since nothing else God did to reconcile sinful humanity to himself appeared to work and the cross did, we may then say that it was necessary. The necessity, however, is a statement from a historical standpoint. It cannot be logically defended. Theoretically, God may have reconciled his creatures in some other way. The point is that God sent his Son whom we crucified, and God so worked within us and history as to make that event the central event of our reconciliation.

The judgment of God means more than condemnation and punishment. God's judgment often means vindication. Also, judgment is a fact of life under God in that we are convicted of our sins, repent, and receive forgiveness repeatedly. This repentance is a part of God's judgment on sin. The doctrine of justification by faith in Romans is an expression of God's judgment. We are guilty before God. Jesus Christ died for our sins. In faith we stand before God acquitted, made right with God.

The cross stands in Christian history as the supreme example of the judgment and justice of God. Our sin is such that we would crucify Christ again. In sin we are at enmity with God. The cross expressed our hostility toward God. God, however, was on the cross in Christ. The cross stands in history as the event in which God proclaimed that his love for his creatures extends through the event of judgment. Our sin is not condoned. When we see the cross for what it is, we repent toward God believing in Christ who died there, and then we confess, "I have been crucified with Christ" (Gal. 2:20).

The Cross and Forgiveness of Sin

However one interprets the crucifixion of Christ, the cross is related to the forgiveness of sin. The conclusion of Peter's sermon which interpreted the cross was "the forgiveness of your sins" (Acts 2:38). The abbreviated summary of the Christian gospel centered on the belief that "Christ died for our sins" (1 Cor. 15:3).

Sin may be seen as a barrier between God and humanity. In this case, sin is a "something." In both the Old and New Testaments and in Christian usage, this is a common way of speaking of sin.

Sin may also be understood in the sense of a broken relationship between God and humanity. In this case, sin is unbelief, pride, sensuality, or rebellion. Sin is viewed in its personal dimension. It is not a "something." Rather, it is the negation of something, the breaking of a relationship.

The forgiveness of sin is understood in terms of one's understanding of sin. If sin is a barrier, forgiveness is the removal of the barrier. If sin is a broken relationship, forgiveness is a reconciliation, the mending, of the relationship. Therefore, forgiveness of sin usually means at least these two things: the removal of the barrier of sin and the restoration of the broken relationship.

The cross of Christ is that event in the Christian understanding at which this forgiveness occurs. If sin is a barrier which men and women have erected between themselves and God, Christ's atonement removes it. If sin is the negation of a faith-relationship with God, Christ's death on the cross restores it and reconciles us to God.

If sin is removed and we are reconciled to God, then Christ's atonement is both objective and subjective. It is objective in historical event, a once-for-all event. It is subjective in that our faith reunites us with God.

The Cross as Victory

Admittedly, we have not explained either sin or the atonement. Our sin is irrational. How can we give a rational explanation for our irrational acts and attitudes—and lives? We have also failed to explain why the death of Christ twenty centuries ago is related to the forgiveness of our sin today. What we have done, however, is to note that this event in history did, in fact, result in the reconciliation of estranged humanity to God. We note that this reconciliation continues today when we hear the message and believe in him.

Gustav Aulen did not explain the atonement, but he did show very clearly that Christ is *Christus Victor* over sin; that victory becomes our victory over sin when we believe in Jesus

Christ. It is the great drama of redemption, greater than any explanation of it.

An anonymous interpreter of the past has compared the beauty of the atonement to that of a diamond. One holds a diamond in the hand, observing facets of its beauty. Then by turning the diamond one discovers facets of beauty from another angle and in other light. After repeatedly turning and admiring, it becomes obvious that one just cannot see all of the beauty from one standpoint. The variety of interpretations of the cross both in the New Testament and since speak of its beauty and meaning. No one of them should be dropped. A single theory of the atonement tends to disregard the others. They all help to illustrate the meaning of the cross. Its full meaning, however, lies beyond our horizon.[11]

Notes

1. C. H. Dodd, *The Apostolic Preaching and Its Development* (London: Hodder & Stoughton, Ltd., 1936), p. 17.

2. P. T. Forsyth, *The Cruciality of the Cross* (London: Independent Press, Ltd., 1909). This volume has been reissued by Chanticleer Publishing Co. of Wake Forest, N.C. in 1983 with an introduction by John E. Steely.

3. F. C. N. Hicks, *The Fulness of Sacrifice* (London: SPCK, 1953), pp. 11-24.

4. Vincent Taylor, *The Atonement in New Testament Teaching* (London: The Epworth Press, 1940), p. 50-51.

5. James E. Tull, *The Atoning Gospel* (Macon: Mercer University Press, 1982), p. 154.

6. Gustav Aulen, *Christus Victor: An Historical Study of the Three Main Types of the Idea of Atonement* (New York: The Macmillan Company, 1951).

7. Vincent Taylor, *The Cross of Christ* (London: Macmillan & Co., Ltd., 1957), p. 71-72.

8. Robert H. Culpepper, *Interpreting the Atonement* (Grand Rapids: William B. Eerdmans Publishing Company, 1966), pp. 73-108.

9. Gregory of Nyssa, "Address on Religious Instruction," Sect. 24. in "Christology of the Later Fathers," *The Library of Christian Classics,* 3 (Philadelphia: The Westminster Press, 1954), p. 301.

10. St. Anselm, *Cur Deus Homo?* (London and Sydney: Griffith Farran Okeden & Welsh, n.d.).

11. Gustav Aulen, *Eucharist and Sacrifice,* trans. Eric H. Wahlstrom (Edin-

burgh: Oliver and Boyd, 1956); William Barclay, *Crucified and Crowned* (London: SCM Press, 1961); James Denney, *The Death of Christ* (London: The Tyndale Press, 1951); J. Z. Mozley, *The Doctrine of the Atonement* (London: Gerald Duckworth & Co. Ltd., 1953); Vincent Taylor, *Jesus and His Sacrifice* (London: Macmillan & Co., Ltd., 1959); J. S. Whale, *Victor and Victim* (Cambridge: Cambridge University Press, 1960).

11
Reconciliation

In the previous chapter, we discussed the atoning work of Christ who died on the cross "for" us. We noted that Christian thinkers have always regarded the cross as the bridge between sinful persons and God. We cannot explain why or how that event long ago is the saving or reconciling event. Interpreters have tried many ways to show the meaning of the cross. We also noted the universal conviction of Christians that in Christ's cross the way opens to us for a victory over sin and a restoration to God.

Sin, with its separation from God, is both an individual and group experience. Salvation from sin is likewise an individual and group experience. When the individual sins against God, it is an individual act for which the individual is responsible. At the same time, however, the individual is aware that his or her sin took place in a community of persons within the family, clan, or community. The same is true with salvation or reconciliation.

The major emphasis in this chapter will be upon the individual's experience of reconciliation to God. This is necessary for the sake of a clear discussion. In almost every emphasis on the reconciliation of the individual to God, we shall anticipate the next chapter in which reconciliation is discussed in terms of its collective character.

In the next chapter, the discussion of reconciliation will be presented to show the other side of the individual's reconciliation to God. It includes the experience within the Christian fellowship of persons who have also made the pilgrimage from the separation in sin to reconciliation with God. An attempt will be made to show that the reconciliation of the individual to God is always a happening that is related to other persons.

A Narrow Gate

When Jesus, in the Sermon on the Mount, invited people from their separation from God back to faith in God, he pointed out that it was a hard way. "Enter by the narrow gate; for the gate is wide and the way is easy, that leads to destruction, and those who enter by it are many. For the gate is narrow and the way is hard that leads to life, and those who find it are few" (Matt. 7:13-14).

The invitation was genuine and apparently universal, but it sounds almost as if Jesus discouraged would-be followers. He knew how deeply they were mired down in self-centeredness and how painful repentance would be. He knew it is hard for a proud person to confess guilt for sin and depend solely on another—Christ who died on the cross—for forgiveness.

If one could compare all of history to an hourglass, Jesus Christ and his cross form that small opening through which all must flow. In Christian faith, there is one way of salvation— the way of the cross.

Many theologians have drawn attention to a simple way of speaking about salvation. They stress: there is one way of salvation, there are two sides of salvation, and, there are three stages or tenses of salvation. My own teacher of theology has recently published a volume which presents this scheme in a very complete and helpful manner.[1]

The one way of salvation appears in many New Testament statements. Jesus said, "I am the way, the truth, and the life" (John 14:6), and "I am the door; if any one enters by me, he will be saved" (John 10:9). Luke said of him, "And there is salvation in no one else, for there is no other name under heaven given among men by which we must be saved" (Acts

4:12). Paul wrote of him, there is "no other foundation" (1 Cor.
3:11) and that there is only one gospel for salvation (Gal.
1:6-9). The author of Hebrews expressed the same belief by
writing, "how shall we escape if we neglect such a great salvation?" (Heb. 2:3).

There are two sides of salvation: one is <u>God's side of grace,</u>
<u>atonement, and forgivene</u>ss; the other side is the <u>human side</u>
which includes <u>hearing the Word of God, repentance, faith,</u>
<u>and confession</u>. Again, these are distinguished for the sake of
understanding, but they are inseparable.

The three stages of salvation are past, present, and future.
The New Testament teaches, and Christian tradition follows,
that salvation may be spoken of as an event realized in the past.
It is right to speak of having been saved in the past, as in
Ephesians, "For by grace you have been saved through faith"
(2:8).

It is also right to speak of salvation as a present and continuing process, as in Philippians 2:12 where the apostle encouraged the readers to "work out your own salvation with
fear and trembling." That statement illustrates the human side;
the following, the divine: "for God is at work in you" (13).

The future, or completion, of salvation appears in numerous
statements such as, "For salvation is nearer to us now than
when we first believed" (Rom. 13:11), and "as the outcome of
your faith you obtain the salvation of your souls" (1 Pet. 1:9).

The Divine Initiative

In the previous discussion of revelation, we noted that God
took the first step in showing himself to his creatures in order
to reconcile them to himself. <u>Revelation</u> is never directed toward any goal but that of re<u>conciliation</u>. In addition to *revelation*,
there are several other terms which speak of God's taking the
first step in our salvation. Examples of these are *grace, calling*,
and *conviction*.

Grace

Grace is the free, unrestricted, and spontaneous love of God. Grace is extended actively to sinful, undeserving humanity because of God's nature and not because of human value or works. It cannot be explained by human reason. God's grace is pure love, an extension of his divine nature.

Grace has its source in the character of God and is made known most fully in the life and death of Jesus Christ. The grace of God and the grace of Jesus Christ are the same. "For you know the grace of our Lord Jesus Christ, that though he was rich, yet for your sake he became poor, so that by his poverty you might become rich" (2 Cor. 8:9). Grace is more than God's attitude of goodwill and love; it is the active expression of this self-giving love as shown in Christ.

Our reconciliation to God is the result of his grace. Christian faith knows that no human works could get the attention of God or deserve his forgiveness. Rather, we know that our reconciliation to God is a matter of pure grace—his work toward, for, and in us. "For by grace you have been saved through faith; and this is not your own doing, it is the gift of God" (Eph. 2:8).

Religion has always wanted to limit God's favor to those who deserve it. Judaism in the New Testament time had so stressed obeying the law that righteousness became an occasion for pride. The Christian church has not escaped the temptation to distort its own faith into a system of works and merit. Righteousness, or justification, in God's sight comes "through faith in Jesus Christ for all who believe" (Rom. 3:22). Since all have sinned, and have therefore failed to achieve righteousness, God has graciously provided for a reconciliation of sinful people on the basis of his grace. Paul wrote, "They are justified by his grace as a gift, through the redemption which is in Christ Jesus, whom God put forward as an expiation by his blood, to be received by faith" (vv. 24-25).

God's grace is more than an attitude of goodwill. It is an

active power at work within the lives of people. It is an environment in which we live and grow. Through faith in Christ, "we have obtained access to this grace in which we stand" (Rom. 5:2). The power of grace abounds and increases to overcome the power of sin (v. 20).

Grace is often related to election and should be if election is understood correctly. God's choosing of people, election, is his gracious act which does not exclude others but includes others. His election of Israel was so that they would obey and would be the means by which others would come to God. When the Old Testament writer dealt with election in terms of why God had chosen Israel, his answer was no reason. He simply stated, "It is because the Lord loves you" (Deut. 7:8).

When Paul attempted to deal with the question of election and grace, he argued that God had not rejected Israel. Israel may have rejected God. God had at the present time those faithful who were "chosen by grace" (Rom. 11:5).

The understanding of grace has not always fared too well in the discussions of those with rigid views of predestination. Augustine did not actually teach that people were predestined to damnation, but his heavy emphasis on the predestination of some to salvation made it easy for others to do so. Augustine's view of the depravity of humanity led him to distinguish between "prevenient grace" (before conversion) and "subsequent grace" (after conversion). His point was that there is a grace of God operating in our lives prior to our faith in God, and this accounts for whatever good one may do.

Thomas Aquinas distinguished between "habitual" grace and "actual" grace. Theologians emphasizing predestination even speak of "irresistible grace,"[2] but these distinctions lead away from an understanding of grace rather than to it.

The grace of God may be mediated by the Word of God, the Spirit of God, worship, prayer, or the ordinances. It is an active, sustaining presence which God gives us. Paul spoke of some malady with which he was afflicted, a "thorn" in his flesh. He besought God to remove it. God's response was, "My grace is sufficient for you" (2 Cor. 12:9).

God took the first step in seeking us for salvation. His salvation is a matter of grace—his free gift. He gives his love and grace to his creatures. When they through faith in Christ are reconciled to God, they uniformly speak of God's gift of grace.

Calling

God calls or invites persons to receive his grace. This is one of the most common expressions of God's taking the first step in our reconciliation and one of the most misunderstood. The misunderstanding comes from interpretations of election, which is a synonym for calling, and predestination. Both of the biblical terms have been devastated by interpreters who went beyond the meaning of the terms in the Bible and sought to answer questions not raised in the Bible and to coerce later concepts into the context of the biblical records. In this volume, the emphasis will be on "calling."

The story of reconciliation as early as the patriarchs stresses that God took the first step and called Abraham. God's purpose was to bless the nations through Abraham's family. The result was that Abraham lived in a special relationship with God and followed a specific life mission. The prophets were conscious of a call from God. He sought them before they sought him. Jesus "called" disciples; he invited them to follow him.

In the New Testament, the verb "to call" is "a technical term for the process of salvation."[3] The verb "to call" and the noun "calling" appear in most of the books of the New Testament.

The expression means simply that God has taken the first step and invited us to be reconciled to him. He does this through his proclaimed Word, the gospel, and through the convicting power of the Holy Spirit. He sends the "Spirit of his Son into our hearts," making it possible to us to address him as "Father" (Gal. 4:6).

Those who have known the reconciliation with God through Christ speak of their experience as a response to God's invitation, his calling. They certainly don't mean to imply that God is not calling others, nor do they think that their "calling" is for an exclusive privilege. Rather, they think of it as something to share with others and a basis of giving glory to God.

The individual thinks his or her present relationship with God is the result of God's call (Rom. 1:1) and that all of the redeemed people are so because they "are called to belong to Jesus Christ" (v. 6). It was God who called us into "the fellowship of his Son, Jesus Christ our Lord" (1 Cor. 1:9; Gal. 1:6,15; 5:13).

The relationship with God and with the church is spoken of as "the calling to which you have been called" (Eph. 4:1). It is a "holy calling" not related to our works but, rather, it is according to God's purpose and grace (2 Tim. 1:9). Peter, while discussing redemptive suffering wrote, "For to this you have been called" (1 Pet. 2:21), and this calling had eternal significance for his readers whom he told, God has "called you to his eternal glory in Christ" (1 Pet. 5:10).

Sometimes *calling* refers to special tasks of ministry, as in the case of Paul who was called to be the apostle to the Gentiles. Usually, however, it refers to the calling which all Christians know—the call to discipleship.

God calls us to salvation in a personal and specific way. It is more than a general invitation. As we hear the gospel, we also sense the Holy Spirit convincing and convicting us of sin (John 16:8).

After estranged persons are reconciled to God, they confess that God took the first step in calling them and convincing them. This in no way nullifies the human response; rather, it makes possible the human response. In an earlier discussion, we noted that a basic characteristic of creatures in the image of God is that they can respond to God.

The Human Response

God took the first step in the reconciliation of sinners, but reconciliation is complete only when they respond by hearing, repentance, and faith.

Hearing

In the Greek mystery religions and in Oriental Gnosticism, more emphasis was placed on seeing than on hearing. In the Mithras liturgy, for instance, the sacred moment came in the vision.[4] In biblical faith, however, the emphasis is on hearing. When visions and theophanies (appearancies of God) occur, they soon fall into the background so that God's Word can be heard. This is because biblical faith is always related to God's Word.

The Hebrew call to worship begins with the summons, "Hear, O Israel: The Lord our God is one Lord" (Deut. 6:4). The prophets' authority was in their "thus saith the Lord," and the people were under condemnation because they would not hear the word of God (Jer. 7:13; Isa. 1:10).

When John the Baptist doubted that Jesus was the Coming One and sent men to inquire, Jesus told the men to return and "tell John what you hear and see" (Matt. 11:4). Jesus spoke of his disciples as being related to him through hearing when he said, "My sheep hear my voice, and I know them, and they follow me" (John 10:27). Jesus' parable of the soils and sower has to do with hearing. He often told his hearers, "He who has ears, let him hear" (Matt. 13:9), as if they had a special responsibility for hearing.

Hearing is necessary to believing. Paul spoke of the need for people to hear the gospel and concluded, "So faith comes from what is heard, and what is heard comes by the preaching of Christ" (Rom. 10:17).

Hearing the Word of God is not a passive experience. The hearer is active, listening. Hearing in the biblical sense means more than merely listening to a message or sound; it spills over into obedience when one is hearing God.

In the process of reconciliation to God, the first human response is hearing, hearing God's call of invitation. This hearing creates an awareness of God and God's claim on human life. It is also the awareness that human beings are the creatures of God. It is an awareness of the conversation which took place before the fall, the memory of a language almost forgotten. The human creature is made to be able to hear God's word and by listening to respond.

Repentance

The call of God to humanity in sin is a call to return to God. This turning is the basic meaning of repentance in the Old Testament. It is turning to God from a life of sinfulness.

There are two New Testament words which are translated by the words *to repent* or *repentance.* One is *metamelomai* which means to change the mind and usually has in it the element of grief or remorse. It appears six times. The other word is *metanoeō,* the verb which means to repent in the sense of changing the mind and attitude toward God. It appears thirty-two times as a verb and twenty-two times as the noun, *metanoia.*

This change of mind, or attitude, toward God results in a rather radical change of life, often called conversion.

John the Baptist preached, "Repent, for the kingdom of heaven is at hand" (Matt. 3:1). Repentance was related to the forgiveness of sins, and John demanded some evidence, or fruit, "that befits repentance" (v. 8).

Jesus' message also was, "Repent, for the kingdom of heaven is at hand" (Matt. 4:17), or as Mark recorded it, "The time is fulfilled, and the kingdom of God is at hand; repent, and believe in the gospel" (1:15).

Peter, in his sermon on the day of Pentecost, proclaimed, "Repent, and be baptized every one of you in the name of Jesus Christ for the forgiveness of your sins; and you shall receive the gift of the Holy Spirit" (Acts 2:38).

In the preaching of John the Baptist and Jesus, the motivation for repentance is not fear but the promise of the kingdom. It is as if they said, "Turn to God because he is coming in his kingdom, and you were created for the kingdom." The call to repentance may be motivated by joy and hope, as well as by fear. A strong warning is in order at the point of mistaking remorse for repentance. Doing penance may encourage an attitude of self-condemnation or remorse without leading to repentance (see Matt. 27:3-5.) Paul knew the difference between two kinds of "sorrow" or grief. One is harmful. Wallowing in guilt is dangerous. The other is healthy. It leads to life. "For godly grief produces a repentance that leads to salvation and brings no regret, but worldly grief produces death" (2 Cor. 7:10).

Repentance is, therefore, a basic response to the Word of God made known in a change of mind toward God and from sin. The change involves a renewing the mind (Rom. 12:2). It is a basic change of the person into a "new creation" with a new relationship to God, reconciliation, and a new kind of life with a ministry of reconciliation to others (2 Cor. 5:17-21).

Repentance is the companion of faith. One does not turn from sin without turning to God. True repentance is accompanied by faith and is a turning to God. Before repentance and faith, a person can be described as living "according to the flesh"; after repentance and faith, that person lives "according to the Spirit" (Rom. 8:4).

Faith

The most complete term for the right response to God is the word *faith*. The Greek verb *pisteuō* is stronger than the English "to believe." By adding the preposition "in" or "on" to the verb "to believe," we come closer to the meaning. Faith is more than believing "that" something is true; it is believing "in" or "on" Christ. Faith includes a personal element of trust or commitment.

When the Philippian jailer asked, "What must I do to be saved?" the answer was, "Believe in the Lord Jesus, and you will be saved, you and your household" (Acts 16:30-31). The theme of Romans is that we are made right with God "through faith in Jesus Christ" (3:22; 5:1). Both sides of salvation are clearly identified in the summary, "For by grace you have been saved through faith; and this is not of your own doing, it is the gift of God" (Eph. 2:8).

John Baillie has written that faith is the only right human response to God's revelation. God's revelation presents to us a strange demand, the demand that we accept a gift.[5] To God, faith is always personal trust. Faith would be simply agreement if revelation were understood as a set of communicated truths.

Faith is a complex term, but in our experience it includes at least three factors: knowledge, assent, and trust. We first hear the Word of God, thereby receiving information. Then we come to accept it as true; that is assent. Both of these involve thinking. It becomes faith, however, only when it reaches the point of personal trust in God. This is will.[6]

Many persons who have lived in a religious environment would readily agree that they believe that Jesus Christ is the Son of God, and they agree to most of the teachings of the Christian church. They know, however, the difference between that general assent "that" something is true and personal trust "in" Christ. Faith is believing "in" God through Christ. Faith is an acceptance and a commitment.

While discussing "How Salvation Becomes Ours," Lesslie Newbigin related the experience of faith to the disclosure of the cross.[7] When we understand the cross, we grasp for the first time the enormity of our sin and the infinite depths of the love of God. When we see the relationship between our sin and Christ's death on the cross, we see the meaning of God's judgment and mercy. Out of this recognition, we accept God. We surrender to him. We trust him. That is faith. It is a response we make to God, but it is not our independent work; it is, rather, a work of the Holy Spirit within us. Thereby we become partakers of Christ.

We previously noted the ever-present element of unbelief in human sin. Whether sin is regarded as pride, sensuality, or rebellion, unbelief is always a part. It is, therefore, quite reasonable that salvation is by faith in Christ.

Reconciliation to God begins with faith precisely at the point of unbelief. God wills that we trust him. If we trust him, he can deal with all of our other ills. He is willing to take us as we are. The message of the cross and the gospel is that God calls us personally to be what we were meant to be. The bond in all personal relationship is trust. It is not strange, therefore, that our relationship with God would be secured by faith.

Repentance is not an event that happens only once. Rather, the person who lives for God in this world is frequently turning back to God after drifting off course. By the same reasoning, faith is not a static reality that can be presumed upon. Faith is an ever-trusting relationship. It grows or it can be weakened. Doubt, however, is not the enemy of faith. Honest doubt can often be the question that causes one to search further and deeper in an understanding of faith. Unbelief, however, is a desperate human situation. It can happen almost innocently by neglect, like wading into deep water. Distrust, on the other hand, is a cultivated unbelief which is malignant and destructive and quite possibly terminal.

The twin experience of repentance and faith mark the beginning of the Christian pilgrimage. The beginning experience of repentance and faith may be compared to the radical turn of an oceangoing ship as it clears the harbor and channel and takes a course plotted to take the ship across the sea. As the ship sails, however, the navigators are always at work. They reckon the position of the ship, affected by wind and wave, in relation to its course to its destination. Regularly along the journey they recommend small course changes to correct for drift. In a similar way, the Christian pilgrim, through worship, hearing the Word, prayer, and conversations with others, becomes aware of the drifting. Then, as at first, repentance and faith mark the turning back to God. The entire journey is marked by these smaller but distinctive turnings and trustings.

Human destiny is to have faith in God and faith in other human beings. The end of faith is faithfulness. God's only requirement of us is faithfulness.

Reconciliation

There are several words in the Bible and in Christian usage which designate the event of God's work of reclaiming sinful persons: *salvation, redemption, restoration,* and *new creation.* Each term is comprehensive and, in most cases, includes or presupposes the others. The selection of the term *reconciliation* is in keeping with the understanding that sin causes separation from God.

Reconciliation with God involves the forgiveness of sins, our restored relationship after the image of God, regeneration, and justification.

The Forgiveness of Sins

The saving work of God on our behalf often speaks of the forgiveness of sins. For instance, in Paul's summary of the earliest gospel tradition, he stated that "Christ died for our sins" (1 Cor. 15:3). As early as Pentecost, Peter related the events of Christ's death and resurrection to human repentance and "forgiveness of your sins" (Acts 2:38).

Several distinctions about sin should be reviewed. Sin may be understood as a "something," a barrier between us and God; it may also be viewed as a broken relationship. Both views appear throughout the Bible and Christian history. Sin is always against God. The psalmist was keenly aware that whatever crime he may have committed against the law, his sin was somehow uniquely against God, "Against thee, thee only, have I sinned" (Ps. 51:4). An offense against the state or a violation of a law is a crime; sin is against God. Therefore, sin and the forgiveness of sin must be understood in purely personal terms. Any legalistic connotation will distort the understanding of forgiveness.

Unfortunately, we cannot maintain a consistent distinction between "sin" and "sins" since both appear in the Bible. It would be easier for us if we could maintain such a distinction. The inclusive singular *sin* would more accurately preserve the concept that sin is a personal and relational matter between

God and human beings. The plural, *sins,* encourages the idea that sins are things or objects and can be dealt with accordingly. Sins do not exist apart from sinners. Therefore, we shall avoid some errors if we carefully insist on keeping the discussion in the personal area.

There are two significant interpretations of forgiveness of sin: the removal of the barrier of sins and the reconciliation of the sinner and the Forgiver. Those who hold to the former view think of forgiveness as "the prelude" to reconciliation.[8] This view tends to put the great terms about salvation in a step-by-step order: forgiveness, reconciliation, etc. The neatness of such an arrangement, however, is not worth the price. Actually each term includes part or all of the meaning of the others.

The other view practically equates the meaning of forgiveness of sin with reconciliation. E. B. Redlich, for instance, states that forgiveness is "full restoration to fellowship."[9] If one considers the parable of the forgiving father, it would be quite artificial to divide the forgiveness into two stages, removing a barrier and restoring the fellowship. Of course, both elements are present but not in a chronological sequence.

Since the biblical sources mention both sin and sins and since forgiveness is also spoken of as both removing the barrier and restoring the relationship, we shall include both emphases but insist that forgiveness is a gracious and personal act of God which issues in full reconciliation. This approach is required because of the way in which the biblical witness speaks both about sin and forgiveness.

Old Testament Terms for Forgiveness. There are four words in the Old Testament which are usually used to designate forgiveness: *halach* means "to send away"; *nasa* means "to lift up a burden"; *kaphar* means "to cover"; *machah* means "to blot out." These expressions about forgiveness mean that sins were viewed as objects. As such they can be removed, covered so as not to be incriminating evidence, or simply blotted out of existence. The idea of "covering" sin, for instance, has nothing to do with concealing evidence. The Hebrews spoke in very concrete terms. When Cain killed Abel, the blood of Abel stained the soil and cried out from the ground. This staining and crying out reflect need of revenge or punishment prevalent in the early Old Testament period. The amazing thing about the forgiveness of God is that it "covered" the sin. God deals with it so that it no longer serves as a basis for the demand for blood revenge. The idea of "blotting out" stresses that sin is real, a barrier. God who spoke the world into being out of nothing can speak such a barrier out of existence. Forgiveness is a creative act of God. Sin stands between us and God. He can will it away. That is forgiveness if sin is seen as a barrier.

Forgiveness in the New Testament.[10] The theme of forgiveness is, for all practical purposes, the same as the idea of salvation in the preaching of John the Baptist (Mark 1:4). Jesus forgave sin (Mark 2:5; Luke 7:48) and was accused of blasphemy because only God can forgive sins.

Jesus introduced a new idea that persons who could not, or would not, forgive others could not be forgiven. He stated, "For if you forgive men their trespasses, your heavenly Father also will forgive you; but if you do not forgive men their trespasses, neither will your Father forgive your trespasses" (Matt. 6:14-15). Jesus did not intend anything like a bargain between persons and God. Jesus was speaking to people who were already acquainted with God's forgiveness but would need to be forgiven repeatedly in the future. His statement appears to mean that those persons who cannot forgive others are incapable of accepting God's forgiveness. The acceptance of free grace depends upon one's ability to abandon pride and to acknowledge helplessness, the need for pure mercy. The person who cannot feel for another person who is in need of forgiveness is unable to accept forgiveness for himself or herself.

One of Jesus' most distinctive sayings on forgiveness is that forgivers do not keep records; they forgive every time they are asked to forgive, as many as seventy times seven times (Matt.

18:21; Luke 17:3). Again, the regard for persons is the context. Legalism is alien to this discussion.

Repentance is related to forgiveness but not as a requirement of the forgiver. It is the condition of the person seeking forgiveness. The forgiver who demands repentance or evidence of repentance has introduced a legalistic element into the process and becomes a judge of the other person. Repentance is a condition of forgiveness (Matt. 18:21; Luke 17:3). Jesus commended the tax collector who beat his breast and cried out, "God, be merciful to me a sinner!" (Luke 18:13). Persons who demand repentance from others before they will "forgive" are probably speaking of an uneasy truce and not forgiveness at all. Persons, however, who seek forgiveness know that they are repenting and that the repentance is itself the condition which makes it possible for them to seek and receive forgiveness.

Forgiveness begets love and not license. Legalistic minds think otherwise. Jesus told a story about two debtors of whom one owed 500 denarii and the other 50. The creditor, when they could not pay, forgave them both. Jesus asked, "Now which of them will love him more?" Simon the Pharisee grudgingly acknowledged, "The one, I suppose, to whom he forgave more" (Luke 7:42-43). Religious persons have always been suspicious of Jesus' teaching and practice of forgiveness. Legalism, or their pride, blinds them. God's forgiveness is sheer grace. It does not encourage the forgiven to go on sinning; rather, it encourages the forgiven to love the Forgiver.

Forgiveness is, or results in, reconciliation. Jesus' story of the forgiving father (Luke 15) needs no clarification. It portrays forgiveness as reconciliation. The parable of the older brother which follows illustrates the legalistic idea, always present, that forgiveness should be preceded by a probationary period, retribution, and so forth. That, however, would not be forgiveness.

In the Acts and the Epistles, forgiveness is a continuing experience for Christians. They continue to seek the forgiveness of God, and they continue to forgive one another. Paul encouraged "forgiving one another, as God in Christ forgave you" (Eph. 4:32; Col. 3:12-13). Forgiveness and being forgiven are so essential in the life of faith that the church has been described as the "community of forgiveness."[11]

Forgiveness is the gracious act of God in which he removes our sins and receives us back into the creaturely relationship with himself. Since our sin broke our prior relationship and destiny with God, forgiveness is correctly understood as our full recovery. For this reason, forgiveness is sometimes used to describe the whole experience with God. It earned a place in the earliest creeds of the church.

Reconciliation as Restoration After the Image of God

If salvation, or reconciliation, is seen as God's work of restoring human creatures, then we should expect the redeemed person to be endowed with the image of God.

Jesus Christ, as Son of God and true humanity, revealed the "image of the invisible God" (Col. 1:15), the "likeness of God" (2 Cor. 4:4), and the "very stamp" of God's nature (Heb. 1:3). In Christ we see what God is like and what human beings ought to be like.

Four New Testament passages speak about the changing of human lives into the image of God or Christ (Rom. 8:28-29; 2 Cor. 3:12-18; 1 Cor. 15:49; Col. 3:9-10). The experience of salvation, as restoration, is "to be conformed to the image of his Son" (Rom. 8:29).

If we try to measure our restoration in terms of identifying and counting evidences of the image of God in ourselves or others, we fail again. If we see the image of God, however, in terms of our dominion over nature under God as a relationship with God which includes freedom and responsibility and a responding trusting dependence on God, we can know the power of Christ's reconciliation.

Regeneration

Regeneration designates in a special way that God makes us over or renews us in the process of salvation. It is related to several other words which are used to describe the change of the sinner into a child of God. Paul tended to use terms like *transformation* (Rom. 12:2), "conformed to the image" of Christ (Rom. 8:29), or "new creation" (2 Cor. 5:17). He spoke of the radical renewal of sinful persons into the children of God.

The most popular expression of regeneration is the "new birth" or being "born again." This biological analogy is very descriptive for the spiritual birth or renewal of the person. It is not mentioned frequently in the New Testament but is a significant contribution toward understanding our salvation.

Jesus said to Nicodemus that a person had to be "born anew" or he could not see the kingdom of God (John 3:3). In clarifying to Nicodemus, Jesus spoke of natural birth and spiritual birth and indicated that this new birth was to be "born of the Spirit" (3:6). The resulting "eternal life" is for "whoever believes in" Christ (3:16). Obviously, the saving experience is realized by faith, and the event is so radical that it can be described as being "born anew" or "from above" or "born of the Spirit."

Regeneration appears in Titus in the context of cleansing and renewal. The letter speaks of the Savior coming because of the loving-kindness of God and "not because of deeds done by us in righteousness, but in virtue of his own mercy, by the washing of regeneration and renewal in the Holy Spirit" (3:5). The emphases are that regeneration is a washing or cleansing and that it is accomplished by the Holy Spirit.

In his summary of Christian beliefs, Peter said that "by his great mercy we have been born anew" (1 Pet. 1:3) and that this new birth has come about "through the living and abiding word of God. [and] That word is the good news which was preached to you" (1 Pet. 1:23,25).

The process of regeneration appears to be accomplished by the work of the Spirit and the Word of God. Dale Moody interprets the Letter of James as teaching this. Desire is born as sin and culminates in death (Jas. 1:15). Parallel to this idea is that the Word of God can be implanted in us and then can grow to our salvation (vv. 18-22).[12]

Since regeneration is the result of the Spirit of God and the Word of God within us, we can understand the transforming power of faith in God. This being born of the Spirit is the same as the baptism of the Spirit.

Justification

The Christian doctrine of justification by faith in Christ is distinctively a doctrine of Paul found mainly in Romans and Galatians. Paul tended to use the word *justification* instead of *forgiveness* when speaking of the unique saving event in Jesus Christ. The two terms are not identical, however, in spite of their use for the same theological idea. *Forgiveness* is a term at home only in the context of personal relationships. *Justification*, on the other hand, is a term whose meaning is partly determined by a legal context.

Paul's doctrine of justification by faith is cast in a legal context (*Justification* is a synonym for *righteousness*.)The terms *just, right, righteous, righteousness, justify*, and *justification* are built on the same root word. Paul understood the righteousness of God as a kind of legal righteousness[13] which demands righteousness of us. Paul, as a true Israelite, had sought the righteousness of God "based on law" but "did not succeed in fulfilling that law" (Rom. 9:31). The incredible realization of Paul was that righteousness, which could not be had through the keeping of the law, came as a gift to those who believed in Christ (Rom. 9:30; 10:3). He spoke autobiographically of his own religious antecedents who were "ignorant of the righteousness that comes from God, and [were] seeking to establish their own, [so] they did not submit to God's righteousness" (Rom. 10:2-3).

The amazing fact that rightness with God comes through faith in Jesus Christ is the theme of Romans. Paul maintained a close relationship with the law and saw Jesus Christ as the fulfillment of that law. "For Christ is the end of the law, that every one who has faith may be justified" (Rom. 10:4).

Paul turned against the legal concept of Judaism but interpreted the salvation event against that background. Paul viewed God as the Judge before whom we all stand, and we are all condemned for our sin (Rom. 2:12). God's righteousness as clearly made known in the law and his demand for us to be righteous are never annulled. Through the cross of Christ, God's righteousness becomes righteousness for us (Rom. 3:22-25).

The justification by faith in Christ must be recognized as a free gift (Rom. 5:1,15; Eph. 2:8). It is based on Christ's death (Rom. 5:9) and reconciles us to God. Justification by faith in Christ must also be understood as a rejection of any view of salvation by works. This awareness, more than any other, inspired Martin Luther. Luther, like Paul, had sought a righteousness of his own through careful obedience to the rules and religious practices of the Roman Catholic Church. Like Paul, Luther had failed. The discovery of rightness with God through faith in Christ was a dominant theme of Luther.

God's justification of the sinner through faith in Jesus Christ is an act in which God takes the first step. Justification is a present experience that implies a time of final judgment. Justification is always conditioned by the responding faith of men and women, and it is always grounded in the atoning work of Christ.[14]

Paul boldly declared that God "proclaims the guilty innocent" and that God declares the "guilty righteous." Paul's use of such phrases makes a legal interpretation of justification possible. But to be true to Paul, one must go on to note that Paul understood justification to be a changing experience because it is made possible by faith. To be justified, declared righteous, by God is to be reconciled to God by faith. In this relationship, a genuine righteousness is realized; but it is always based upon God's grace on the basis of Jesus Christ's sacrificial, vicarious, and representative death on the cross and realized through the human response of faith.[15]

Deliverance from Sin

When persons turn from God to sin, they actually come under the tyranny of evil powers. They are not free. The biblical writers witnessed to this mystery of evil in numerous ways.

Sinners are under the "dominion" of sin (Rom. 6:14) and the dominion of death (v. 9). Persons in unbelief are in the "dominion of darkness" (Col 1:13). Sinners are "slaves" to sin (John 8:34; Rom. 6:17; Gal. 4:3). Evil forces are the masters of sinful persons. They are the "principalities and powers" (Col. 2:15) who rule sinful persons' destinies.

Human sin is associated with unbelief, self-centeredness, idolatry, sensuality, rebellion, and ungodliness. It results in a slavery or a bondage. In the discussion with his opponents, Jesus referred to freedom and slavery. He told them that "the truth will make you free." They denied ever having been "in bondage to any one." Jesus stated, "who commits sin is a slave to sin" (John 8:31-34). We are "sold under sin" (Rom. 7:14).

Biblical faith speaks of this bondage to sin in many ways. One way is that sinners are serving the devil instead of God. Jesus told his adversaries, "You are of your father the devil, and your will is to do your father's desires" (John 8:44). Following the sin of Adam and Eve, there was a "curse" on the serpent. For the man and woman, the curse took the form of suffering. Even the good ground came under the curse and bore "thorns and thistles." How else, except in poetic language, can we speak of the tragedy which follows men and women who leave God?

Death also became the cruel tyrant as a result of human sin. Death is always more serious than the coroner's report. Death has to do with separation from God just as life has to do with the presence of God. Ultimately, "the wages of sin is death" (Rom. 6:23). We were formerly "slaves of sin," and "the end of those things is death." After faith in Christ, however, we "have been set free from sin and have become slaves of God." The "return" is "sanctification and its end, eternal life" (Rom. 6:20-23).

In the discussion of the cross of Christ, we noted that Gustaf Aulen summarized the atoning work of Christ as victory through conflict over sin, death, and the devil. These are the powers which threaten, rule, and destroy men and women who are away from God. Christ defeated those powers for us.

Reconciliation, or salvation, has more than the positive side of forgiveness and restoration to God. On the other side, there is the defeat or destruction of the powers of darkness. Just as repentance is positively turning to God and turning from sin as a result, reconciliation is also the reunion with God and the victory over the former powers which held us in slavery.

To overlook this deliverance from sin is to forget its seriousness for human existence. It is right to speak of the joy of repentance, faith, and reunion with God. It is disastrous, however, to forget that in this world there is a power of darkness and destruction at work. It is dangerous to live in this world. One can go to hell from this world if not in it. The Christian view of salvation is that in Christ we have victory over these evil powers as we are reconciled to God.

The Consequences of Sin

It is quite natural to ask what effect salvation has on sin in terms of its consequences. Persons often ask this question in connection with the forgiveness of sins. They often reflect the notion that God's forgiveness would in some way remove all of the consequences of their previous sinful acts.

Some of the consequences of sin are separation, lostness, loss, bondage, irresponsibility, depravity, and death.

It is obvious that reconciliation to God removes the separation and the lostness. The believer now has been freed from the bondage of sin and acknowledges Christ as Lord. Slavery to sin gives way to service to God. The sinner denied his responsibility to God. In repentance, one assumes responsibility again both for sin and accountability to God. Depravity exists in varying degrees. Reconciliation to God leads to sanctification, the saving of the life, but this does not occur instantly.

It is in the area of loss that sin claims a permanent payment. Even God does not rewrite history; he does not turn back the calendar. The Christian believer has accepted the forgiveness of God, and hopefully, that of his or her fellow human beings. One should also "forgive" oneself, that is, accept the forgiveness of God and live in the joy of the new relationship rather than in the regret of lost years and opportunities. There remains, however, the awareness that the days spent away from God were evil, uncreative days. In those days, people injured others and denied themselves the destiny which God has ordained. There is no way to go back and undo many of those wrongs growing out of sin. This is dealt with by forgiveness. God "forgets" our sins. Jeremiah stated, "I will forgive their iniquity, and I will remember their sin no more" (Jer. 31:34). The psalmist worded it, "as far as the east is from the west,/so far does he remove our transgressions from us" (103:12).

When God reconciles us to himself, he "forgets" our past.[16] We start over. He bids us to forget the past and make the new beginning. Death "no longer has dominion over" Christ who was raised from the dead (Rom. 6:9). His resurrection has given us the victory over death and the fear of death (1 Cor. 15:54-58).

A New Beginning

Reconciliation through Christ restores human beings to the original state which was lost in sin. There is now freedom and responsibility, relationship with God and with fellow human beings. By faith, a new birth, a new creation, has happened. Instead of pride, sensuality, idolatry, and unbelief, there is faith in God, worship of God, and love for God. This is the meaning of the Christian life, "life according to the Spirit." Its identifying marks are faith, hope, and love.

Notes

1. Dale Moody, *The Word of Truth* (Grand Rapids: William B. Eerdmans Publishing Company, 1981), pp. 308-313.
2. See articles on "Grace" in IDB, 2, pp. 463 *ff.; The Oxford Dictionary of the Christian Church* (London: Oxford University Press, 1958), p. 576-577.
3. TDNT, 3, p. 489.
4. TDNT, 1, p. 217.
5. John Baillie, *The Idea of Revelation in Recent Thought* (New York: Columbia University Press, 1956), p. 84.
6. Ibid., p. 85-86.
7. Lesslie Newbigin, *Sin and Salvation* (Philadelphia: The Westminster Press, 1956), pp. 97-100.
8. William Klassen, *The Forgiving Community* (Philadelphia: The Westminster Press, 1956), p. 212.
9. E. B. Redlich, *The Forgiveness of Sins* (Edinburgh: T. & T. Clark, 1937), p. 104.
10. Morris Ashcraft, *The Forgiveness of Sins* (Nashville: Broadman Press, 1972), pp. 24-36.
11. Klassen, "Forgiveness and the Community of the Forgiven."
12. Moody, p. 318-319.
13. TDNT, 2, p. 202.
14. Vincent Taylor, *Forgiveness and Reconciliation* (London: Macmillan & Co., Ltd., 1960), pp. 35-39.
15. See also TDNT, 2, pp. 178-225; IDB, 2, pp. 1027-1030; Hendrikus Berkhof, *Christian Faith: An Introduction to the Study of the Faith,* trans. Sierd Woudstra (Grand Rapids: William B. Eerdmans Publishing Company, 1979), pp. 432-445; Otto Weber, *Foundations of Dogmatics,* 2, trans. Darrell L. Guder (Grand Rapids: William B. Eerdmans Publishing Company, 1983), pp. 258-314.
16. Ashcraft, p. 23.

12

The Church

The early confessions of Christians included a statement, "I believe in the church." Many different organizations, clubs, churches, and radio and television programs today answer to the name "church." One wonders what "church" the early Christians believed in.

The word translated *church* in English Bibles is the Greek word, *ekklēsia. Ekklēsia* is a compound word consisting of the preposition *ek* and the noun *klēsis* ("calling") from the verb *kaleō,* "to call." As such, it named a gathering or congregation of people. It was used in the New Testament to translate an Old Testament word with the same meaning, "congregation" or "assembly of people."

Within the New Testament, the word was used for the local congregations of Christians and the body of Christians as a whole. It was also used for the church as an institution, and in one case, a mob at Ephesus (Acts 19:32). Many interpreters have been tempted to extract from the word *ekklēsia* more meaning than it has to offer—"the called out," etc. Several other terms in the New Testament are used for the church and should be considered.

The English word *church* came by way of Latin and German from the Greek word *kuriakos* which means, "belonging to the Lord," and appears as *Kirche, kirk,* and *church.*

In this discussion, we shall look more to the meaning of "belief in the church" at the time of its origin, hoping thereby to understand what the church is. Less attention will be given to the various historical interpretations and manifestations of the institutional churches.

Jesus of Nazareth came "not to be served but to serve, and to give his life as a ransom for many" (Mark 10:45). One would assume that the church which claims to be "his body" would also be characterized by serving, giving, and giving itself.

The New Testament writers spoke of the church in a great many ways. Paul S. Minear listed and discussed thirty-two "Minor Images of the Church," before even getting to the major images.[1] In another discussion, he pointed out that the New Testament does not actually portray a technical doctrine of the church; rather, it portrays a "gallery of pictures."[2]

The following steps will be helpful to our understanding the church: (1) the origin of the churches in the New Testament; (2) the discovery of "the church" in the New Testament; (3) New Testament reflections on the nature of the church; (4) the identifying marks of the church in later history; and, (5) the mission and ministry of the church.

The Origin of the Churches in the New Testament

The New Testament word *ekklēsia* is the Greek translation of the Hebrew word meaning "congregation" (*qahal*). In the Septuagint, the Greek translation of the Hebrew Old Testament, the word *ekklēsia* was used. For that reason, and several others, some scholars speak of "the church in the Old Testament." The word *church* became so specifically identified with the Christian congregation that it should not be used any longer in any other way. To avoid confusion, terms like *congregation* or *assembly* (as the RSV translation does in Acts 19:32) will be used here to mean assemblies in a general sense. The term *church* will be reserved for the Christian assembly and congregations.

Jesus Christ—The Origin

Jesus Christ was the origin of the reality known as the church. Before he came, there was the Hebrew covenant people of God. This people had a long heritage of worship and learn-

ing. The people later to be known as the church were participants in the Hebrew community. There were remarkable differences, however, between the congregation of Israel and the
church. The congregation of Israel was primarily a racial group;
the church which originated in the life, death, and resurrection
of Jesus Christ is universal. Their messages were related but
were very different.

In a previous chapter, the uniqueness of Jesus Christ, the
"once-for-allness" of his revelation of God, and reconciliation
of humanity were noted. Who can say when the church began?
Scholars have argued over whether Jesus really founded the
church. We can say with assurance that the church had its
origin in the cluster of events surrounding the life, teachings,
death, and resurrection of Jesus.

In both the teachings and actions of Jesus, we encounter a
new Israel, a nucleus of a new people, a new sustaining message, a mission, and certain practices which later became the
focus of Christian worship. If Jesus did not establish the
church, we must conclude that it was the result of his deliberate teaching and work.[3] Scholars vary in their conclusions as
to when the church began. Some would say it began when
Jesus called the disciples; others would say it could not have
been until Christ had completed his redemptive work in the
cross and resurrection; others would look to the great outpouring of the Spirit at Pentecost as the beginning of the church.[4]

Jesus Christ stands at the beginning, center, and end of any
discussion of the church. Any organization that does not so
regard Jesus Christ should choose a name other than church.
His life, teachings, wonders, presence, revelation, death, and
resurrection left the disciples saying such words as, "Did not
our hearts burn within us while he talked to us on the road,
while he opened to us the scriptures?" (Luke 24:32).

After the crucifixion and resurrection of Jesus, the disciples
waited expectantly while they worshiped, broke bread together, prayed, and enjoyed fellowship within the group. They

were held together by an expectation based on a promise Jesus had made.

The Holy Spirit—The Continuation of Jesus' Ministry

Jesus had indicated to his followers that after his departure the Holy Spirit would come as Teacher, Counselor, and Guide. The great event on Pentecost convinced the disciples that this had happened and that the Holy Spirit's presence would continue. The Holy Spirit, as Christ's Spirit, was now the supreme leader of their group, even though men like Peter, James, John, and later Paul would emerge as leaders. This belief about the Holy Spirit, despite misunderstandings and misuses in later times, was a decisive factor in the origin of the church.

The leadership of the Holy Spirit in the church is another way of speaking of God's providence. The awareness of God's presence, sustaining power, and guidance gave power to the young church. The church of today, like the early church in Jerusalem, lives by his presence in its life.[5]

The Word of God—The Emergence of the Gospel

Jesus, as had John the Baptist before him, preached a message of repentance. Jesus proclaimed, "The time is fulfilled, and the kingdom of God is at hand; repent and believe in the gospel" (Mark 1:14). Biblical faith, wherever one encounters it, always stresses the Word of God. The mission or purpose of the people of God is always related to that Word.

The promises of Jesus regarding the message and the kingdom appeared to have been fulfilled in the events of his life, death, and resurrection and in the outpouring of the Spirit on the day of Pentecost. We have no way of knowing how much the disciples discussed this message. But Peter proclaimed a message on Pentecost which has within it a fulfilment of the old promise, as well as a remarkable new element. The death of Jesus—a crime of men—and the resurrection of Jesus—an act of God—were proclaimed as "according to the definite plan and foreknowledge of God" (Acts 2:23). This message of good news included the promise of forgiveness of sins to those who repented and were baptized in the name of Jesus Christ (v. 38).

This message is essential for the church. This is what Paul passed on to the church in Corinth (1 Cor. 15:3-8) and told the Romans that the gospel "is the power of God for salvation to every one who has faith, to the Jew first and also to the Greek" (Rom. 1:16). The gospel has marked the life of the church. This "power" for salvation is the message for the whole world. The church often uses words when setting apart its ministers such as "for the gospel ministry" or "for the ministry of the Word."

A New Community—Called into Being

The disciples had formed a community during the ministry of Jesus. We don't know its exact size. One reference at a time shortly after the resurrection, but before Pentecost, mentions that "the company of persons was in all about a hundred and twenty" (Acts 1:15). We don't know if this included the women and children. A few weeks later there was a phenomenal growth, but the point is not size. Rather, the point is that the believers were aware that they were a new people, a new community. They met, worshiped, shared food, and shared their property.

A significant thing about the church is that members did not organize this movement; it was not of their planning. They had been called together by Jesus and were held together by their faith in him. This "calling" acknowledged that they were in the group because of his initiative, not theirs. Paul understood this and, although his missionary efforts resulted in numerous congregations, saw the church as the community of those "called [by God] to be saints" (Rom. 1:7).

The "whole church" of Acts 5:11 may be only the congregation in Jerusalem (Acts 8:1). Almost immediately thereafter, however, we hear about the "church throughout all Judea and Galilee and Samaria" (Acts 9:31). The church was mentioned in the singular even though three provinces were included. We may safely assume that this "church" was the result of the scattering of the Christians following Saul's persecution of the church (Acts 8:4). "Churches" in the plural, however, appear in great numbers after the beginning of the missionary journeys (Acts 15:41).

Persecuted Christians Witnessing as They Went

After the stoning of Stephen, a "persecution arose against the church in Jerusalem" and the members who were "scattered went about preaching the word" (Acts 8:1,4). The purpose here is not to discuss persecution as a missionary strategy; persecutions tend to kill off leadership and eventually destroy movements. Persecutions which do not last long and are not intense may serve as a temporary prod, but that is beside the point.

The churches in Galilee and Samaria emerged in response to the witnessing of those who fled the persecution in Jerusalem. This incidental witnessing is probably the basic strength of the ministry of the church. The early Christians were witnesses. Witnesses are those who were there, who saw, who heard, or who experienced something worth telling others. Origen later responded to Celsus who had denounced Christianity because it spread its faith through workers in wool and leather and its missionaries were uneducated men and women teaching other uneducated people.[6]

The churches emerged in localities in which these witnesses told about Jesus' death and resurrection for the forgiveness of sin. This speaks not only about the origin of churches and missionary work but also of the nature of the church. The church is composed of witnesses—people who have heard, seen, and experienced Christ.

The Holy Spirit in Mission

The Book of Acts, usually published in Bibles as *The Acts of the Apostles,* is literally filled with statements about the Holy Spirit's leading the churches and the Christians in their decisions and ministry. For this reason, some think the book should be named "The Acts of the Holy Spirit." Whatever the title, the writing acknowledges the faith of this early Christian movement that the Holy Spirit was in charge.

We cannot understand the church apart from the leading and empowering role of the Holy Spirit. Ours is not a faith that merely remembers Jesus who died long ago; rather, it is a living belief that Jesus Christ is living today with us as Holy Spirit.

Planned Missionary Efforts

To our knowledge, the first planned missionary activity was carried out by the church in Antioch. This congregation felt guided by the Holy Spirit to "set apart . . . Barnabas and Saul for the work to which [God] called them" (Acts 13:2). Then the members fasted and prayed and "laid their hands on them and sent them off" (Acts 13:3). This is often seen as "ordination"; but there was certainly no privilege involved, no governmental tax exemptions, no status or power, or even salary, which appear to be associated with ordination today.

This event speaks not only to the origin of the churches but also to their nature. When the Holy Spirit is at work in churches, he guides and empowers them to "give away" the good news of salvation to others. There is no suggestion in this narrative that the missionaries were to organize "missions" which would send money to and report converts to be counted by the "mother" church.

In this quiet but significant event in Antioch are several important facts. The individuals had been called by the Holy Spirit; the Holy Spirit led the church in the decision to affirm that call; the congregation participated in "sending" them; and, later the missionaries reported back to the church. This speaks of the nature of the church.

Emergence of Christian Communities

Wherever the witnessing Christians or the appointed missionaries went with their message, people responded. Those who responded felt "called" to the Lord. They also felt "called" together. Congregations of "called" people are communities of persons who have been reconciled to God and to one another, and that is the nature and purpose of the church and the churches.

The Discovery of "the Church"

The Book of Acts tells the story of the origin of the church in Jerusalem and of its expansion from Jerusalem to Rome, from the Jews to all peoples. Many of the letters of the New Testament were written to specific churches. Most of the references are to "the churches," or local bodies of believers. In Ephesians and Colossians and perhaps in another place or two, however, the church appears in the singular and appears to mean all the churches as a whole.

One Church and Many Churches

Three or four decades of Christian history had passed by the time Ephesians and Colossians were written. Our records are, unfortunately, too limited to give us a full account of the expansion of the church, all of the persons involved in it, and the understanding of many questions about the church. The records are, fortunately, complete enough to give us some insights that appear reliable. We began with a church in Jerusalem. It may have included other congregations in Judea. Soon, there were churches in Judea, Samaria, Galilee, and Syria. When the journeys of Paul were complete by AD 64, there were churches scattered over Asia Minor, Greece, and Italy. There were almost certainly churches in Egypt, if not in other parts of Africa, and in Syria beyond Damascus. We know very little about the relationship of these congregations to one another.

In Ephesians and Colossians, however, we encounter the church, in the singular. Jesus Christ has been exalted and is "head over all things for the church which is his body" (Eph. 1:22-23). Believers hold membership in "the household" or family of God which is "built upon the foundation of the

apostles and prophets, Christ Jesus himself being the corner-
stone, in whom the whole structure is joined together and
grows into a holy temple" (Eph. 2:20-21). The great mystery
now revealed is that Christ wants "all men [to] see what is the
plan of the mystery hidden for ages in God who created all
things; that through the church, the manifold wisdom of God
might now be made known" (Eph. 3:9-10).

In one section, "the church" is related to Christ as a wife is
related to the husband (Eph. 5:23 ff.).

In Colossians, Christ "is the head of the body, the church"
(Col. 1:18), and in this new relationship with Christ all human
barriers are broken down because "Christ is all, and in all"
(Col. 3:11).

The Unity of the Church

The greatest single passage on the unity of the church is in
Ephesians (4:1-6). This kind of unity is not achieved by seeking. It is not uniformity. The discussion continues with references to the diversity of gifts (v.11). Unity consists in certain
universal characteristics which all Christians know. The vast
differences among churches have come as a result of geographical isolation, language barriers, imported cultural changes,
mixtures of other religions, political and governmental forces,
and so forth. The failure to note the difference between these
influences and the faith results in great confusion. There is,
however, an underlying unity in the church, which just is. It
requires no promotion—only recognition. The unity is derived
from the oneness of God.

One Calling (Eph. 4:1). This "calling" is the act of God through
the proclamation of his Word. The Holy Spirit along with the
gospel brings about an awareness within the hearer. Through
repentance and faith, the one who responds has a sense of
being called by God. This is quite different from being enlisted
by members of a religious group to do something religious.

One Spirit (Eph. 4:4). Nothing happens until the Spirit moves.
The Spirit is involved in the "calling." The Spirit gives power

to the Word as Christians grow toward sanctification. The Spirit gives the energy. He is the evidence of God's providence. Above all, he is the Presence of God. This Presence is the source of unity.

One Hope (Eph. 4:4). Christian faith is a remembrance. It is also an expectation. Christians believe that God who came in Christ to reconcile us to himself will come again to complete our salvation. Christians believe that God has great things in store for his children now and after death—the resurrection. This hope binds Christians together. The joyful anticipation of Christ's future coming is as strong a motivation as the memory of his previous coming.

One Lord (Eph. 4:5). Jesus spoke often about the kingdom of God or the kingdom of heaven. He was misunderstood by those who wanted another kingdom like those of this world. His kingdom, however, is his reign in the lives of those who believe and obey. His kingdom is not like kingdoms of this world (John 18:36).

All Christians confess, "Jesus is Lord." The statement means nothing unless it means that the confessor recognizes Christ as King and seeks to obey. These are the children of the kingdom. There is only one Lord whom Christians confess.

One Faith (Eph. 4:5). Our faith is that commitment of trust in Jesus Christ on the basis of his death and resurrection. There is no other way of salvation. All of us who wear his name entered by that door. Consequently, we share a common faith; thus, we are "one." That faith is stated in beliefs and, then, doctrines which expose our diversity, prejudice, nationalism, political biases, etc. These statements are many and varied, but our "faith" is one.

One Baptism (Eph. 4:5). The controversies about who should be baptized, when, how, and by whom, and what relationship that should have to church membership have all but destroyed the meaning of baptism to many people. Baptism, as immersion in water of one who has died to sin but is now alive to God in Christ (Rom. 6:1-11), is a beautiful confession of the death, burial, and resurrection of Jesus. At the same time, the confession is made that "our old self was crucified with him," "buried," and "raised" for a "newness of life." There is only one such confession of faith in Christ even though people in different traditions and cultures practice the rite in a variety of ways.

One God and Father of Us All (Eph. 4:6). This is the meaning of all Christian theology. The reconciling work of God in Christ knows no boundaries of any kind. The oneness of God gives unity to the church. Religious groups (by whatever name or tax-exempt status) can tell if they are the church by whether they believe in God in this way and have the resultant love and respect for all of God's other children wherever they may be or in whatever organizations and governments they find themselves.

New Testament Reflections on the Nature of the Church

The theologians of the church have pointed out several New Testament ideas or symbols which seem to point to the nature of the church: it is the people of God; it is the body of Christ; and, it is the community, or fellowship, of the Holy Spirit.[7] To these three, I wish to add three more which deserve notice: the church is a priesthood of all believers; it is the community of reconciliation; and, it is a community of witnesses to the Word of God.

The church, in the sense found in Ephesians and Colossians, may be called the universal church as many have done. The congregations located everywhere would then be called "the local churches." If we do so, it needs to be noted that the church is not the organization of, nor the sum total of, all of the churches. The church is the living body of those who believe in Jesus Christ which transcends boundaries between nations, cultures, races, and centuries. The churches, however, if they are churches at all, are the local manifestations at this time of all that the church is or ever was. Or, to put it another way, a church is the church at this place in the present. It partakes of all of the characteristics of the church.

The Church as the People of God

The church is often spoken of in its relationship to God. It is "the church of God" (1 Cor. 1:2; Gal. 1:13), and they are the "churches of God" (1 Cor. 11:16). After a lengthy summary and rationale of Christian faith, Peter referred to the church as "a chosen race, a royal priesthood, a holy nation, God's own people" (1 Pet. 2:9).

The expression, the people of God, in the New Testament maintains the continuity with the covenant people of the Old Testament. One of the most affectionate statements in the Old Testament attributed to God expressed his love for Israel, "I will be your God, and you shall be my people" (Jer. 7:23). The well-known "new covenant" passage of Jeremiah, after speaking of the old covenant, states, "I will put my law within them, and I will write it upon their hearts; and I will be their God, and they shall be my people" (Jer. 31:33).

Paul's reasoning in Romans (9—11) was that the Hebrew nation is no longer God's people but that those who hear the gospel and believe in Christ are. The Christians are called "Israel of God" (Gal. 6:16). They are the "new covenant people."

The Epistle to the Hebrews (8:10) restates this new covenant which has been realized through Christ as the fulfilment of the Jeremiah prophecy: "I will be their God, and they shall be my people." The ultimate fulfillment of this hope was stated by John in the Apocalypse, "Behold, the dwelling of God is with men. He will dwell with them, and they shall be his people, and God himself will be with them; he will wipe away every tear from their eyes, and death shall be no more" (Rev. 21:3-4).

The same idea of "people of God" appears in the symbolism of the temple. The church is compared to the temple of God (2 Cor. 6:16; 1 Cor. 3:10-17; Eph. 2:11-22). This last passage also introduces the idea of the church as the "household" or family of God (Eph. 2:19).

The nature of the church consists of at least two realities and a relationship between them. The church is the people; and, the people are distinct because they are specifically called by and dedicated to God. The church is made up of those people living in this relationship with God.

The Church as the Body of Christ

The relationship of the church to Christ is best described by the phrase "the body of Christ." At the Last Supper, Jesus took bread, blessed it, broke and distributed it to the disciples, and said, "Take; this is my body" (Mark 14:22). Paul's stated the tradition, "This is my body, which is for you" (1 Cor. 11:24). Consequently, the word "body" suggests the meaning of the Last Supper.

The human body (the whole person) is the temple in which God's Spirit dwells (1 Cor. 6:19), and our bodies are "members of Christ" (1 Cor. 6:15). Paul spoke to the Roman Christians in these terms, "You have died to the law through the body of Christ, so that you may belong to another, to him who has been raised from the dead" (Rom. 7:4). This last passage, speaking of Christ's death on the cross, includes believers in that death according to the interpretation of baptism in the previous passage.

The church is compared to a human body. "For as in one body we have many members, and all the members do not have the same function, so we, though many, are one body in Christ, and individually members one of another" (Rom. 12:4-5). Paul expressed the same idea in correspondence to the church in Corinth, "Now you are the body of Christ and individually members of it" (1 Cor. 12:27). The idea of the vine and the branches in John is similar (John 15:1 *ff.*).

The church is repeatedly compared to a body in Ephesians and Colossians (Eph. 1:23; 2:3,16; 3:6; 4:4,12,16; 5:23,30; Col. 1:18,22,24; 2:19; 3:15). In these passages, the church is the body of Christ; people are members of the body; Christ is head of the church; the diversity of function among the members is unified by the head.

To speak of the church as the body of Christ means that: (1) the church is totally dependent on Christ who was crucified and raised and (2) living in the body of Christ is a daily bodily life in which we manifest our love to others.[8]

The analogy speaks to the nature of the church as a unity with diversity within it, and it says in an unchangeable way that the church belongs to Christ.

The Community of the Holy Spirit

The phrase "fellowship of the Spirit" appears only twice in the New Testament (2 Cor. 13:14; Phil. 2:1), and the subject in each place was not specifically the church. Dale Moody summarized the fellowship of the Spirit as "the baptism of the Spirit, the gift of the Spirit, and the unity of the Spirit.[9]

We have already noted that, in Acts, the church moved under the guidance and power of the Spirit. We have also noted that the Holy Spirit is the Spirit of Christ who leads the church as Christ led the disciples. It is fully correct to describe the nature of the church as a community of persons in fellowship with the Holy Spirit.

The Holy Spirit is the agent who introduces each Christian to conviction and faith. The individual and the church are the temples in which the Holy Spirit dwells. The Holy Spirit builds each individual church, and the whole church is the building of the Spirit (Eph. 2:17-22). The church lives under the rule of the Spirit who creates the church by his calling people to repentance and renews the church by his presence.[10]

In our age, it is not easy to understand the meaning of Spirit. Scientific thought, which is objective oriented, is seriously influenced by a general suspicion of religious thought. This influences people to turn toward those realities which are more obvious and usable. A vast majority of modern persons think very little about the intangible realities and values. Even within many churches there is a reluctance to speak about the Holy Spirit.

The uneasiness which people experience in talking about the Holy Spirit has been partly the outgrowth of irresponsible claims on the part of others about the Spirit. This is tragic because the Holy Spirit is God with and within us.

The church, and that means the churches, is a community of people who march to the cadence of the Holy Spirit. It is not the church at all unless the Holy Spirit is present, recognized, and followed.

Church as Priesthood of All Believers

Within the Protestant tradition, and now in Roman Catholicism, the church is often spoken of as "the priesthood of all believers." This phrase surfaced in the writings of Martin Luther to counter the authoritarian "priesthood" which ruled within the Roman Catholic Church at the time. The doctrine essentially means that (1) every believer in Christ has direct access to God through Christ without a human mediator and (2) every Christian believer is to serve as a priest on behalf of all others.

The Hebrew faith included official priests who related to God on behalf of the rest of the people. These priests had access to God, offered sacrifices, and probably blessed the rest of the people.[11]

Some passages in the Old Testament indicate that all of the people formed a kind of universal priesthood. "You shall be to me a kingdom of priests and a holy nation" (Ex. 19:6); "you shall be called the priests of the Lord" (Isa. 61:6). The idea is not dominant in the Old Testament, probably because of the existence of the official priesthood.

In spite of Martin Luther's emphasis, the idea of the priesthood of all believers is not prominent in the New Testament. The prominent idea is that Christ himself is the priest and, therefore, the basis of any Christian priesthood.

Jesus is "a high priest for ever after the order of Melchizedek" (Heb. 6:20). As our priest, Jesus is "a high priest, holy, blameless" and he offered himself for us (Heb. 7:26 *ff.*). Jesus' high-priestly role is dominant in Hebrews.

Only two New Testament writers speak of the church as a priesthood of all believers. The most important passage reads, "But you are a chosen race, a royal priesthood, a holy nation, God's own people" (1 Pet. 2:9). While addressing the seven churches, John wrote, "and made us a kingdom, priests to his God and Father, to him be glory and dominion for ever and ever" (Rev. 1:6).

The New Testament writings give a general support for the contention of Luther that within the New Testament Christian community, all participants were priests and the only mediator was Christ. The passages do not, however, provide the kind of direct support one would expect in light of the fact that most lists of "Protestant Distinctives" include "the priesthood of all believers."[12]

The belief in the priesthood of all believers has been grossly misunderstood and taught. Some understand it to mean that there is no difference between ministers and laypersons in the church. Others understand it to mean that every believer has the right to do anything that the church does. It is even distorted to mean that we don't need priests. Occasionally, someone indicates that every person is a priest in his or her own family and, therefore, says grace at the table.

Within the Free Church tradition, some persons understand it to mean that Roman Catholics need priests to mediate between them and God, to hear their confessions, but we don't need priests. Every person is his own priest.[13] T. W. Manson pointed out that, in popular usage, the doctrine often came to mean something like the priesthood of no believers at all, or "the non-priesthood of all believers." Such disregard can lead to the rejection of not only a priestly order within the church but also of any ministerial order.[14]

There has been a tendency among Baptists and Congregationalists to overlook the "all," thereby stressing the individual and forgetting the universal aspect.[15] In the Western democracies with their equalitarian political emphases, the doctrine often degenerates into a rejection of authority and a notion of "every man for himself."[16]

The idea of the priesthood of all believers was developed by the early church fathers. Justin Martyr, Irenaeus, Tertullian, Clement of Alexandria, Polycarp, Origen, and Clement of Rome spoke of the doctrine in keeping with the implications of the New Testament passages.[17]

The belief in the priesthood of all believers has several important implications for understanding the nature of the church: (1) the so-called "clergy" and "laity" should not be so distinguished; (2) the ministry of the church cannot be delegated to a few; (3) every Christian serves as a priest on behalf of others, as well as having direct access to God in one's own right; (4) the church looks to Christ and the Word for its authority, rather than to an official priestly caste; (5) ministers are chosen on the basis of their call and the congregational affirmation and are God's gift to the churches; (6) the government, or order, of the church involves all of the members.

Although the phrase has been confused by controversy, it designates something meaningful for understanding the churches of the New Testament. It indicates that all of the members are equal participants, with equal access to God and his grace, and serve as priests for others. It is certain that all believers should serve one another in areas such as private confession, counseling, guiding, and comforting.

Church as Community of Forgiveness

In Peter's Pentecostal sermon, the whole gospel came to focus in the forgiveness of sins. Paul's summary of the gospel included the theme, "Christ died for our sins" (1 Cor. 15:3). The Apostles' Creed includes this theme.

The Keys of the Kingdom and Forgiveness of Sins

After Peter's confession at Caesarea Philippi, Jesus stated:

You are Peter, and on this rock I will build my church, and the powers of death shall not prevail against it. I will give you the keys of the kingdom of heaven, and whatever you bind on earth shall be bound in heaven, and whatever you loose on earth shall be loosed in heaven (Matt. 16:18-19).

Throughout much of its history, the Roman Church interpreted this passage so as to give primacy to Peter, and many understood it to give the Roman Church the power to forgive sins or to refuse to do so. Naturally, non-Roman church groups who opposed this particular interpretation tended to ignore the passage or find other interpretations which were more acceptable.

The question of authority was raised by the disciples who asked, "Who is the greatest in the kingdom of heaven?" (Matt. 18:1). Jesus responded by calling a small child and indicating that the greatest was the humblest. In a similar case (Matt 20: 20-28), Jesus said, "The rulers of the Gentiles lord it over them. . . . It shall not be so among you." These statements about authority were made in the context dealing with forgiveness.

The "keys of the kingdom" passage talks about binding and loosing. This theme of binding and loosing appears again in Matthew 18. There it falls in the discussion of forgiveness of sins and includes the church in such removal and reconciliation. On another occasion, after the resurrection, Jesus said to the disciples, "If you forgive the sins of any, they are forgiven; if you retain the sins of any, they are retained" (John 20:23).

These passages indicate that the decisions of men and women in matters of response to the message of God have eternal consequences; they are binding. This does not necessarily mean that the church has the arbitrary power to forgive or refuse to forgive sins. That would violate Jesus' teaching about authority and greatness in the immediate context of the passages.

The church is not an authoritarian institution which admits some and rejects others. It does not have the franchise on forgiveness. The church is the people of God, the body of Christ, and the community of the Holy Spirit. It has been entrusted with the gospel of forgiveness. When the church does its ministry, the doors of the kingdom are open and people are admitted; when the church fails, people remain in their sins. This is the meaning of the "keys of the kingdom."

Martin Luther saw the relationship between the keys and the forgiveness of sins in the passages cited.[18] John Calvin understood these passages to teach that the forgiveness of sins takes place in the church through its ministry.[19] This is a common interpretation in Protestant Christianity.[20]

It is not enough to indicate that one of the tasks of the church is to proclaim the gospel of forgiveness; rather, it is necessary to note that the very nature of the church is that of being a community of forgiveness. William Klassen wrote a volume on the church entitled *The Forgiving Community*.[21] The church, however, is more deeply involved in forgiveness than being the forgiv*ing* community.

The church is the forgiv*en* community. Admission to the church is by forgiveness only. We were the sinners alienated (Eph. 2:11-22) from God but are now members of God's family. We entered by way of the door of forgiveness. Life within the church is one of forgiving and being forgiven (1 John 1:9; Eph. 4:32; Col. 3:13). We are the examples of the forgiven. Our forgivenness serves as encouragement to our neighbors who can see Christian forgiveness being practiced by the forgiven.[22] The church not only exhibits forgiveness but also teaches and offers the forgiveness of sins to others.

The church can be reasonably well perceived as a community of the forgiven, forgiving, and offering forgiveness of sins through its living and proclamation of the gospel.

The Church as a Community of the Word

Space will not permit adequate discussion of the church as a community of the Word, but a reminder is necessary. It is easy to fall into the notion that the church somehow owns or is in control of the Word. Appeals of ministers and missionaries to proclaim the Word seem to suggest that the church has an option. The church has no option if it is the church. The truth of the matter is that the church is by nature a community of the Word of God.

The church is composed of the witnesses who have heard the Word of God and responded. They naturally and inevitably bear their witness in one way or another. The witness always includes a telling of what happened—a message.

Within each church, the constant emphasis is on the Word. Worship consists of proclaiming and hearing the Word in the sermon, instruction, and discussion.[23] The sermon and the teaching present the message of God on which the church is nourished, lives, and grows. The discussion, whether formal or informal, is a vital part of that proclaiming and hearing the Word. Those who hear, question, ask for clarification, differ, and learn. The very nature of the church is to be in constant dialogue with the Word of God. It goes without saying that the Bible is the primary source of that Word of God for us, but the *Word of God* is a broader term than *Bible.* God spoke his Word before there was a Bible, and quite effectively.

At this point, contemporary Christians may be missing a part of the Word of God. The living God speaks his living Word within a living church. The Bible will forever remain the textbook of the church, and rightly so, but a warning is in order. Those seeking to honor the Bible can easily forget the living Word God is speaking through the Bible and within the church in every age.

The church, as a community of the Word, is responsible for translating the Scriptures and interpreting them to the contemporary generation. Yes, indeed! The task of interpretation, however, involves the demonstration of understanding and love within the human community. The church transmits its message not only to its own generation but also serves as the link which transmits the message throughout the ages.

A local community of believers meets in worship and hears the Word of God and then shares that with others. It is not only "doing" what churches do but is also "being" the church. It is distressing that a generation of "doers" asks what we in the church ought to do and assumes that we can do it. The first question is, What is the church? or Who is the church?

A Local Church and the Universal Church

One who knows the church at all knows it in the present, local, and tangible form of a congregation of believers. This very visible, and very human, assembly is a local manifestation of all that the church is. It is impossible for one to believe in the universal church and hold the local church in disdain. Although the universal church is often spoken of as the invisible church, it should not be idealized at the expense of its humanity.

The church of the ages, in whatever culture, language, or political setting is the people of God, the body of Christ, the community of the Holy Spirit. It is forgiven and forgiving, serving as priests under God on behalf of others, hearing, proclaiming, and living by the Word of God. The local church, by whatever name, structure, language, political or governmental sanction or prohibition, is nothing less and nothing more. All that the church is, a church is. And this raises the question of recognizing the church.

The Identifying Marks of the Church

There is a risk in talking about the identifying marks of the church. It may suggest that we sit in judgment on "whether or not" a particular organization is, in fact, a church. If it is possible to do so, let's forget that aspect and discuss positively the marks of a true New Testament church.

Martin Luther spoke of the "external marks" by which one can recognize the true church on earth. In one writing, he listed three: baptism, the sacrament, and the gospel.[24] In other writings, he listed others. These may be summarized as follows: (1) the true church exists where the Word of God is faithfullly preached, believed, confessed, and obeyed; (2) the church is identified by its faithful practice of the sacrament of baptism; (3) the church is recognizable in its faithful practice of the sacrament of the altar; (4) the church is identifiable by its faithful use of the keys of the kingdom, the forgiveness of sins; (5) the church is known by the fact that it calls and consecrates ministers for its offices; (6) the true church is recognizable by its practice of prayer, public thanksgiving, and praise to God; (7) the church is recognizable by its possession of the holy cross, which means that it suffers for Christ's sake.[25]

John Calvin spoke of the marks of the church as two: (1) the faithful preaching and hearing of the Word of God; and (2) the faithful observation of the sacraments according to Christ's institution.[26]

Emil Brunner, writing in the Protestant tradition in the New Reformation theological movement, identified five "Essential Marks of the Church According to the Apostolic Witness of Faith."[27] These marks are (1) "Apostolica," (2) "Catholica," (3) "Sancta, (4) "Una," and (5) "Credo." Hans Küng, in his treatment, includes the first four as "The Dimensions of the Church."[28]

For the church to be apostolic, it must stand on the foundation of the apostles who were the eyewitnesses of Jesus Christ on whom everything depends.

While some Protestants have difficulty with the word *catholic,* because of its common association with the Roman Catholic Church, the universality of the church is what is meant by the term and cannot be discarded.

To speak of the church as (*sancta*) "holy" is to draw attention to the New Testament "called to be saints," the *communio sanctorum.* The church as the people of God are those called by the

Word into a community. The point is not moral achievement but dedication to God.

The unity of the church is clearly taught in Ephesians but is hard for a modern to grasp because of the bewildering chaos of so many "churches" on the scene.

Jesus Christ who is the origin of the church was noted for being the Servant of all. His authority was also related to his servanthood. It may be that the church in its true form may be recognizable by its servanthood rather than by some of the other characteristics cited.

The Mission and Ministry of the Church—Reconciliation

> Therefore, if any one is in Christ, he is a new creation; the old has passed away, behold, the new has come. All this is from God, who through Christ reconciled us to himself and gave us the ministry of reconciliation; that is, in Christ God was reconciling the world to himself, not counting their trespasses against them, and entrusting to us the message of reconciliation. So we are ambassadors for Christ, God making his appeal through us. We beseech you on behalf of Christ, be reconciled to God (2 Cor. 5:17-20).

The mission and ministry of the church is the living out of its nature. It is not something else. It is not something the church does in addition to being the church. It is the actual "being" of the church. A separate discussion is offered for the sake of clarity and emphasis.

We have noted that the church, known as local churches, is the people of God, the body of Christ, the community of the Holy Spirit, hearing and obeying the Word of God, forgiven and forgiving, serving as priests to God on behalf of others. This is what the church is; this is what its mission is, and this is its ministry. Several characteristics of the church are obvious in its practices which illustrate its ministry of reconciliation. The following list is not exhaustive but illustrates this point.

Worship

The word *worship* means to acknowledge God's worth. Numerous ideas are included. It is to give glory to God, to praise God, to prostrate oneself before God, to celebrate and enjoy God's presence.

Worship is, of course, both private and public, formal and informal. Worship may be defined as "a graced response" by means of "symbolic activities" which "celebrate God." As a response to God, worship focuses on God. We acknowledge God, rehearse God's previous actions for us, and we proclaim what God is and has done.[29]

The acknowledgment of God may be expressed in meditation, confession, awareness of God's presence both in revelation and mystery, song, praise, or commitment.

The response to God known as recitation or rehearsal includes some kind of declaration of God's previous gifts, blessings, and actions. The Hebrews were instructed to assemble their children and rehearse the mighty acts of God. Christians recite God's wondrous works in reading the Scriptures, proclamation, personal testimony, song, baptism, Lord's Supper, and prayers of thanksgiving.

Responding to God through proclamation is a form of worship associated both publicly and privately with the telling of the "message of reconciliation" (2 Cor. 5:19). We tell this message in the form of a personal testimony, in the instruction within the church, in the sermon, and in response to the sermon.

Worship is the private or public acknowledgment of God. We recognize and confess his presence, respond in repentance and confession, rejoice in his forgiveness and acceptance. We also recall his previous mercies, enjoy his presence and the company of others who worship, and proclaim in word, song, and ceremony God's saving work.

Worship, therefore, includes among many other experiences, a conversation with God's Word, prayer, fellowship in reconciliation, baptism, and the Lord's Supper.

Conversation with God's Word. Worship begins in the awareness of God's presence. Whether we speak of Moses in Midian before the burning bush or Isaiah in the Temple or Paul on the road to Damascus, worship in the Bible began in the awareness of God's presence.

God's primary means of communicating with his human creatures is through his Word. When the individual or the church worships, there is the hearing and responding to God's Word. Most often this begins in the reading of the Bible or the singing of a hymn whose words are closely related to, if not directly derived from, Scripture. The responses to hearing God's Word include awe and reverence, conviction of sin and its confession, inspiration and encouragement, calling to service, and commitment to God. The call experience of Isaiah (6:1-8) is the most beautiful outline of worship in the Old Testament. It included: a previous preparation, an awareness of God's presence which was awesome, an awareness of personal and corporate sin, a confession of sin, cleansing and forgiveness of sin, a call to service, and a response of commitment.

Celebrating God's presence always includes hearing and obeying his Word. One may proclaim God's Word to those who do not respond. But in worship, the proclamation of the Word includes a response, thus transforming proclamation into conversation.

Christian worship inherited much from the Hebrew faith which had a similar emphasis on the Word of God which was read or recited, and included an element similar to the sermon. Hebrew worship included the Psalms. Christian worship is deeply indebted to its Hebrew background for this praise of God through song. No section on music and worship appears in this discussion because the psalm or hymn is another presentation of God's word.[30]

The reading and proclamation of God's Word must remain a vital part of worship. It is through the Word that God calls sinners to repentance and saints to growth, commitment, and service.

Prayer. The discussion on prayer would be appropriate in the discussions of several beliefs such as God, humanity, salvation, Spirit, one's personal Christian life, or in the doctrine of the church. It is included in this discussion of worship because it is so vitally related to the larger theme of our direct relationship with God in worship.

Prayer is more than talking to God. Prayer is a conversation with God which involves listening, as well as speaking. Prayer is an indispensable element in the Christian life. Whether or not our prayers are formal, we walk the Christian way only in the conversation with God known as prayer. Those who speak of prayer tell of their personal conversations with God which happened as they worked, traveled, or listened during the sacred moments of being alone with God.

Prayer has been called a "means of grace" by some because God's very saving power and keeping power have come to us by this means. Others object to this phrase on the grounds that it would make prayer dependent on God's initiative rather than humanity's. Prayer, however, is not simply an act of a human being. It is that, but it is also a response, directly or indirectly, to God who has addressed us first.[31]

Prayer is a conversation with God which includes both the individual and the church. The individual believer does not live his or her life apart from the church; he or she lives as a participant in the community life of the church. Prayer is a conversation with God which may be individual at one moment, or it may, and often does, include the family.

Prayers may be statements of thanksgiving. Even though begun by the one praying, these prayers are responses to God. Prayers may be adoration of God; if so, they express an awareness of God's prior acts. Prayers may be petitions asking for faith, forgiveness, help for self and others, guidance in a decision or strength for the day. In every instance, these prayers are responses to God in the light of a memory of what God has done in the past and an anticipation of God's willingness and ability to answer. Persons sometimes pray to God asking nothing but the joy of his presence. This, too, is a kind of response and a conversation.

Prayers in the worship service of the church are most likely to be more formal and to take the form of statements in prose. This is not always the case because some of the greatest prayers are sung. Many individuals find that their most meaningful times of prayer consist of meditation, reading published prayers and works of devotion, and sometimes through writing poems. There is a mystical element involved when we speak of a conversation with God, and we may do injury if we probe too prosaically into this sacred area. Jesus, however, did give a number of teachings on prayer which give practical guidance.

The Gospels note that Jesus prayed often. We have at least part of his prayers from the Sermon on the Mount and from Gethsemane.

Luke noted that it was after Jesus had been praying that the disciples said to him, "Lord, teach us to pray" (Luke 11:1). Jesus responded with what we call the Lord's Prayer. Luke's version (11:2-4) is shorter than Matthew's.

In Matthew's account of the Lord's Prayer, several features are important since this is a model prayer given in response to the request, "Teach us to pray." (1) Prayer is addressed to God who is "Our Father." (2) The holiness of God's name is acknowledged. (3) The prayer is that God's reign will be acknowledged by persons on earth and that they will do his will which is being done in heaven. (4) Persons in prayer acknowledge that God is the source of their daily bread. (5) The prayer for forgiveness is accompanied by a pledge of having forgiven others. (6) Those who pray ask for victory over temptation and deliverance from evil.

Prayer seems not so much intended to change God's will as to change our wills so that God's will can be done. In Gethsemane, the prayer of Jesus was that the forthcoming death be avoided; but he prayed "not what I will, but what thou wilt"

(Mark 14:36). This is not to imply that prayer is to get us into an attitude of accepting what is going to happen anyway. Jesus also taught the disciples to pray to God (Matt. 7:7), indicating that our "Father who is in heaven" gives "good things to those who ask him" (Matt. 7:11).

Prayer is also our approach to God. We address him in prayer when we sense our need for his love, strength, and guidance. We go to him in our loneliness. We go to him in our joy. When we are aware of the goodness of life and creation and the persons we know, we go to God in prayers of thanksgiving.

In this sense, prayer is a part of worship which is a vital element in our reconciliation to God.

Baptism. Most churches have practiced a form of baptism and have observed a sacred meal following the Last Supper tradition of Jesus and the practice in the early church. Many in the Free Church tradition do not call these *sacraments* because the word appears to imply that there is saving value in the rites themselves. Many, however, are quite comfortable with that word. For some believers, the term *ordinances* is less descriptive and seems too weak to denote these two most important occasions of worship.

The word *baptize* in the Greek meant to dip or plunge or immerse; few scholars would argue that point. The New Testament concept of baptism, however, means much more than being immersed in water.

In the Jewish faith, there were ceremonial rites related to cleansing or purification which probably provide an antecedent for understanding Christian baptism. The first New Testament appearance of baptism had to do with the baptism of John the Baptist. All of the Gospels refer to the baptism of John the Baptist. Mark, Matthew, and Luke quote John who contrasted his baptism in water with that of the one coming after him who would baptize people with the Holy Spirit, and in some cases with fire (Matt. 3:11; Mark 1:8; Luke 3:16). The Fourth Gospel does not use the same words but does feature the coming of the Spirit at the time of Jesus' baptism.

The rite of immersing in water (baptism) has been so variously interpreted and practiced that the "baptism of the Holy Spirit" has been largely neglected or misinterpreted as some kind of additional event. We noted that the new birth resulted from the agency of the Spirit and the work of the Word. The believer is born of the Spirit. This is the "baptism of the Spirit" about which the Gospel writers spoke.

The immersion in water, baptism, is a beautiful dramatic portrayal and confession of that spiritual experience. Baptism was practiced commonly in the early church (Acts 1:5; 2:41; 9:18; 10:44 *ff.;* and 16:15).

Paul interpreted its meaning as a confession of belief in Jesus' death, burial, and resurrection on our behalf (Rom. 6: 3-11). Baptism, however, is much more than a confession of belief in Christ's death, burial, and resurrection. It is our confession of faith that we, through baptism, have died with Christ, been buried with him, and have been raised already so that "we too might walk in newness of life" (Rom. 6:4).

Baptism, therefore, is an act of worship not only to the one being baptized but also for the whole church in which the rite is observed. We all confess our common faith in Christ's death, burial, and resurrection, the new spiritual birth of the person being baptized. All of us confess that we believe that our future death and burial will be followed by a resurrection to be with Christ.

As such, baptism is a dramatic proclamation of the gospel of Christ. It is, therefore, a message of reconciliation to both the lost and the reconciled.

Although many churches have observed baptism in a variety of ways and have baptized infants, many Christians believe that only those who have believed in their own decision (spiritual baptism) should be baptized and that the water rite should be by immersion of the believer.[32]

Paul interpreted the spiritual meaning of baptism as being clothed in Christ. He wrote the Galatians, "For as many of you as were baptized into Christ have put on Christ" (3:27). The context suggests the new covenant of faith versus the old covenant of law. Consequently, some have seen a parallel between circumcision, the seal of the old covenant, and baptism as the seal of the new covenant. The two rites appear together in Colossians (2:11-12). Some have taken this as a basis for justifying infant baptism by the argument that circumcision was an infant rite. The context, however, along with the Galatians passage, makes me think that in both instances the author was speaking of the spiritual significance of the two rites in relationship to their respective covenants. The meaning of baptism, therefore, is in its symbolic meaning with reference to the covenant of which it is the seal and symbol.

When a church convenes to baptize a new believer, it proclaims the gospel and confesses its faith in worship.

The Lord's Supper. The celebration of a sacred meal is a universal practice among Christian churches. The expression, that Jesus "when he had given thanks" (1 Cor. 11:24; Matt. 26:27; Mark 14:23), includes the Greek word *giving thanks (eucharisteo)*, which has led some churches to refer to the meal as the Eucharist. In 1 Corinthians, Paul wrote, "The cup of blessing which we bless, is it not a participation in the blood of Christ? The bread which we break, is it not a participation in the body of Christ?" (10:16). The word translated "participation" is the word *koinōnia*, which means "fellowship" or "communion," leading some groups to speak of the Lord's Supper as Communion.

In the Roman tradition, the meal has been called the Mass from the Latin word used at the end. Others use the simple title, the Lord's Supper, as found in 1 Corinthians (11:20). The common name sacrament has been used by many; it came from the Latin word *sacramentum* and may or may not suggest saving power within the supper itself. It is used by many groups whose views do not regard the supper as having saving efficacy in itself.

The Lord's Supper dates from Jesus' observance of the Last Supper on the night of his betrayal. The Synoptic Gospels record the Last Supper as having been held in the upper room in a house in Jerusalem (Matt. 26:26-30; Mark 14:22-26; Luke 22:14-20). Paul wrote to the church in Corinth the tradition which he had received (1 Cor. 11:23-26). The accounts vary in length and details, but there can be no doubt about the basic content of the meal.

The elements were bread and wine. Jesus gave thanks and shared the bread with those present, saying, "This is my body." Then, he took the cup of wine, blessed it, gave it to them, and said, "This is my blood of the covenant" (Mark 14:24).

The supper is a _remembrance_ of Christ; we look back to him when we observe it. He used the word _remembrance_ (_anamnēsis_) twice in Paul's account (1 Cor. 11:24-25). The Nestle Text of the Greek New Testament includes this statement in Luke (22:20), but obviously the translators of the Revised Standard Version followed the variant reading and omitted it. The references to the covenant are also references related to remembering.

The supper also is an _anticipation_ of the future coming of Christ and the kingdom. Jesus indicated at the Last Supper that the next time he ate and drank with the disciples it would be in connection with his coming and the kingdom of God (Luke 22:16-18; Mark 14:25). Paul included in his account the future hope expressed in the words, "For as often as you eat this bread and drink the cup, you proclaim the Lord's death until he comes" (1 Cor. 11:26).

The present meaning of the supper is in connection with the _communion_ with Christ and _fellowship_ in the Christian calling.

The supper is a _proclamation_ of the gospel. No service of worship in the church compares with the Lord's Supper in terms of its theological content unless it is baptism. In the supper, Christ has assembled the church as guests at God's table. Christ's body and blood speak of the costly salvation from sin which is ours through Christ. Eating together symbolizes the communion among the believers. We look back to the saving events, and we look forward to the coming of the Lord. We see rather clearly what God is like, how serious our sin is, how much God loves us, the costly redemption, the glorious reconciliation, and the joyful anticipation of God's final victory for and within us.

During much of its history, the Roman Church regarded the supper as a sacrifice to be reenacted with the bread and wine being changed into the body and blood of Christ. Martin Luther held to a real presence of Christ's body in the Eucharist and adamantly rejected Zwingli's attempt to maintain some kind of spiritual presence while he held to the supper as a "Memorial" with only a symbolic presence of Christ.

The supper, as a form of Christian worship, means more than a mere "memorial." Memorials are something we do or say on behalf of the dead and departed. The kind of *remembrance* indicated in the Lord's Supper includes our participation in some spiritual sense. The Lord's Supper is not to be understood in a magical sense; at the same time, Christians do know the presence of God and a renewal of their faith in its celebration.

The churches of the modern period have experienced considerable achievement in terms of breaking down some of the artificial barriers which have separated them. Participation in the Lord's Supper indicates the kind of communion suggested in the New Testament. Wolfhart Pannenberg, while writing about "The Lord's Supper-Sacrament of Unity," has probably been too optimistic in his appraisal of this ecumenical advance.[33] Churches, bound more by their historical traditions than by the teaching of the New Testament, still make the Lord's Supper the dividing line between them instead of the participation in the body and blood of Christ.[34]

Mission

The mission of the church was repeatedly stated or implied in the discussion of the nature of the church and its worship. The mission is not something separate from the nature of the church and its worship but is rather the expression of it.

Being the Church. The mission of the church is *to be* the church. The community lives as the people of God and the body of Christ under the power and guidance of the Spirit while it proclaims and hears God's Word. The church, through prayer, is in conversation with God. Through worship, including baptism and the Lord's Supper, the church proclaims its message and is nourished.

Being the church is a ministry not only to those within the church but also to those outside the community. The church, because of what it is, responds to human need and gives itself for others. Churches, with varying degrees of commitment, give themselves to helping the poor, healing the sick, caring for those people without power, the widows, orphans, prisoners, and the oppressed.

As God's people, the church should be alert and sensitive to the persons in the world and to those yet to be born. As God's people, the church should respond by being the advocate for justice, peace, and an environment in which God's children can live and achieve their destiny. The church, if true to its nature and mission, must give itself to clear thinking and action in the realm of ethics.

Ministry of Reconciliation. The entire belief in salvation was summarized in terms of reconciliation: (1) God "reconciled us to himself" through Christ, (2) "gave us the ministry of reconciliation," which is (3) "God was in Christ reconciling the world to himself," (4) "entrusting to us the message of reconciliation," and (5) "we are ambassadors for Christ" (2 Cor. 5:18-20).

The ministry of reconciliation begins when one individual is reconciled to God or to one other person. It extends to other individuals, families, and other human collectives. Those who follow Christ are committed to being peacemakers. They serve to reconcile persons to one another by love, understanding, and forgiveness.

A statement of Jesus recorded by Matthew is often called the Great Commission. It reads, "Go therefore and make disciples of all nations, baptizing them in the name of the Father and of the Son and of the Holy Spirit, teaching them to observe all that I have commanded you; and lo, I am with you always, to the close of the age" (28:19-20). A reaffirmation of that Commission appears in the beginning of Acts, "But you shall receive power when the Holy Spirit has come upon you; and you shall be my witnesses in Jerusalem and in all Judea and Samaria and to the end of the earth" (1:8).

Churches organize in different ways to take this ministry of reconciliation to the rest of the world. The key words are *making disciples, teaching,* and *witnesses.* It is obvious that proclaiming and teaching the Word are central. It is not always recognized, however, that this can be done only by the "witnesses," those who have themselves known this experience of reconciliation. As noted earlier, the Christians who fled Jerusalem during the persecution witnessed wherever they traveled. This illustrates that the "mission" of the church is "being" the church wherever it is.

Much could be said about missions and missionaries, and that is important. But it would be pointless unless the church, and those who are the church, know who they are and what they are about. If they are the church, then they have unlimited possibilities in a world like this to carry out their ministry of reconciliation.

Serving and Giving. Jesus, whose life and ministry are continuing in the life of his body, the church, stated his own purpose, "not to be served but to serve, and to give his life as a ransom for many" (Mark 10:45).

The ineffectiveness of many modern church groups may well be the result of having fallen, unknowingly, into the contemporary craze for being served and getting. The nature and mission of the church is to serve and give itself away. There is no need for a list of ways in which this can be done. The church which is willing to serve and give will never lack opportunity.

The Ministers of the Church

If indeed the church is a priesthood of all believers, then all of its members are ministers. Some groups take this quite literally, while others who take it seriously still find adequate justification for special ministers who have been called and affirmed for ministry. There is no adequate ground for such distinctions as "full-time" or "part-time" ministers. Nothing related to the Christian life or ministry is "part time." In most cases, people are distinguishing between ministers who receive salaries and those who do not. The New Testament presents a great variety in its references to the ministers in the church.

The Ministers in the New Testament. Jesus chose twelve disciples whom he taught during his earthly ministry. When the church began as a result of his life, death, and resurrection, these disciples naturally occupied a place of leadership in the Christian community.

The first order of Christian ministers was the *apostles.* These were the twelve who had been with Jesus since the day of his baptism and had witnessed his resurrection (Acts 1:21-22). After the death of Judas, the group chose Matthias as a replacement, but he was never mentioned again. Paul, who popularized the name "apostle" in his missionary journeys, was somehow acknowledged as one of the apostles by many. Paul's inclusion is an interesting fact for which no explanation was offered. He had not been with Jesus during his ministry, but his Damascus road experience may have qualified him as a witness of the resurrection.

The apostles were the primary witnesses. They enjoyed great respect because they had been with the Lord. Their authority was recognized in the early community. Strictly speaking, there could be no successors to the apostles.

Elders were ministers in the early church. Following the Jewish custom, Christians spoke of their leaders as elders in Acts (11:30; 14:23, etc.). By AD 49, when the conference in Jerusalem was held, elders and apostles appear to have been a council within the church having significant authority.

Bishops, or overseers, appear to be the same as elders. The Greek word *episkopos* appears to be more understandable in churches which did not have the Jewish background for understanding elders. The term appeared in Paul's speech to the leaders of the Ephesian church (Acts 20:28), although the Revised Standard Version translated it "guardians." When Paul wrote the letter to the Philippian church, he addressed the "bishops and deacons" as if they were the ministers of the church (1:1).

Bishops and *deacons* appear in 1 Timothy as if they were the two orders of ministers. Qualifications for bishops are given (1 Tim. 3:2-7). Qualifications for deacons follow with a mention of "women," which is not altogether clear (3:8-13). The references to "widows" (1 Tim. 5:3 *ff.*) suggest more than their enrollment for charity since qualifications and limitations are mentioned. Elders are also mentioned (1 Tim. 5:17).

Gifts for Ministry. Of greater significance than the titles just listed are the gifts for ministry as they were recognized and practiced in the early churches.

When a need arose in the early church for someone to care for the needs of the Hellenistic widows, the "Twelve" assembled the people. They designated seven qualified men who performed the ministry. They were not called deacons in Acts (6:1-6), but some see them as the first deacons.

The question of spiritual gifts prompted Paul to write about the church as the body of Christ in which "God has appointed in the church first apostles, second prophets, third teachers, then workers of miracles, then healers, helpers, administrators, speakers in various kinds of tongues" (1 Cor. 12:27-28). One would gather that God called these or gave them to the church, and the church recognized and accepted them. A similar list appears in Ephesians. "And his gifts were that some should be apostles, some prophets, some evangelists, some pastors and teachers, to equip the saints for the work of ministry, for building up the body of Christ" (Eph. 4:11-12).

The New Testament pattern contains variety. The emphasis is upon gift or calling to ministry.

Call and Affirmation. There is nothing in the New Testament quite like ordination in modern churches. Ordination has a long history and numerous implications. Confusion in our time has resulted from a mixture of cultural and legal matters into "setting apart" for ministry. Ordained persons have certain rights, authority, and privileges, even including exemptions from military service, tax benefits from the government, and so forth. There was nothing like this in the New Testament.

When the church in Antioch (Acts 13:2-3) commissioned Saul and Barnabas, the dedication may be the nearest event to ordination to be found in the New Testament. The Holy Spirit called Saul and Barnabas and led the church to affirm them. The affirmation included prayer and fasting. Then they "laid their hands on them," probably with prayers of dedication, and "sent them off."

Within Protestant Christianity, there has been a twofold calling to "the ministry." In writing about "Non-Episcopal Ministries," T. W. Manson noted that there is always a two-fold emphasis: (1) ministers are called by God; and (2) they are affirmed by the church which accepts Christ's gift in a formal recognition.[35] John Calvin spoke of a "secret" or "inner" call of which the minister was conscious, and the "outer" call which had to do with church order, the selection and affirmation by the church.[36] This view of ministry is discussed ably in the section "The Congregationalist Ideal" in *The Apostolic Ministry.*[37]

The ministry of the church shows great variety both in the New Testament and in subsequent history. The guidelines are: the nature of the church determines the shape of its ministry and ministers; the minister of the Word is called by God and affirmed by the church; no calling is complete until the church has recognized and affirmed the gift and call of the minister.

Church Order. Generally speaking, churches have understood three types of church government: episcopal, presbyterial, and congregational.

The Roman and Anglican churches in the West followed the idea of government by bishops. Within this general category, there is a wide range of authority. In the present day, bishops exercise less control over the churches than was the case in the Medieval period. There is more involvement by the laity in all churches of the episcopal type.

Presbyterial government is by council, the presbytery. This dates from the group of "elders" in the church in Jerusalem.

Congregational government is the type in which authority is lodged within the membership. Within this category, churches manifest considerable variety. Some state their order as "majority rule," or "democratic government." These are oversimplifications and not entirely correct. If it is the church, Christ is the head and rules in the church. The majority does not rule. Decisions are made by polling the congregation, but the theory back of the action is the view of the church. The idea of the church is that it is a body of regenerate members who prays, thinks, and then votes in keeping with what they understand to be the will of God.

Congregational-type churches often give great power to individuals whose authority is like that of Medieval bishops. They also delegate responsibilities to boards, councils, and committees. Presbyterial-type churches have ways of involving all of the members, as do episcopal-type churches.

Church order or government is an expression of the nature of the church as understood by its members.

Notes

1. Paul S. Minear, *Images of the Church in the New Testament* (Philadelphia: The Westminster Press, 1977), pp. 28-65.

2. IDB, 1, p. 616.

3. R. Newton Flew, *Jesus and His Church* (London: The Epworth Press, 1938), pp. 35-88.

4. For a discussion of these views, see J. Robert Nelson, "The Origin of the Church," *The Realm of Redemption* (London: The Epworth Press, 1951), pp. 1-36.

5. G. W. H. Lampe, *God as Spirit: The Bampton Lectures, 1976* (Oxford: Clarendon Press, 1977), p. 228.

6. Origen, *Contra Celsus*, 3, p. 55.

7. H. Jackson Forstman, *Christian Faith and the Church* (St. Louis: The Bethany Press, 1965), pp. 59-84.

8. Eduard Schweizer, *The Church as the Body of Christ* (London: SPCK, 1965), p. 76-77.

9. Dale Moody, *The Word of Truth* (Grand Rapids: William B. Eerdmans Publishing Company, 1981), p. 447.

10. Hans Küng, *The Church* (New York: Sheed and Ward, 1967), pp. 167-179.

11. Cyril Eastwood, *The Priesthood of All Believers* (London: The Epworth Press, 1960), p. 261.

12. Robert McAfee Brown, *The Spirit of Protestantism* (New York: Oxford University Press, 1961), p. 97; Arthur W. Mielke, *This Is Protestantism* (Westwood: F. H. Revell Company, 1961), p. 37; Wilhelm Pauck, *The Heritage of the Reformation*, rev. ed. (Glencoe: Free Press, 1950), p. 31.

13. Robert McAfee Brown, *The Spirit of Protestantism* (Oxford: Oxford University Press, 1961), p. 97.

14. T. W. Manson, *Ministry and Priesthood: Christ's and Ours* (Richmond: John Knox Press, 1958), p. 40-41.

15. Eastwood, p. 161.

16. J. Robert Nelson, *The Realm of Redemption* (London: The Epworth Press, 1951), p. 144.

17. See Eastwood, pp. xi; also, Manson, pp. 64 *ff.*

18. Martin Luther, "On the Papacy in Rome," *Luther's Works*, ed. Eric W. Gritsch, (Philadelphia: Fortress Press, 1970), Vol. 39, p. 86-87.

19. John Calvin, *Institutes of the Christian Religion*, "Library of Christian Classics" (Philadelphia: The Westminster Press, 1960), book 4, chapter 1, section 20.

20. Paul Tillich, *A History of Christian Thought*, ed. Carl E. Braaten (New York and Evanston: Harper & Row, 1968), p. 232-233.

21. William Klassen, *The Forgiving Community* (Philadelphia: The Westminster Press, 1956).

22. H. R. Mackintosh, *The Christian Experience of Forgiveness* (London: Nisbet and Company, Ltd., 1927), p. 271; on the theme of church and forgiveness see also Küng, p. 330-331.

23. Hendrikus Berkhof, *The Christian Faith: An Introduction to the Study of the Faith*, trans. Sierd Woudstra (Grand Rapids: William B. Eerdmans Publishing Company, 1979), p. 346-347. Berkhof has an interesting list of elements that are essential to the church's transmission of its life.

24. Luther cited by ed. Hugh Thomson Kerr, Jr., *A Compend of Luther's Theology* (Philadelphia: The Westminster Press, 1943), p. 126.

25. Ibid., pp. 126-130.

26. John Calvin, *The Institutes of the Christian Religion*, "Library of Christian Classics" book 4, chapter 1, section 9.

27. Emil Brunner, *The Christian Doctrine of the Church, Faith and the Consummation, Dogmatics III*, trans. David Cairns and T. H. L. Parker (Philadelphia: The Westminster Press, 1952), p. 117.

28. Küng, pp. 263-359.

29. John E. Burkhart, *Worship* (Philadelphia: The Westminster Press, 1982), p. 28-29.

30. See Franklin M. Segler, *Christian Worship: Its Theology and Practice* (Nashville: Broadman Press, 1967), pp. 92-108.

31. Gustaf Aulen, *The Faith of the Christian Church* (Philadelphia: The Muhlenberg Press, 1948), p. 401-402.

32. John Baillie, *Baptism and Conversion* (London: Oxford University Press, 1964). This small volume presents very brief summaries of "Baptism in the New Testament," "The Roman Teaching," "The Lutheran Teaching," "The Teaching of Calvin," "The Teaching of the Reformed Churches," and "The Teaching of the Baptist Churches."

33. Wolfhart Pannbenberg, *The Church*, trans. Keith Crim (Philadelphia: The Westminster Press, 1983), pp. 116 *ff*.

34. See Jean-Jacques von Allmen, *The Lord's Supper* (Richmond: John Knox Press, 1969); I. Howard Marshall, *Last Supper and Lord's Supper* (Grand Rapids: William B. Eerdmans Publishing Company, 1980); William Barclay, *The Lord's Supper* (Philadelphia: The Westminster Press, 1967).

35. T. W. Manson, *The Church's Ministry* (London: Hodder and Stoughton, 1948), p. 95 *ff*.

36. John Calvin, *Institutes of the Christian Religion*, 4, 3, 11.

37. Kenneth E. Kirk, ed., *The Apostolic Ministry: Essays on the History and the Doctrine of Episcopacy* (London: Hodder and Stoughton, 1946).

PART V
Belief in the New Creation

Then Jesus told his disciples, "If any man would come after me, let him deny himself and take up his cross and follow me. For whoever would save his life will lose it, and whoever loses his life for my sake will find it."

—Matthew 16:24-25

I have been crucified with Christ; it is no longer I who live, but Christ who lives in me; and the life I now live in the flesh I live by faith in the Son of God, who loved me and gave himself for me.

—Galatians 2:20

But we would not have you ignorant, brethren, concerning those who are asleep, that you may not grieve as others do who have no hope. For since we believe that Jesus died and rose again, even so, through Jesus, God will bring with him those who have fallen asleep. For this we declare to you by the word of the Lord, that we who are alive, who are left until the coming of the Lord, shall not precede those who have fallen asleep. For the Lord himself will descend from heaven with a cry of command, with the archangel's call, and with the sound of the trumpet of God. And the dead in Christ will rise first; then we who are alive, who are left, shall be caught up together with them in the clouds to meet the Lord in the air; and so we shall always be with the Lord. Therefore comfort one another with these words.

—1 Thessalonians 4:13-18

13

The Christian Life as New Creation

The seriousness of human sin resulted in separation from God and a degradation of human life to such a degree that any mention of "image of God" in humanity seems incredible, if not irreverent. The infinite love and power of God, however, not only made human restoration a possibility but also lead to the redemptive suffering which made it real for those who believe in Christ.

In the chapter on "Reconciliation," many of the terms indicating how the individual believer comes to know this salvation and what it means in human life were discussed. The discussion of "The Church" noted that the individual believer's salvation involves a relationship with the other believers, the people of God. Salvation, like sin, has a personal and individual dimension, but it also involves everyone else.

The present discussion of "The Christian Life as New Creation" may appear to be repetitious. The Christian life is not something added to reconciliation but is the expression of it. Participation in the Christian community is not optional for one who believes in God through Christ. Otherwise we would miss the personal meaning and practical changes in our lives when we believe in Christ.

Let us consider the Christian life in the following dimensions: (1) a new creation, (2) a new freedom in belonging, (3) discipleship, and (4) participants in the kingdom of God.

The Christian Life as a New Creation

There are rich terms in the New Testament and in Christian tradition for describing the change which faith in Christ makes. None is more meaningful in the theological sense than this term *new creation.* Consider the inspiration and motivation within the believer who learns the inner meaning of this New Testament image.

The apostle Paul wrote, "Therefore if any one is in Christ, he is a new creation; the old has passed away, behold, the new has come" (2 Cor. 5:17).

The Nonexistence of the Old

God's redeeming work is a radical remaking of each human being. The creature in sin remembers the bondage to sin which caused a divided feeling within the person. This feeling was expressed by Paul when he said, "For I do not do what I want, but I do the very thing I hate. For I do not do the good I want, but the evil I do not want is what I do" (Rom. 7:15,19).

The inward contradiction of knowing what is right and good but doing what is wrong and evil is the torment of human beings created in the image of God but living in alienation and self-centeredness. God through Christ has so transformed the believer that this contradiction is replaced by an inner integrity, peace.

In the concrete language of the Old Testament, God willed creation into existence. The account reads, "And God said, . . . and it was so." In a similar way, the Hebrews spoke of our sin as a "something," a barrier, separating us from God and an inward depravity out of which we do injustices to our fellow human beings. Now, God has willed our sins out of existence. The old sinful self died with Christ on the cross (Rom. 6:6; Gal. 2:20).

When God forgives sins, he forgets them. We place such a high premium upon remembering that we forget the virtue of forgetting. One of the Hebrew words meaning "to forgive" is the word meaning "to blot out." Jeremiah understood God's forgiveness as a willing sin out of existence, leaving neither trace nor memory, "I will forgive their iniquity, and I will remember their sin no more" (Jer. 31:34).[1] The psalmist spoke of God's forgiveness by saying, "as far as the east is from the west,/so far does he remove our trangressions from us" (Ps. 103:12).

The forgiveness of sins, from God's standpoint, means literally that they no longer exist—not even in memory and certainly not on a record. A common error, evidently related to a view of human responsibility, is that God keeps a list of all human sins and will open the books at a final judgment. That is a denial of the meaning of forgiveness and regeneration. God wipes out the past; he gives us a new beginning. The old has passed away. What is forgiven will not appear on God's books at the final judgment.

The Reality of the New Creation

The Christian life is a new creation. Since it is a specific work of God, it gives human life a new outlook and introduces eternity into the present.

A Creation of God. The Christian life is not an achievement of human beings. It is a creation of God. God has done something new. The new "is from God, who through Christ reconciled us to himself" (2 Cor. 5:18). Grace is God's free gift to his creatures. His work of recreating human beings into his image is motivated by his love, not human worth or potential. His new creation of us is like the first creation. He, of his own will, has chosen to create. No reason is needed or possible. Consequently, the Christian life which owes its origin and continuation to a gracious work of God can be lived in meaning, joy, and thanksgiving.

A New Outlook. The Christian life is quite distinct because it has a new direction, a new focus, a new center, a new outlook. In the original creation, men and women lived for God. He was the center of reality. In sin, persons became self-centered; they lived for themselves. Now, the person in Christ lives a life directed toward God. When one loves God with all of the self, it is possible to love one's fellow human beings. Genuine human existence is both vertical toward God and horizontal toward other persons. The new life is a radical new creation. It was so distinctive that quite early it was spoken of as "The Way" (Acts 22:4; 24:14,22).

A New Age. One of the earliest Christian realizations was that in Christ the new age had dawned. This new age—in contrast to the old age of Adam, sin, and death—is the age of Christ, faith, and life. Christ has come to deliver us "from the present evil age" (Gal. 1:4) and introduce us to the age to come. In the Christian life, one already lives in the eternal. John stated this present tense idea of the eternal, "This is eternal life, that they know thee the only true God, and Jesus Christ whom thou has sent" (John 17:3).

The Christian life takes place in two worlds. The Christian is a citizen of this world and the world to come. In a sense, the world to come is already here. A strong word of warning, however, is in order at the point of the attitude of "other-worldliness." Some Christians have neglected their responsibilities in this world and have spoken of salvation as being saved out of this world for the next one.[2] Christian hope is the companion of faith and love, and as such, is restrained from an overemphasis on the next world.

A New Freedom in Belonging

Human beings were created in the image of God. Freedom, therefore, is a basic human characteristic. Human existence in unbelief became a bondage to sin. The redeeming work of Christ set us free from the tyranny of sin so that we can be the creatures we were created to be. Freedom, in the biblical sense, is liberation from false masters. We are free, as new creatures, to be the servants of God—our destiny in creation. In biblical faith, the human being is always a creature of God, living dependently upon God.

We know from theology, psychology, sociology, history, and philosophy that human beings are not genuinely human apart from their relationships with others. In biblical faith, these relationships are the structure of human existence. The Christian life, as restored in the image of God, is the new experience of freedom in the appropriate relationships.

Belonging to God

Belonging is a strong yet tender word of relationship. What human being would want to be severed from ties of belonging? As creatures, and new creatures, we belong to God. This is the basic outlook of the life of faith. We have been called "to belong to Jesus Christ" (Rom. 1:6). Paul said, "You are not your own; you were bought with a price" (1 Cor. 6: 19-20). We are recognized as "those who belong to Christ Jesus" (Gal. 5:24). It is natural to speak of "the God to whom I belong and whom I worship" (Acts 27:23).

This belonging to God is the relationship of creature to Creator. It gives meaning, direction, and security to life. It also equips a person with ready assistance in times of being tempted to do the base, mean, or the ignoble. In those times one remembers that belonging to God has a bearing on one's life and actions. God expects more of us.

Belonging to Others

The present craze for a distorted kind of personal freedom makes it difficult to appreciate what it means to belong to others. *Belonging* names an intimate relationship with others. It can be said we belong to our families, to our churches, to other persons to whom we give ourselves in a human relationship. The early Christians were described as "belonging to the Way" (Acts 9:2).

The richness of human life is found in the human relationships we share. The more we give ourselves to others the more we live. This can be illustrated among those who do not have faith. The reverse can also be illustrated in that those who try to get and keep for themselves lose themselves (Matt. 16:24).

The Christian life is one of belonging, living in relationships with others, which calls for giving, helping, and caring.

Serving and Giving

Those who follow Jesus Christ have learned the secret that life is in serving and giving. The whole theme of redeeming and being redeemed is captured in these words.

Jesus stated his own life purpose as "serving" and "giving" (Mark. 10:45). He indicated the need for serving only one master (Matt. 6:24). He told the disciples that among their group "whoever would be great among you must be your servant . . . slave" (Matt. 20:26-27). The great Christological passage of Philippians begins with an ethical admonition, "Have this mind among yourselves, which you have in Christ Jesus, who, though he was in the form of God, . . . emptied himself, taking the form of a servant" (2:5-11).

The Christian life includes a mind-set of serving and giving. Paul identified himself and Timothy as "servants of Christ Jesus" (Phil. 1:1) and elsewhere indicated that we should all be regarded as "servants of Christ" (1 Cor. 4:1). Peter equated "free men" with "servants of God" in his statement, "Live as free men, yet without using your freedom as a pretext for evil; but live as servants of God" (1 Pet. 2:16).

The Christian life is radically different from the life of the person outside of faith. It sounds strange to speak of giving and serving in a world and country of grabbing and greed.

A New Commandment

The Christian life is a new creation because of a new kind of love which comes into human life. All other kinds of love have a motivation or value, potential or expected return. Christ's love is unmotivated; he loves us simply because it is his nature to love. He introduced *agapē* to us. His new commandment is "that you love one another; even as I have loved you, that you also love one another" (John 13:34).

This new commandment goes beyond the prior rule, "You shall love your neighbor as yourself" (Mark 12:31). That requirement was just. It provided equal treatment for others as for the self. Jesus, however, made it clear that the neighbor was not the person who necessarily lives next door, not the person of our choosing. The parable of the good Samaritan stresses that the neighbor is chosen for us as we cross paths on the journey of life. We don't get to choose our neighbor; rather, we must respond to any person who needs us (Luke 10:29-37). Berkhof says that the "neighbor" may be one who encounters me, confronts me, irritates me, disturbs me, and, in the process, reminds me that my relationship to God includes other persons.[3]

The new commandment for Christians is to love others "as Christ has loved us." This goes more than half way. This requires loving the unlovely, the undeserving. It speaks of caring for others because of who we are rather than because of who they are. This kind of love is self-giving, sacrificing care for other persons—not even of our choosing. To live this way in a world like this is to be a new creation.

Discipleship

A disciple is a learner or student who accepts and follows a doctrine or teacher. The New Testament word for those who followed Jesus Christ is *disciples.* The term indicates that one has understood well enough to commit oneself to following the teacher and learning more fully. The Christian life is one of discipleship—following Jesus Christ.

Following Christ

Jesus called disciples to follow him, taught them what was involved, warned them of the cost of discipleship, and led the way. Disciples must be aware that they face the same dangers as did their teacher, must be prepared to forsake home, family, and possessions (Luke 14:26,33), and must take up their crosses and bear them (Luke 14:27).

Discipleship involves commitment to Christ and his way of life in this world. In short, it involves Christlikeness. That is what is meant by the statement to "be conformed to the image of his Son" (Rom. 8:29).

Discipleship, therefore, is the meaning of Christian life as a new creation. The disciple follows Christ, believes in Christ, and lives according to the purpose of Christ.

Life Under Judgment

There are two common misunderstandings about the judgment of God: one is that judgment is always negative or condemning; the other is that judgment is something in the future. Neither is correct. God's judgment on us may either vindicate or condemn. As such, it may be negative. It may also be an affirmation.

The Christian life is a life lived daily under the judgment of God. Entrance to the Christian life is by repentance. In repentance, one acknowledges guilt and accepts forgiveness. Repentance, like faith, is the constant companion of the one who walks the Christian way. Through prayer, reflection, study, worship, and conversation with others, the disciple learns of his or her errors or sins, repents to God, and goes on. The disciple opens all of life to God's judgment now and seeks to know and do the will of God.

This kind of judgment is not destructive; nor is it resented. It is a part of discipleship, part of learning and following. This also makes the human being a new creation.

A Company of Disciples

The decision to become a disciple may appear to be personal and lonely, but it involves an intimate fellowship with other disciples. One cannot discuss reconciliation with God apart from reconciliation with other persons. From its beginning, the church has been a fellowship of saints, a *communio sanctorum*.

314

Persons following Jesus Christ walk in the company of others who also believe in him.

The Christian grows in grace and learns the Christian graces only in the community of believers. God continues his redeeming work in our lives as we, along with others, serve him and our fellow human beings. These acts of service are not, however, exercises in spiritual growth. They are the genuinely human and earthly tasks in which persons engage because they are needed. The growth is the by-product of the service which is done for its own sake.

Those who have been disciples for many years pay tribute to those companions who have shared the toil and the burdens for their contributions to the pilgrimage.

"Life According to the Spirit"

Human beings can be accurately seen in two groups: (1) those who live "according to the flesh" and (2) those who "live according to the Spirit" (Rom. 8:5).

The sharp contrast in this passage is intended to focus on the direction and commitment of one's life. Of course, all human life is lived in a fleshly body, and even the most degraded person is not totally devoid of spirit. The difference is in the loyalty or commitment or the aim and purpose of one's life.

The persons who live "according to the Spirit set their minds on the things of the Spirit" (Rom. 8:5). They earn their livings in the marketplace. They are susceptible to diseases and accidents. They struggle with economic, political, and other human issues. The difference, however, is that the direction of their lives is set by a commitment to God who, as Spirit, is with them.

Those who live "according to the Spirit" are new creatures in Christ.[4] They are radically different from those who set their minds "on the flesh." These people may be upright and moral, but their lives are focused on themselves or some goal, even a good one, of their own choosing. They live their lives for something which lacks ultimate meaning.

Struggle, Suffering, and Sanctification

Usually, theologians discuss justification (which makes us right with God) and then discuss sanctification (which is the continuing process of God's saving grace applied to human lives as we grow toward full salvation). The natural sequence of justification and sanctification may tend to obscure the fact that the new creation of God does not move automatically from one stage to another. The struggle with sin remains a kind of contradiction in the lives of all Christians.

Paul spoke of this inward contradiction so well in Romans (ch. 7). Some interpreters take the chapter to be autobiographical, describing Paul's own situation before his faith in Christ. Others, however, recognize the continuing agony even after faith.

The person of faith in the Christian life is still a sinner and still struggles with self-centeredness, which is the meaning of Jesus' statement "deny [yourself]" (Matt. 16:24). The disciples of Jesus disappointed us all in their question about who would be the greatest in Christ's kingdom; but among the saintly, the desire for power and recognition dies slowly, or rather thrives. Each Christian scarcely dethrones one idol until another even more attractive and deceptive appears.

The author of Hebrews acknowledged the struggle when he wrote, "In your struggle against sin you have not yet resisted to the point of shedding your blood" (12:4). Timothy was reminded that in his ministry he should "wage the good warfare" (1 Tim. 1:18). The entire Apocalypse of John features the conflict and promises ultimate victory for those who are faithful to Jesus Christ, who through suffering and death has won the victory over evil.

Suffering is a theme in Christian literature. Christ's redemptive work was through his suffering on our behalf. The early Christians considered themselves honored if they were called upon to suffer for Christ (Acts 5:41). Somehow, faithfulness to Christ results in suffering in this world (Rom. 8:17). The closer one's identification with Christ, the greater is the likelihood that one will be called upon to suffer for him (Phil. 1:29).

Most suffering is the result of human wrongdoing against others. As such, it has no justification and produces nothing but injury and destruction. The person who wants to suffer may be ill. Some early Christians sought martyrdom thinking that would provide them a special honor with God. Suicide is not discipleship.

Those, however, who commit themselves deeply and seriously to Christ are very likely to be subjected to suffering not of their own choosing. Christ stood for truth against false religion; he stood for justice and against oppression; he stood for the dispossessed in the presence of those with power. He suffered for it.

When suffering comes to us as a result of our clear stand on the right side of legitimate issues, it may be redemptive suffering. Paul, who had suffered in a good cause, could write, "we rejoice in our sufferings, knowing that suffering produces endurance, and endurance produces character, and character hope" (Rom. 5:3-4.). For Paul, and in the context in which he wrote, this speaks a profound truth. Many, however, miss it. Paul was a committed apostle suffering as a result of his work for Christ, and he was a veteran with many scars. Some suffer and are defeated; their lot is resentment and bitterness. Suffering of itself is only the occasion. God's grace, mentioned in the previous sentence by Paul, sustains persons through suffering, thereby producing endurance and character.

Sanctification is God's work of changing persons into their true selves. It begins in the new birth of God's saving grace. It continues through all the encounters of the human life. Sanctification means "holy" or "dedicated." It may be regarded as the continuation, or completion, of justification. Most, however, do not regard sanctification as completed in this life.

Common misunderstandings of sanctification include ideas such as sinless perfection and unusual spiritual blessings. Sanctification is progressive but not necessarily inevitable.

While it is a work of God within us, it is possible only if we willingly cooperate. It is more nearly correct to say that we don't work to achieve sanctification but that we have committed ourselves to serving the Lord. In the struggle, suffering, rejoicing, working, praying, and living, we discover that he has reclaimed more of our lives than we had anticipated.

Living by Faith, Hope, and Love

Discipleship consists of living by faith, hope, and love. The classic statement of the central virtues of the Christian life is in 1 Corinthians 13, but they appear in several other New Testament texts also (1 Thess. 1:3; 5:8; Gal. 5:5-6; Col. 1:4-5; Rom. 5:1-5; and Heb. 10:22-24). These are very different from the four central virtues of Greek thought: wisdom, temperance, justice, and courage.

Faith is the term which names a present trust in and commitment to God through Christ. It is a present fact but has one element of remembrance in it—an element which points back to those occasions in the past when God has been faithful. This backward look or historical remembrance introduces an element of gratitude into commitment.

Hope is, in a way, faith pointed toward the future. It, too, is grounded in God's previous acts; but it looks toward tomorrow with joyful anticipation of those great things God has in store for his creatures. Hope is trustful and patient; it waits. Hope is not gullibility or blind optimism; rather, hope is a realistic, trustful, confident outlook on the future because of what God has done. The ultimate Christian hope is grounded in the resurrection of Jesus Christ from the dead.

Love is the Christian attitude toward others, a caring that is based on the character of the one who loves, rather than on the character of the beloved. It is a Christlike concern for others with no concern for reward, repayment, or value. It is not often found in pure form among us, but we have a perfect example: "God shows his love for us in that while we were yet sinners Christ died for us" (Rom. 5:8).

In every conscious moment of human existence, there is the past, present, and future. Our motivations and decisions in the present are influenced by our heritage and memory of the past. Likewise, we decide and act in anticipation of the future. Insofar as we know, no other creatures live in this threefold dimension of tense (past, present, and future). The Christian virtues of faith, hope, and love relate us not only to past, present, and future but also to God, others, and self.

Assurance

The Christian life is a matter of faith. Persons often ask if they can know that they are really saved. The Reformers spoke of the certainty of grace and the certainty of salvation. The term "assurance" or "full conviction" does appear as "fully convinced" about God (Rom. 4:21). The term "full conviction" (1 Thess. 1:5) has to do with the gospel. There is a prayer for this assurance (Col. 2:2) and the hope expressed in Hebrews that "each one of you . . . show the same earnestness in realizing the full assurance of hope until the end" (6:11). A similar hope is expressed in a later passage (10:22).

There are primarily two reasons for Christians to feel confident about their relationship to God: the witness of the Holy Spirit and their own love for others.

In Romans, we read, "When we cry, 'Abba! Father!' it is the Spirit himself bearing witness with our spirit that we are children of God" (Rom. 8:16). In the essay on love, John reasoned that we can have assurance of our salvation if we love others. "We know that we have passed out of death into life, because we love the brethren" (1 John 3:14).

It should not be difficult for those who have rested their eternal hope on Jesus Christ to trust him without guarantees or arguments. We have the two witnesses stated earlier. If these do not make the doubts go away, one might look into one's own worship or service. Often, assurance comes only by doing the daily tasks as one has done them before, believing that God will give enough confidence to go on.

Security or Perseverance

The doctrine of the "security of the believer," or the "perseverance of the saints," indicates that one who has been truly saved will not completely fall away. These doctrines may be developed in various ways. If one adopts a premise and rationalizes about it, then one can reach a very valid conclusion—whether it is true or not. The doctrine is opposed by those who advocate apostasy which is the doctrine that one can be lost again. For a presentation on the subject of apostasy see Dale Moody's volume *The Word of Truth*.[5]

Paul, who advocated the theology that our salvation is a work of God's grace realized through faith in Christ, advocated a strong position of security. Since our salvation depends on God, Paul concluded, "For I am sure that neither death, . . . nor anything else in all creation, will be able to separate us from the love of God in Christ Jesus our Lord" (Rom. 8:38-39).

One could argue that, since our faith is involved, we could change our minds to unbelief and thereby forfeit God's grace. I find this rather unconvincing in the light of what reconciliation is: restoration through repentance and faith, a new creation which is a work of God.

If salvation is on the basis of God's grace, and faith is trusting God who then makes us new creatures, one is hardly in the context in which it makes sense to say, "I believed but I don't anymore," or "I have changed my mind." The statement "for I know whom I have believed, and I am sure that he is able to guard until that Day what has been entrusted to me" (2 Tim. 1:12) does not strike me as being unreasonable or erroneous.

The Kingdom of God

The kingdom of God, or the kingdom of heaven which is the same, is usually discussed in the concluding chapter of Christian theology under the heading of eschatology, the study of last things. This is because *the kingdom* is a term related to the end of time. There is just cause, however, for discussing the kingdom in connection with the present "New Creation" or "The Christian Life" because the kingdom is also a present reality.

The kingdom of God designates the kingly rule or sovereignty of God rather than a realm. The kingdom of God is the reign of God. Biblical faith speaks of this reign as an eternal fact (God is sovereign), as a present reality on earth among those who serve God, and a future reality to come with the consummation of the age.

Kingdom as Present Reign

Most of the references to the kingdom point to the future, but some designate a present reality or a present reality that will be made complete in the future. After the casting out of the demons, Jesus said "But if it is by the finger of God that I cast out demons, then the kingdom of God has come upon you" (Luke 11:20). This almost certainly means that the kingdom has arrived in some sense. There is no doubt but that Jesus spoke of the present reality of the kingdom while speaking about John the Baptist, "yet he who is least in the kingdom of heaven is greater than he" (Matt. 11:11).

One of the clearest statements about the kingdom was made by Jesus to the Pharisees. They had asked "when the kingdom of God was coming." Jesus answered, "The kingdom of God is not coming with signs to be observed; nor will they say, 'Lo, here it is!' or 'There!' for behold, the kingdom of God is in the midst of you" (Luke 17:20-21).

Many of the parables dealt with the kingdom. Especially those about growth, while pointing toward a future, speak of a reality already present.

To understand the Christian as a "new creation," it is important to understand the present reign of God in the lives of those who have been freed from the bondage to sin. God's ultimate sovereignty over creation has never been in question; that he will ultimately bring all creation under judgment and sovereignty is an expectation related to the end of the age that is

common both to Hebrew and Christian; but, the present reality of God's reign is a vital part of the beginning of the new creation.

Jesus Christ was and is called Lord. Those who acknowledge him as Lord confess that his reign has begun. The kingdom of God must not be equated with some earthly historical kingdom, neither can it be relegated to some future possibility. His lordship has been fulfilled and his final reign is an object of anticipation.[6]

The kingdom of God and participation in it are important to those who are living the Christian life. When they pray, "Our Father who art in heaven,/Hallowed be thy name./Thy kingdom come,/Thy will be done,/On earth as it is in heaven" (Matt. 6:9-10), they are not looking to the distant future. They are praying that the reign of God will be acknowledged by men and women now on earth. To John the Baptist, the kingdom may have been limited to the future; but to Jesus, it was already present.

Through faith in Christ, a new creation has begun. He has established his reign in the lives of those who believe. He is their King because they have learned the beauty of obedience, one of the Christian virtues close to faith, hope, and love.

Providence and the Will of God

God's providence means his sustaining and guiding relationship to creation. It designates that an action of God may not be recognized by persons at the time. Jeremiah, for instance, noted that after his call he could look back and see that God had a hand in his life from his birth. Paul made the same confession after his call experience.

The providence of God then is his reign over the lives of persons and events in ways known only to him at the time. Some of them may be recognized later; probably, most of them are never so recognized.

The phrase "will of God" describes the purpose of God in human life and history. In Jesus' prayer, the kingdom and the

will of God are related. "Thy kingdom come,/Thy will be done,/On earth as it is in heaven" (Matt. 6:10). These two are almost the same. The prayer for the kingdom to come is the prayer that God's reign will be recognized and accepted. The prayer for God's will to be done points to the purpose of God for human lives.

The Christian life can well be described as knowing and doing the will of God.[7] The apostle Paul wrote, "Do not be conformed to this world but be transformed by the renewal of your mind, that you may prove what is the will of God, what is good and acceptable and perfect" (Rom. 12:2). In Ephesians, the teaching is that we may be "servants of Christ, doing the will of God from the heart" (Eph. 6:6).

Notes

1. Morris Ashcraft, *The Forgiveness of Sins* (Nashville: Broadman Press, 1972), p. 23.
2. Amos N. Wilder, *Otherworldliness and the New Testament* (New York: Harper & Brothers, 1954).
3. Hendrikus Berkhof, *Christian Faith: An Introduction to the Study of the Faith,* trans. Sierd Woudstra (Grand Rapids: William B. Eerdmans Publishing Company, 1979), p. 461.
4. Rudolf Bultmann, *Theology of the New Testament,* trans. Kendrick Grobel (New York: Charles Scribner's Sons, 1955), 2 pp. 330 *ff.*
5. Dale Moody, *The Word of Truth* (Grand Rapids: William B. Eerdmans, 1981), pp. 348-365.
6. Jürgen Moltmann, *The Church in the Power of the Spirit* (New York: Harper & Row, Publishers, 1975), pp. 189 *ff.*
7. Morris Ashcraft, *The Will of God* (Nashville: Broadman Press, 1980), pp. 132 *ff.*

14

Hope and Life Everlasting

Of all the terms which must appear in a study of eschatology (last things) *hope* and *everlasting life* appear to be the most expressive, "Christian," and comprehensive.

Hope is more than a central Christian virtue, along with faith and love. Hope is an essential element in the Christian understanding of reality and life. Hope is the forward-looking companion of faith. Hope is grounded in faith in God. Since it is fixed on God, it has a joyful confidence about the future, a trust in God's providence, and a willingness to wait even if suffering is involved.

Hope is more than an attitude; it is a faith-conviction that embraces, or almost embraces, the whole Christian commitment. It can be used in place of the word *faith* when referring to the whole: "Always be prepared to make a defense to any one who calls you to account for the hope that is in you, yet do it with gentleness and reverence" (1 Pet. 3:15). When the author of Hebrews wrote, "Now faith is the assurance of things hoped for, the conviction of things not seen" (11:1), he almost said, "Now faith is hope."

Hope is the correct word to use to speak of the Christian doctrine of eschatology for several reasons: (1) it is a personal word; (2) it is an acknowledgment of creatureliness in which the creature depends on and waits for God; (3) it is consistent with the other Christian beliefs about God, his goodness, and providence for his creatures; (4) it acknowledges that the future is in the hands of God, and (5) it confesses that God has

323

given us life with purpose and meaning and has more in store for his creatures.

The words "Life Everlasting" have been chosen for part of the chapter title because together they express that toward which hope looks. Everlasting life is neither a refusal to die nor a wish for endless time. What could be more boring than more and more and more time? And what worse despair than to live with no prospect for "an end"?

The belief in everlasting life is based upon two convictions: this life is the greatest gift God has given us and must have permanent meaning, and eternity must be different from time in quality as well as quantity.

Both hope and everlasting life are distinctively Christian beliefs. They are based on faith in God who raised Jesus Christ from the dead. Christians believe in hope and life everlasting because they believe God was in Christ and that in raising Christ from the dead, God established a foundation for the hope that we, too, will be raised from the dead (1 Cor. 15:20 ff.). Hope includes much more than resurrection, but this is a crucial part.

Eschatology is the doctrine of last things. The word is another combination of the Greek words logios, which means generally a study or knowledge of, and eschatos, which means last things. The broad term eschatology would, therefore, include those subjects belonging to a study of the end for individuals, the world, and history. The term will be limited in this study to the Christian beliefs related to the ultimate destiny of the individual, humanity, and the rest of creation.

Eschatology is not an optional doctrine. Occasionally, one will be heard to say, "I have no interest in another world. One world at a time, please."

Eschatology is the logical companion of creation. If one thinks of creation as an act of God, and it would not be creation otherwise, then one has no choice but to raise the question of the purpose or goal of creation—and that is eschatology. If this were not the case, there are only two possibilities: the world and life in it are not the creation of God, or God created without purpose, or abandoned his purpose. Both alternatives deny God. Our study has acknowledged a beginning point in the revelation of God in Jesus Christ. Creation as beginning and eschatology as consummation are logically and theologically necessary.

There are two other preliminary questions that need to be addressed briefly. One has to do with eschatological ideas in other religions or systems of thought. The other has to do with the question of individual eschatology, cosmic eschatology, or both.

Any living religion with a belief in God or gods has, or will develop, some kind of eschatology. There is a contradiction between what is and what ought to be. Religion thinks about reality and looks for something better. If the "dream" is so designated and considered an illusion, then, of course, one has denied God. If faith in God is adequate, the belief will include present struggle and suffering and anticipate a "future eschatology." In this case, the belief in God will determine what the hope will be.[1]

The Hebrew faith, although it did not develop a view of the resurrection from the dead until quite late, included a strong eschatological content. Any Old Testament theology will discuss this eschatological hope, the Day of the Lord, judgment, vindication, and the meaning of history. The message of the prophets which always spoke of God's role in history led to the belief that something was soon going to happen and required such eschatological thought.[2]

Other religions have eschatological ideas about life after death or the end. Buddhism, for instance, envisions release from the continuous reincarnations in a kind of Nirvana, but this escape is nothing like eternal life. Other religions feature teachings which are eschatological, in a sense, but are not comparable to eschatological thought in Hebrew and Christian faith.[3]

Eschatological hope is original to the Hebrew and Christian

faiths because of their linear view of history. The cyclical view of history, characteristic of Greek and Oriental thought, does not lend itself so readily to eschatological hope.

The question of individual eschatology is interwoven with the matter of cosmic eschatology. This is particularly difficult in biblical faith. During the early part of the Old Testament, the individual was not the center of life; the community was. In that setting, eschatological thought tended to focus on the nation or the whole covenant people. After Jeremiah and Ezekiel, who stressed individual responsibility and judgment, there was a considerable increase in the eschatological thought related to the individual.

In the New Testament teachings, individual and community eschatology are intertwined. In spite of some confusion, this is necessary. We noted that reconciliation, or salvation, is never merely an individual experience but rather is always one that involves the whole community. In a similar way, eschatological hope includes both individual and community fulfillment. Sometimes they can be discussed separately, but they are always interrelated.

Christian eschatology can be approached in many ways.[4] One could list and then categorize all eschatological statements in the Bible. This discussion will look at the biblical teachings in the light of the norm of Jesus Christ and attempt to deal with the questions which have arisen in the life of the church trying to understand the hope.

We shall look at the following subjects: hope, death, after death, Parousia, resurrection, judgment, kingdom of God, and life everlasting.

Christian Hope

In facing the future, one experiences both anxiety and hope. Without hope, anxiety would deteriorate into despair. In purely secular life, hope is a necessity in the human consciousness. One must have something worthwhile to look forward to.

Hope is the positive attitude toward the future, whereas anxiety is the negative.[5]

Christian hope is that joyful anticipation of, or patient waiting for, the future on the ground of faith in God. By faith in God, who has been faithful in the past, the Christian faces the future with confidence.

Hope that is fixed on God has three elements: it is an expectation in the future, it is trust, and it results in patient waiting.[6] Christian hope embraces not only the entire future but also is an important fact in the present. With reference to the future, hope believes in the resurrection from the dead, the ultimate victory over sin, the coming of Christ, the full realization of God's kingdom, and life everlasting.

With reference to the present life, hope is an attitude based on beliefs related to faith in God. For instance, the joyful expectation is based on faith in God's faithfulness. The waiting is a sign of accepted creatureliness, dependence on God. The joyful aspect is related to the nature of God as good, and a creation which is not only destined to an ultimate purpose, but is also good now.

The term *hope* is so important in Christian thought that it not only includes all of the elements of Christian eschatology[7] but also is acceptable as a complete term for the entire Christian outlook on life. To make a defense for one's hope (1 Pet. 3:15) is the same as making a defense for one's faith.

Hope should not be confused with optimism, the idea of progress or otherworldliness. *Optimism* is a secular term which slants one's interpretation in the most favorable light. It assumes that this is the best of possible worlds or that reality is essentially good or that the good outweighs the evil. It is a tendency to anticipate the best possible outcome. The Christian understanding of evil imposes a realistic awareness that the world as we know it is beset by evil. While pessimism is also forbidden, a casual optimism is unwarranted.

The idea of progress which prevailed in the early twentieth century in the West was really the idea of inevitable progress.

Many thinking people assumed, by analogy with Darwin's theory of evolution, that the human race was getting better and better. The idea was the offspring of the Enlightenment, nourished by German idealism and the natural sciences. The devastating wars and incredible atrocities of the last fifty years have destroyed any semblance of this optimism or idea of progress.

Otherworldliness is an exaggerated longing for the next world. It results in the neglect of this world and this life. Occasionally, we read of some small sect whose members so long for the "Second Coming" that they have worked out the date and have sold their property to await the blessed event. The Christian cares for this world and human life in it. Few people really want to die. Life is a gift from God; and despite the excesses of a few would-be-martyrs, is to be enjoyed as long as it can last. It is the preparation for eternity, or rather, the first stage of eternity.

Death

In Christian belief, death has several shades of meaning. It sometimes means only the normal end of life as certified by the coroner. In the Old Testament period, after a long life of useful years one went to be with his or her "fathers in peace . . . buried in a good old age" (Gen. 15:15).

Sometimes, however, death is seen as the opposite of life in such a way that one might be regarded as dead even though still biologically alive. Persons who have not come to faith in Christ do not have "life" in the fullest sense and, therefore, are described as "dead through the trespasses and sins" (Eph. 2:1).

There is a positive way of looking at death in terms of relationship to sin and Christ. Paul, contrasting spiritual life with death, said that believers are "dead" to sin or "crucified" with Christ so that they might be alive spiritually (Rom. 6:1-11).

Death is also an enemy and destroyer. Biblical faith associates sin with death. The conversation in Eden covered this subject; the final word appears in "the wages of sin is death"

(Rom. 6:23). In Jesus Christ's triumph through the cross and resurrection, "the last enemy to be destroyed is death" (1 Cor. 15:26). In his vision on Patmos, the seer reported that the exalted Lord identified himself by saying, "I am the first and the last, and the living one; I died, and behold I am alive for evermore, and I have the keys of Death and Hades" (Rev. 1:17-18).

The destructive power of death appears in its most awful expression as "second death" (Rev. 20:6,14; 21:8). These three verses depict a place of ultimate and eternal destruction that will never end. Death is a continuing reality according to the traditional teachings of the church. This kind of death is in contrast with life, and neither term has to do with the records in the hospital, the coroner's office, or the bureau of vital statistics.

For those who believe in Christ, death may be compared to sleep (1 Thess. 4:13). Many Christian grave markers employ the word *asleep,* and survivors derive some comfort from the hope which is expressed in the word. Death, however, is not sleep. It stalks the human being from conception until it wins. Death has time to wait; persons don't.

Death does not always appear so deadly to young persons who are so filled with life. Those who deal in death must steel themselves with reference to the death of others. Those of us who lived through World War II, or have read about the scores of wars since, have often read reports issued from a commanding general's headquarters, "Our casualties were light." They were not light for some. Ask the mothers, fathers, brothers, sisters, sons, daughters, and friends of those few to whom the telegrams were sent. The telegrams did not mention light casualties.

A child of eighteen months had died. A minister made a professional visit and was later quoted as having said to another person, "It was only a baby." There never was "only a baby." That baby was my son.

There was also a man of eighty-four. He had known the love

of a good woman and several children, enjoyed the respect of the community, had good health most of his years and died at a good old age. He left a void, a black hole of inner space. <u>When a human being dies there is no replacement.</u>

The Christian faces death differently from those "who have no hope" (1 Thess. 4:13) because of his hope that beyond death will be a resurrection.

Death, however, is almost never a welcome guest. Life is the gift of God. With full justification, we hold on to it and cherish it.

What Happens After Death?

Since we are not able to think without time-bound limitations, we project our time line beyond death. We know that individual death takes place at a certain date. We expect the coming of Christ at the end of the age at which time the resurrection of the dead, final judgment, and so forth will take place. The question has to do with this time in between individual death and the final consummation.

There is no clear answer to the question. The general words *intermediate state* have been used to designate that time and/or place in which those who die wait for the consummation. It is possible that our misunderstanding is due to this projection of time into eternity and that no such place is necessary. In that case, those who die would enter eternity at the point of death.

The persistent belief that Christ will return to conclude history, however, leaves this gap which has been filled with the intermediate state. Purgatory is a Roman Catholic doctrine which interprets this intermediate place as one in which the status of persons can be changed by works done on their behalf.

Hades (Old Testament Sheol) is the realm of the dead in the New Testament. It could be viewed as death; it may be a place. Paradise would then be the part of hades reserved for the righteous. When Jesus said to the thief on the cross, "Truly, I say to you, today you will be with me in Paradise" (Luke

23:43), he would have been designating this intermediate place. There are interpreters, however, who insist that this paradise is heaven itself and that there is no intermediate waiting place.

There are New Testament teachings which suggest that at death the believers depart to be with Christ (Phil. 1:23; 1 Thess. 5:10; Luke 23:43). Other passages imply that the wicked are already in a place of suffering (Luke 16:23; 2 Pet. 2:9). These implications would be no less true, however, if this refers to an intermediate state with the full heaven and hell to come at a later time.

Purgatory is objectionable to Protestants because of the single teaching that one's status there can be changed by deeds done by others on that person's behalf. Protestants believe that we make our decisions for eternity in this life.

An important issue involved is the body-soul division. Those who believe that at death the soul survives separately from the body are likely to speak of "The Disembodied State."[8] This simplifies the problem and makes an intermediate state quite natural as the waiting place until the final resurrection when, presumably, resurrection bodies are provided. Luther apparently thought that death would be like sleep, and we would awake on resurrection morning. Those who hold to an intermediate state see it as a place in which a distinction between the righteous and wicked has already taken place, a place of consciousness with final judgment still in the future. Ray Summers insists that it is a conscious, fixed, and incomplete state for both the righteous and wicked.

The believers in Christ have the hope that when they die they will depart to be with the Lord. It should be no great disappointment if their being with the Lord is in some intermediate place or state awaiting the others who will follow. The wicked, on the other hand, could not complain if they have an intermediate period before final separation from God.

We know so little that it is not wise to speculate on what the immediate situation after death will be. Our clearest insight is the resurrection of Jesus, and I don't see how that answers this question.

Parousia

The word *Parousia* means "presence." In popular usage, people speak of the "second coming," but that term does not appear in the New Testament. The idea is taken from two passages: Jesus' statement, "I will come again" (John 14:3) and "so Christ, having been offered once to bear the sins of many, will appear a second time, not to deal with sin but to save those who are eagerly waiting for him" (Heb. 9:28).

Two other words, meaning "appearing" and "revelation," are also used of Christ's appearance. The more common word is *presence* or *Parousia* in the New Testament. The New Testament writings suggest that the early Christians expected Christ to return quite soon. The passage in Thessalonians (4:13-18) appears to have been prompted by the death of some of the believers who had expected Christ to return during their lifetime. This theme was advanced in the writings of the early church and has remained a strong basis of hope among Christian believers. The time of Christ's coming is, of course, not disclosed. The manner of his coming is described with apocalyptic terminology including the shout, the clouds of heaven, and the like.[9]

The early writers of the church kept alive the expectation that Christ who had come would come again. This has continued to be an inspiring element of Christian expectation.

The Parousia is related closely to the kingdom and to the judgment so it will be discussed in that connection. The speculation as to the date of the coming and the charts seeking to chart the related events have all but destroyed the hope for many modern persons.

The expectation of Christ's return, in whatever way, continues to be a genuine and well-grounded eschatological hope. When he comes, in whatever way, we shall know the fullness of the salvation he has begun and the victory he has promised.

The Resurrection

The cross and the resurrection receive more attention in the New Testament than any other specific subjects. This dual event is the central focus of the Christian faith and message. The earliest summaries of that faith in the New Testament writings include this declaration: (1) Peter's sermon on Pentecost, "But God raised him up, having loosed the pangs of death" (Acts 2:24); (2) Paul to Corinth, "For I delivered to you as of first importance what I also received, . . . he was raised on the third day" (1 Cor. 15:3-4); and (3) 1 Peter, "By his great mercy we have been born anew to a living hope through the resurrection of Jesus Christ from the dead" (1:3). The earliest creeds which came after the New Testament writings also include the affirmation of belief in the resurrection.

The creedal statements about the resurrection go beyond the affirmation of Christ's resurrection; they express faith in the hope of our own resurrection.

The General Idea of Life Beyond Death

There is strong evidence for the assertion that most peoples, both ancient and modern, primitive and advanced, have held to a belief, or hope, or wish for life beyond physical death. Ludwig Feuerbach, of course, spoke of this and the Christian doctrine of the resurrection as wishful thinking which should be abandoned along with our other superstitions.

Survival as shades or ghosts is a common form of the idea. Please note, however, this is quite different from the Christian idea of resurrection. John Baillie, in one of the most delightful books on Christian hope, *And the Life Everlasting,* has traced this idea from "Ghostly Survival Among Savage Peoples" through "The Classical World and in Israel." He concluded that it was a "scientific rather than a religious dogma" because it grew out of experience rather than religious beliefs.[10]

If one feels compelled to explain the idea of ghostly survival on a scientific basis, the most likely approach is through dreams in which the departed loved ones reappear or the departed feared ones continue to threaten the living. The dead live on in our memory, consciously or unconsciously, and perhaps that "explains" it.

The immortality of the soul, however, is a philosophical notion whose classical form was the achievement of Greek philosophers. The idea is that the soul or mind of a person does not die when the body dies because the soul is either a part of divinity or has its existence in the nonmaterial realm which cannot die. The body, which is physical, obviously dies and deteriorates.

The idea of an immortal soul, as in Platonism, is related to a concept of reality in which our lives are only a shadow of the real. The soul was imprisoned in the body, hence merely limited for a time. At death, the soul was freed to resume its participation in the real world above. The soul in Platonism was both preexistent and immortal.

The similarity between the immortality of the soul and the biblical view of resurrection appears quite impressive at first, and many theologians accept this view as a reason-based parallel to the biblical belief. There are remarkable differences, however, between the two. The Greek view leads to a notion that the body is evil; in biblical faith the body is God's good creation. The Greek view sees the soul as divine or partly divine; in biblical faith, human beings are altogether creatures and only God is divine. Scholars vary on the relationship of the immortality of the soul and the resurrection.[11]

The Hebrews did not believe in the "immortality of the soul." They believed that at death the person died. The idea of Sheol, the place of the dead, was not a place for souls that could not die. It was the dark, nether world of death.

The idea of resurrection from the dead was a late development in the Old Testament. It is usually dated in the Hellenistic period on the assumption that Daniel is related to that period. There is only one very clear and definite reference to a belief in the resurrection in the Old Testament. "And many of those who sleep in the dust of the earth shall awake, some to everlasting life, and some to shame and everlasting contempt" (Dan. 12:2). Another verse in the Old Testament in which some interpreters find the resurrection is, "Thy dead shall live, their bodies shall rise" (Isa. 26:19).

Job raised the age-old question in a haunting way when he asked, "If a man die, shall he live again?" (14:14). He went even further in his confession, "For I know that my Redeemer lives,/and at last he will stand upon the earth;/and after my skin has been thus destroyed,/then from my flesh I shall see God" (19:25-26), but interpreters are not sure that he was talking about a resurrection.

The Psalms provide some statements suggesting what is later a resurrection hope. Is there some implication in the statement, "the wicked will not stand in the judgment" (1:5)? What about, "I shall dwell in the house of the Lord for ever" (23:6)? Scholars do not usually think these verses teach an individual resurrection, but they voice a thought and inward longing.

There was considerable development of the resurrection idea during the interbiblical period, as evidenced in the writings of the Apocrypha and Pseudepigrapha. The idea of a resurrection, however, was not universally accepted in Judaism in New Testament times. In general, the Pharisees believed in the resurrection of the dead, but the Sadducees did not.

Jesus' Teaching on, and Raising the Dead

Apparently Jesus believed in and taught the resurrection of individuals from the dead. In chapter 11 of John's Gospel, Jesus told Martha who lamented the death of her brother, Lazarus, "Your brother will rise again" (v. 23). There seems to be little doubt but that the resurrection belief was common by this time. The following statement of Jesus, "I am the resurrection and the life" (11:25), while very meaningful to Christians, is very difficult to interpret in its context.

Mark noted that on three occasions Jesus predicted his forthcoming death and resurrection (8:31; 9:31; 10:33-34). Some scholars would see this as having been influenced by the resurrection event as an interpretation at the time of writing rather than a statement of Jesus at the time. Numerous other statements, however, in other settings indicate that Jesus foresaw his vindication (Luke 13:35).[12]

In the response to the question of John the Baptist about whether Jesus were the "Coming One," Jesus instructed the messengers to tell John what they had seen and heard of Jesus' ministry, which included "the dead are raised up" (Matt. 11:5; Luke 7:22). The words *raised up* are not the same as the term for the resurrection of Jesus.

The Gospel writers reported that Jesus raised from the dead the son of a widow of Nain (Luke 7:11-17) and Lazarus (John 11:43 *ff.*). The daughter of Jairus was apparently dead (Mark 5:35); but before restoring her, Jesus said, "The child is not dead but sleeping" (v. 39).

Luke reported a raising from the dead of one named Dorcas of Joppa (Acts 9:36-43) by Peter. Eutychus was probably not dead because Paul said "his life is [still] in him" when he was restored (Acts 20:10).

In all of these cases, Jesus had power over death, but those who were raised died again. The resurrection of Jesus was a different kind of event; Jesus was raised to the eternal realm, never to die again.

The Resurrection of Jesus

The Gospels stress the crucifixion of Jesus, his death on the cross, his burial, the guard at the tomb (Matt 27:62-66), the empty tomb, and the appearances of the risen Lord. The other New Testament writers spoke often of the resurrection of Jesus because it is a vital part of the gospel.

The Gospel writers gave adequate details to certify that Jesus was really dead. The guard at the tomb (Matt. 27:64) appears to have been a guarantee against the removal of Jesus' body, but many interpreters see this narrative as a later addition.

The case for Jesus' resurrection rests on (1) the certainty of his death, (2) the empty tomb, (3) the appearances after the burial, and (4) the changed lives of his followers.

There are those who would call in the witnesses and prove, as if in a courtroom, that Jesus was raised from the dead. It remains a fact, however, that no one saw him rise from the dead, and all of the witnesses of the resurrection were believers. The resurrection of Jesus cannot be *proved,* as that word is usually used, nor can it be *disproved.* It is a precious belief of Christians based upon the reliability of the numerous witnesses and upon the fact that faith in this resurrected Christ still changes lives. One of the strongest recent statements on the importance of the resurrection appears in the theology of Wolfhart Pannenberg.[13]

The resurrection appearances are the strongest case for the belief in Jesus' resurrection. We have some difficulty in determining if the different sources are reporting different or the same appearances, but it seems that there were eleven appearances apart from Paul's claim to have seen the risen Lord. He appeared to the following: (1) to the women (Matt. 28:9-10), (2) to Mary Magdalene (John 20:11-18), (3) to Peter (1 Cor. 15:5; Luke 24:34), (4) to two disciples on the way to Emmaus (Luke 14:13-31), (5) to the eleven and other disciples (Luke 24:36-49: John 20:19-23), (6) to Thomas and some others (John 20:24-29), (7) to the eleven in Galilee (Matt. 28:16 *ff.*), (8) to disciples (Acts 1:6-9), (9) to some of the disciples at the sea of Tiberias (John 21:14), (10) to the crowd of over five hundred people (1 Cor. 15:6), and (11) to James (1 Cor. 15:7).[14]

The Meaning of Jesus' Resurrection

Since the Christian faith as a whole stands or falls with Christ, it would be impossible to state adequately how much the resurrection of Jesus really means. Several themes are clear.

Jesus, who is now the risen Lord, is identified with Jesus of Nazareth who had taught and led the disciples. This continuity is vital in the understanding of the incarnation and the person of Christ.

God had vindicated Jesus the Christ and affirmed the disciples' faith in him.

The defeated disciples were changed into victorious proclaimers of Jesus' message.

The new age had dawned. The defeat of sin and death had been demonstrated.

The human hope for life beyond death has a sure foundation in the resurrection of Jesus the Christ.

He is Lord and is alive forevermore.

The Christian Hope for Resurrection

The resurrection of Jesus Christ from the dead is the foundation of the Christian hope for resurrection and life everlasting. We believe that after death, "we shall certainly be united with him in a resurrection like his" (Rom. 6:5). This will apply both to those who have died before his coming and those who are still alive (1 Thess. 4:14).

This resurrection hope is a vital part of our lives today in that it gives daily life purpose, meaning, and direction. It means "newness of life" now (Rom. 6:4). The hope of the resurrection is a "power" in daily life and a goal or expectation which inspires the best from life (Phil. 3:10-11).

The speculation about when the resurrection will occur and what the resurrection body will be like is almost infinite, but the information is almost nonexistent. Paul devoted a long chapter to this question from the Corinthian Christians. His conclusion was that it is a "mystery." Christ will return, we will be raised, we will be changed, and death will have been finally defeated.

He repeated the questions addressed to him, "How are the dead raised? With what kind of body do they come?" (1 Cor. 15:35). Then he said, "You foolish man!" (v. 36). His answer drew attention to the change anticipated and concluded, "it is raised a spiritual body" (v.44). That is the whole context of our knowledge.

The Judgment

The word *judgment* has an ominous sound, but it really should not be so. April 15 holds no fear for those who pay their income taxes and have records to prove it. It is otherwise for those who could not withstand the checking of the records. We have heard the threat of judgment from our context of guilt and have not thought through our beliefs after forgiveness. As a result, people cringe at the sound of the word.

To be sure, the biblical records speak often of judgment and often in a negative way to those in guilt. It should be remembered, however, that even if the theme of judgment were not even mentioned, we would have to invent it ourselves because we are creatures in freedom and responsibility. Our own natures would require it even if God did not. He does however.

Judgment can result in vindication as well as condemnation. In the parable of the plumb line (7:7-9), Amos taught that God measures the wall by the plumb line to see if it is perpendicular. If so, the plumb line vindicates it and predicts that it will stand. If it is not perpendicular, the judgment says that it will fall. Jesus, in his parables, indicated that some would be vindicated with the "well done. You have been faithful," whereas others would be rejected (Matt. 25:14-30).

In biblical faith, judgment is both a present reality and a future expectation.

Judgment as Present

When a person repents toward God in faith, he or she has willingly been judged. The Christian lives under the daily judgment of God through study, reflection, and prayer. The Christian seeks to know God's will and one's shortcomings so as to make changes and do the will of God now. This kind of judgment is discipline, wholesome, and productive.

Judgment also appears as the consequences of sin. This theme recurs repeatedly in the Old Testament. The nation turns from God, stands the judgment of God, and suffers at the hands of enemy peoples. One should be careful about attributing to God any arbitrary action in the suffering. It is the judgment in that we through rejecting God incur the suffering. The "wrath of God" in Romans is in facing the consequences of constantly rejecting God for idols. Reluctantly, "God gave them up in the lusts of their hearts to impurity, . . . dishonorable passions . . . base mind" (Rom. 1:24-28). God does not will these evils. God, like a patient parent, tried to get them to do his will, but they would not. God refuses to coerce people into compliance. Their rejection of God results in this debasement; that is "indirectly" a judgment of God.

Judgment as a present reality is clearly taught in the Fourth Gospel. The basis of judgment, as elsewhere, is what people do in response to Jesus Christ.

> He who believes in him is not condemned; he who does not believe is condemned already, because he has not believed in the name of the only Son of God. And this is the judgment, that the light has come into the world, and men loved darkness rather than light, because their deeds were evil (John 3:18-19).

The Basis of Judgment

In the parables of Jesus on judgment, the theme is that people are judged or to be judged on the basis of their responses to God and persons in the human situation. One parable spoke of a man to whom others were in debt. One debtor, in great distress, begged for mercy and received it. Then that forgiven debtor treated his lesser debtor unmercifully. This failure to respond with justice and mercy was the cause of his condemnation (Matt. 18:23-35). Other parables speak of judgment on the basis of what persons do with what is entrusted to them and the opportunities they have (Matt. 24—25).

Since Jesus Christ is the full revelation of God, the ultimate judgment will be on the basis of what response persons make to him. Response to him includes responses to others.

The Future Judgment

The biblical writings expect a future judgment. The author of Hebrews spoke of certainties in his statement, "And just as it is appointed for men to die once, and after that comes judgment, so Christ, having been offered once to bear the sins of many, will appear a second time, not to deal with sin but to save those who are eagerly waiting for him" (Heb. 9:27-28). Note the vindication.

There are several apocalyptic descriptions of final judgment or judgments. These are related to the idea of a return of Christ to earth and a final event to conclude history. There are those who see all of these descriptions as illustrations of the fact of judgment and the certainty that we shall stand before God but not a chronological listing of several judgment scenes.

The Christian, however, does not stand in fear of a final judgment because the judgment is already a fact in the Christian life. Final judgment is the last word on human responsibility and freedom in light of our being the creatures of God. It holds no fear for the believer, or should not.

Hell

The biblical teachings are clear on the point that not all persons will be saved. The word *hell* and its synonyms stand for the ultimate abode for those who reject God. The apocalyptic descriptions of hell include details of fire and incredible sufferings. The most terrible aspect, however, would be to be separated from God and God's people forever.

In modern times, there has been a tendency for theologians to move toward, or to, universal salvation. Karl Barth spoke of hell as an "impossible possibility." Emil Brunner, who wants to take both God and man seriously, found the traditional view of hell repugnant and the doctrine of justification finding "its crown in a proclamation of universal redemption" but could not come to a conclusion. He saw both as the voices of God's

Word. God wills to save all. Would God settle for a partial victory? Both alternatives are beset with misgiving.[15]

If heaven is the eternal abode of God and those who trust him, then hell would be the ultimate separation from God.

The belief in universal salvation not only has the weight of biblical teachings against it but also has to face the logical problem of human freedom. If every person will ultimately be saved anyway, then is a person free? Does not that belief mean that one can never say no to God? Does not the Bible teach and reason support the idea that God has endowed us with the freedom even to say no. If we are ultimately all to be saved, then it appears that we can only say not yet.

The Kingdom of God

The kingdom of God, or the kingdom of heaven, is the acknowledged and accepted reign of God. Since God is Creator of the world, his sovereignty stands without justification. God, however, created human beings in freedom and responsibility. When they turned from God, he began his work of reconciliation or salvation. God always willed that his creatures should trust him, obey him, and receive their meaning in life from him. This is his nature and theirs. God imposed a limit upon himself, however, when he gave freedom to creatures. He refuses to coerce us into compliance; he gave us genuine freedom. His entire work of reconciliation was intended to bring his human creatures back into that relationship. That is the meaning of the kingdom of God. Their return, however, must be their willing return. God is faithful in his realm and honors the freedom of his creatures.

The kingdom is the reign of God in the lives of his creatures, accepted willingly and joyfully. It is not something human beings build. It is of God's doing. People enter the kingdom.

Jesus and the Kingdom of God

The subject of Jesus' preaching was the kingdom of God. After John the Baptist had preached, "Repent, for the kingdom of heaven is at hand" (Matt. 3:2), Jesus came preaching, "Repent, for the kingdom of heaven is at hand" (4:17). Mark did not give John the Baptist's reference to the kingdom but reported that "Jesus came into Galilee, preaching the gospel of God, and saying, 'The time is fulfilled, and the kingdom of God is at hand; repent, and believe in the gospel' " (Mark 1:14-15).

The motivation for repentance and faith is the message that the time has come for the promises to be fulfilled and the kingdom of God is at hand. This coming of the kingdom inspires faith. Evil has reigned, but now God's reign is to be established in the lives of people who will accept him.

Jesus presented the kingdom as a present reality (Luke 17:20-21), as the beginning of a kingdom and as a future hope. The future hope will be fully realized when the kingdom comes to the extent that the will of God is done on earth as it is in heaven (Matt. 6:10). In the Last Supper, Jesus pointed into the future and his next eating and drinking with the disciples "in the kingdom of God" (Mark 14:25). Jesus emphatically denied any exact knowledge as to the time of the future consummation of the kingdom (Mark 13:32).

Other New Testament Ideas on the Kingdom

In spite of Jesus' concentration on the kingdom of God, New Testament writers spoke more often about Christ himself. This appears to be due to the fact that they have acknowledged him as King and Lord. They realized that faith in him is participation in his reign. The great Christological passage of Philippians ends, "that at the name of Jesus every knee should bow, in heaven and on earth and under the earth, and every tongue confess that Jesus Christ is Lord, to the glory of God the Father" (Phil. 2:10-11).

The revealing work of Jesus Christ was done to bring eternal life to those who believe in him to the glory of "the King of ages, immortal, invisible, the only God" (1 Tim. 1:17). The concluding appeal to Timothy was to keep the commandment "until the appearing of our Lord Jesus Christ; and this will be made manifest at the proper time by the blessed and only Sovereign, the King of kings and Lord of lords" (6:14-15).

The cosmic conflict over evil has been won through the death and struggle of Christ, the Lamb, who has defeated the forces of evil and now "is Lord of lords and King of kings, and those with him are called and chosen and faithful" (Rev. 17:14; also see 19:16).

The kingdom of God and Christ has prevailed and the new age dawns in this consummation of his kingdom.

Questions About the Kingdom and Earth

There are two questions which command attention with reference to the consummation of the kingdom and this earth. Will this earth share in the full salvation of human creatures? Will there be a millennial reign on earth?

A New Earth. John spoke of "a new heaven and a new earth" (Rev. 21:1). He indicated that the former earth and heaven had passed away. This raises the question for some about the renovation of this earth. Isaiah had spoken about creating a new heaven and a new earth (Isa. 65:17). In 2 Peter, the author spoke of the heavens being destroyed on the Day of God but indicated a hope for "new heavens and a new earth in which righteousness dwells" (3:13).

The sin of man in Eden resulted in a curse on creation with thorns and thistles. It stands to reason that the full restoration of human beings would have a bearing on earth if that full restoration takes place on this earth. The literature of the period in which the New Testament was written has numerous ideas of the transformation of the earth.[16]

Paul's passage in Romans has led to much speculation. He indicated, "For the creation waits with eager longing for the revealing of the sons of God; for the creation was subjected to futility" (8:19-20). The "[whole] creation" groaning in travail, "will be set free from its bondage to decay and obtain the glorious liberty of the children of God" (vv. 21-22). What can this mean?

Present concerns about the earthly environment have increased interest in the Christian's responsibility for creation and properly so. The question about the coming kingdom of God and the renovation of the earth, however, cannot be answered with the information at our disposal.[17]

A Millennial Reign? In the twentieth chapter of Revelation, there are references to a reign of Christ of a thousand years' duration. Those who interpret Revelation as history, or literally, rather than as an apocalpyse, tend to place this reign of a thousand years here on earth. The literature on the subject is almost limitless.[18]

An earthly reign of Christ in a world in sin would place him on the kind of throne he rejected when he was on earth. No other biblical writer speaks of such a millennial reign. Jesus spoke on eschatological subjects rather fully, and Paul wrote the Epistles to the Thessalonians to answer questions about the end. He did not mention such a millennial reign. Furthermore, the apocalyptic nature of Revelation would suggest an interpretation other than this kind of reign.

The Meaning of the Kingdom of God

The future kingdom of God is nothing more or less than the full realization of the purpose of God and the destiny of humanity.

When God created free beings, he imposed a limitation upon himself. He refuses to coerce these creatures. When the human creatures of God rebelled against him, he set out to reconcile them to himself without repealing their freedom. It cost him the life of Jesus Christ, his Son.

The entire work of reconciliation is consummated in the future kingdom of God. God's sovereignty will be freely and joyfully acknowledged. Human destiny will be achieved in its fullest, in freedom and responsibility. Human beings will be reconciled to one another as they are completely reconciled to God.

The harmony of individual reconciliation and the entire

human family of God under his lordship is the kingdom of God.

Life Everlasting

Eternal life is not life with no end of time; rather, it is an existence different from time, a changed existence. The qualitative difference is often overlooked.

Life everlasting is regarded as endless but is not entirely future. The eternal life is the quality of life known in Christ by faith and is a present reality (John 17:3).

Life, in the biblical sense, is more than biological existence. It means a kind of existence under God and with other persons in meaningful relationships. This kind of "life" may not be measured by clocks and calendars; it certainly cannot be controlled by them. Rufolf Bultmann, for instance, spoke of the life of faith as "authentic existence." Other existence was partial or counterfeit. With his particular view of existentialism and history, which I think is inadequate, he equated "authentic existence" with "eschatological existence." In other words, all that the biblical faith says about a future life with God can be known now. While I don't think that is true, I think it illustrates that quality of existence is the meaning of life in Christian faith.

The life everlasting is the ultimate realization of human destiny. Human beings are creatures of God, free and responsible, capable of responding to and trusting God, capable of a lasting relationship with God and persons. Heaven is the ultimate fulfillment of all these potentials.

We shall be completely liberated from the bondage of sin. Without hindrance, we can respond to God and others.

We shall be completely free, liberated from the shackles which inhibit full humanity.

We shall enjoy our creatureliness in the presence of our Creator.

We shall trust God completely. Faith is our nature. Unbelief is an illness. Distrust is a disaster to human beings.

There are those who long for "rest." Will heaven be a place of continual rest? God works, creates. Human beings are in the image of God, and they work too. Perhaps there are tasks for us to do in God's creation. There are those who long for God's presence, and they shall see God. We tend to think of heaven in terms of what we already love, and that may be all right. Heaven will be characterized by the presence of God. We shall be with him. All will be right then. P. T. Forsyth began the concluding chapter of his splendid little book *This Life and the Next* with these words, "To live is Christ, to die is more Christ. We pass into a genial native land."[19]

Notes

1. T. W. Manson, *The Teaching of Jesus* (Cambridge: Cambridge University Press, 1948), p. 247.

2. Gerhard von Rad, *Old Testament Theology,* 2, trans. D. M. G. Stalker (New York and Evanston: Harper & Row, Publishers, 1965), p. 115.

3. Baron Friedrich von Hügel, *Eternal Life, a Study of Its Implications and Applications,* 2nd. ed. (Edinburgh: T. & T. Clark, 1913), pp. 7-14: See also John Noss, *Man's Religions* (New York: Macmillan Co., n.d.), for related ideas in religions.

4. Otto Weber, *Foundations of Dogmatics,* 2, trans. Darrell L. Guder (Grand Rapids: William B. Eerdmans Publishing Company, 1983), pp. 656 *ff.*

5. Emil Brunner, *Eternal Hope,* trans. Harold Knight (Philadelphia: The Westminster Press, 1954), p. 7.

6. TDNT, 2, p. 531.

7. Dale Moody, *The Hope of Glory* (Grand Rapids: William B. Eerdmans Publishing Company, 1964); Brunner, cited in note 5 comprises the entire eschatology; see also Howard Clark Kee, *The Renewal of Hope* (New York: Association Press, 1959).

8. Ray Summers, *The Life Beyond* (Nashville: Broadman Press, 1959), pp. 15 *ff.*

9. J. A. T. Robinson, *Jesus and His Coming* (New York and Nashville: Abingdon Press, 1957); see also Summers, pp. 95-146; Moody, pp. 193-232.

10. John Baillie, *And the Life Everlasting* (London: Oxford University Press, 1934), pp. 62 *ff.*

11. Oscar Cullman, *Immortality of the Soul or Resurrection?* (London: The Epworth Press, 1958).

12. IDB, 4, p. 45.

13. Wolfhart Pannenberg, ed. *Revelation as History* (London: The Macmillan

Company, 1968); *History and Hermeneutic* (New York: Harper & Row Publishers, Inc., 1967); *Jesus—God and Man* (Philadelphia: The Westminster Press, 1968).

14. For listing see IDB, 4, p. 47.

15. Brunner, pp. 179-184.

16. Martin Rist, "The Revelation of St. John the Divine," *Interpreters Bible,* 12 (New York and Nashville: Abingdon Press, 1957), p. 528-529.

17. Dale Moody, "The New Creation," *The Hope of Glory,* and "Cosmic Eschatology," *The Word of Truth.*

18. On "Millennialism" see commentaries on Revelation 20; The Scofield Reference Bible for a dispensational form of the view; D. H. Kromminga, *The Millennium in the Church* (Grand Rapids: William B. Eerdmans Publishing Company, 1945) gives a comprehensive discussion of the subject, as do hosts of others in any library of biblical and theological materials.

19. P. T. Forsyth, *This Life and the Next* (London: Independent Press, 1918), p. 84.

INDEX

Apollinarianism, definition of, 60

apostles, 298

Arianism, definition of, 59

assurance, definition of, 318

atonement

and forgiveness of sins, 227-228; biblical teachings on the, 222-229; definition of, 221; historical theories of the, 229-234; interpretations of the, 226-229; Old Testament Teachings on, 222-225; various theories of the, 230-234

authority, revelation and, 85-88

beliefs, definition of, 13, 28-29

belonging

definition of, 310; to God, 310; to others, 310-311

Bible, formation of, 18-19

bondage, 196

calling, 245-246

Christ

as contemporary, 62; cross of, 220-239; millennial reign of, 345; the deity of, 57-58; the finality of, 63-65; the humanity of, 55-57; virginal conception of, 55-57

Christian faith, distinction of, 13

Christian hope, 216

Christianity

church and, 16-17; definitions of, 17; expansion of, 17-18; expressions of, 19-26; origin of, 15-16

Christology

Chalcedonian, 60-61; definition of, 221

church

a new community, 268-269; and Christianity, 16-17; as body of Christ, 276-277; as community of forgiveness, 280; as community of the Holy Spirit, 277-278; as community of the Word, 283-284; as people of God, 275-276; as priesthood of all believers, 278-280; belief in, 264; characteristics of the, 286-301; definition of, 264-265; discovery of the, 271-274; emergence of, 270-271; Holy Spirit in, 267; identifying marks of the, 284-286; local and universal, 284; ministers of the, 298-301; ministry of, 300; mission and ministry of the, 286-301; mission of the, 295-297; missionary efforts of the, 270; New Testament reflections on nature of the, 274-284; one and many, 271-272; order, 301; origin of, 16-19, 265-271; sanctification in the, 273; unity of the, 272-274; Word of God in the, 267-268; worship in the, 287-295

commandment, a new, 311-312

conviction, 95

createdness, world as, 130-131

creation

a theological belief, 121; belief in, 120; biblical teachings, 121; Creator and,

349